OPPOSITE
POLES

OPPOSITE POLES

Immigrants and Ethnics
in Polish Chicago,
1976–1990

Mary Patrice Erdmans

The Pennsylvania State University Press
University Park, Pennsylvania

Library of Congress Cataloging-in-Publication Data

Erdmans, Mary Patrice.
    Opposite Poles : immigrants and ethnics in Polish Chicago, 1976–
1990 / Mary Patrice Erdmans
    p.   cm.
Includes bibliographical references and index.
ISBN 0-271-01735-X (cloth : alk. paper)
ISBN 0-271-01736-8 (pbk. : alk. paper)
    1. Polish American—Illinois—Chicago—History—20th century.
2. Immigrants—Illinois—Chicago—History—20th century.   3. Chicago
(Ill.)—Ethnic relations.   I. Title
F548.9.P7E73   1998
977.3'110048185—dc21   97-17949
                                                                   CIP

It is the policy of The Pennsylvania State University Press to use acid-free paper for the first printing of all clothbound books. Publications on uncoated stock satisfy the minimum requirements of American National Standard for Information Sciences— Permanence of Paper for Printed Library Materials, ANSI Z39.48-1992.

To my grandmother,
Helen Frances Grasinski,
for her elegance and strength

Contents

Ackowledgments

I did not work or write in isolation, so there are of course many people I need to thank. I am grateful to my friends, colleagues, and teachers in Chicago who encouraged me in the early stages of this work: Celia Berdes, Leyla Gungor, and Wayne Severson, for having plucky souls and being damn good friends; Anna Domagala and Mariusz Szajnert for help translating; and Carol Heimer, Albert Hunter, and Arthur Stinchcombe for their shrewd questions, playful discussions, and incisive criticisms.

My understanding of the Polish community in Chicago would not have been possible without the generosity of all those who shared their memories, musings, and files. Getting to know the Polish immigrants and Polish American ethnics has given me a greater appreciation of home and kinfolk. In Poland, the gracious hospitality of Halina Gala, Jurek and Krystina Przystawa, and Marysia Kowalska fed my love for this indomitable nation.

I am indebted to those who helped me manage my life and thoughts while writing the manuscript in Greensboro: Jeanne Jones and John Malone, for their open refrigerator, and special thanks to Jean, for her gutsy piano playing and her directive to write about my work with as much passion as I talked about it; Janice Tulloss, for Ernie-sitting; Andy Brod, for long hikes and late-night editing; David Mitchell, Bill Markham, and Rebecca Adams, for their comments on sections of the manuscript; Steven O'Boyle, for suggesting the title; and Julia Capone, for helping me get it wrapped up and out the door.

I would also like to thank those who helped me turn the pages of words into a finished product: Stanislaus Blejwas and Mary Kelly, for their insightful reviews; Ewa Wolynska, the special collections archivist at Central Connecticut State University; Robert Gaines, documents librarian at the University of North Carolina at Greensboro; and Peter Potter and Patricia Mitchell at Penn State Press.

And then, there are those I would like to thank for a lifetime of support: the Erdmans clan—Jim, Rosemarie, Andrew, Diane, Curt, Evan, Veronica, Rachel, David, Kathy, Matthew, Michael, Laura, Chris, Jeremiah, Elizabeth, Hannah Rose, Paul, and Vicky—for reminding me that I am simply one among many; special thanks to Jimmy, for bringing me supplies and teasing me into laughter; my parents, James and Angel Erdmans, for their steadfast love, strong faith, and for giving me the cabin when I needed it most; to my buddy, Eddy—though I promised a dedication I am at least delivering an acknowledgment; and finally, my aunts, the Grasinski girls, for just being beautiful and reminding me that my grandmother is always with us, through them.

List of Tables

Introduction: Immigrants and Ethnics

In August 1980, Polish workers locked themselves inside the gates of the Lenin Shipyard in Gdansk. Surrounded by flowers, rosaries, and pictures of Pope John Paul II, the workers framed their struggle in *solidarność* (solidarity) with workers across Poland. The strike led to the formation of the *Niezależny Samorządny Związek Zawodowy* (Independent Self-Governing Trades Union), and the opposition movement in Poland became known to the world as Solidarity. In Chicago, thousands of Polish Americans and Polish immigrants responded with their own demonstrations, marching in front of the Polish consulate, burning a replica of the Soviet flag, singing the (noncommunist) Polish national anthem, and chanting "*Solidarność*" in unity with the Polish workers. The opposition activities in Poland rekindled homeland sentiments for many third-generation Americans of Polish descent and reconnected many Polish immigrants to their country of birth.

On December 13, 1981, the communist regime in Warsaw imposed martial law and declared illegal the Solidarity union. Fifty thousand Polish Americans and Polish immigrants marched in angry protestation. Over the next few years, thousands of Solidarity activists who had been imprisoned during martial law emigrated to America, where they carried on the fight for Poland's independence. Throughout the 1980s, the Chicago demonstrations in front of the Polish consulate continued but the number of protesters dwindled. During the cold winter months in the mid-1980s, the chilling Lake Michigan wind and early evening darkness mirrored the despairing social landscape in Poland. The Warsaw regime harassed and imprisoned opposition activists, and people who only a few years earlier had openly supported Solidarity were now afraid to look the activists in the eyes when they passed on the street. The economy deteriorated, the physical environment decayed, and hopes for a better life crumbled. Life was, in short, miserable, and consequently an increasing number of Poles chose to emigrate, tens of thousands to Chicago. A new wave of strikes broke out in Poland in 1988, and the communist government, forced into negotiations with the Polish opposition, eventually agreed to hold partially free elections for the first time since World War II. The changes in Poland reverberated in

Polish Chicago. In June 1989, the former protesters came to the Polish consulate to cast their absentee ballots for Solidarity candidates, who won all but one of the seats open to them. The new government immediately began to dismantle the state-owned economy. The gears also shifted in Chicago as organizations once mobilized for Poland's political independence now worked to help "jump start" Poland's new free-market economy.

In America, "land of immigrants," where ethnic identification and links (at least sentimental ones) with the old country are fundamental aspects of social identity, no region was more active in fighting the revolution from abroad than Chicago Polonia (Polonia is the name for the Polish community abroad). With roughly 900,000 people claiming Polish descent in the 1980s, Chicago is reputed to have the second largest population of Poles in the world, second only to Warsaw. The community includes century-old and newly formed organizations, dozens of schools teaching Saturday morning Polish classes, annual citywide Polish festivals, and a multitude of restaurants, churches, stores, newspapers, TV stations, and radio programs. In the heart of Polonia people work, shop, pray, drink, and buy gravestones speaking Polish.

The swell of support for Poland during the 1980s came from this community composed of older-generation Polish Americans and newly arrived Polish immigrants. These groups were linked by a common purpose and a seemingly common heritage. Nonetheless, there were divisions in Polonia that led to mistrust, miscommunication, and bitterness. At times, Polish Americans and new Polish immigrants expended more energy on internecine struggles than on fighting against the Polish communist regime. At one point, Polish American leaders branded the immigrants' activities as "hooliganism" and urged people not to participate in demonstrations. At another time, Polish immigrants characterized Polish American leaders as weak and ineffective and described established Polonia as a place where "stupidity is rampant." People filed lawsuits against each other, wrote editorials to the *Chicago Tribune* maligning each other, and ridiculed and denounced each other in the Polish media. What caused these divisions? What borders within Polonia disrupted collective action and undermined group solidarity?

The most important division was between ethnics (native-born Americans of Polish descent) and immigrants (foreign-born Poles). Common collective goals made the two groups think they "ought" to work together. One Polish activist wrote that "various emigrant generations and emigrant organizations can readily cooperate with each other if they are united by the same aim" (Wlodarczyk 1980, 40). Yet, the adjective "Polish" did not always serve as an inclusive identity. The nouns—"immigrant" and "ethnic"—represented distinct cultural and social identities that overrode the tenuous and debatable Polish link. The contrasts between the groups became salient in the arena of collective action to support the opposition in Poland. The period of collective activity that this book examines (1976–90) corresponds with the period of oppositional activity in Poland. I focus on those organizations and groups in Chicago Polonia that actively supported the opposition movement in Poland from 1976 (during the incipient stage of the movement) through the peak Solidarity era of 1980–81, the low period of underground activity in the mid-1980s, the partially free elections in 1989, and the opening up of Poland's market in 1989–90. Support for these activities gave Polish Americans and new Polish immigrants a common collective goal. Focusing on this arena of political action for the homeland, this book analyzes differences between immigrants and ethnics in order to explain both conflict and cooperation in the community. Given their common goal, why did they have problems working together? And conversely, given their differences, what made cooperation possible?

Communities are as heterogeneous as they are homogeneous. Yet, we often think of ethnic and racial communities as monolithic groups. We homogenize groups, smoothing over differences within groups in order to compare differences between groups. This heuristic device is useful for comparing two communities, but it denies internal diversity. It is for this reason that Werner Sollors (1986) criticizes John Shelton Reed's study *The Enduring South* (1974). Reed compares white Southerners in America to all non-Southern whites in America, thereby making the "it" (the South) and "not it" (non-South) cases more distinct. "What happens in such polarizing comparisons is the forced homogenization not only of the nonregion not studied but also of the investigated region itself" (Sollors 1986, 177). This forced homogenization can be undone when we acknowledge and examine the diversity within groups. In fact, Sollors contends that ethnic identities are catch-all identities that people invent as a device for uniting a hetero-geneous group. Ethnicity creates a dominant paradigm under which the diverse group can be unified. For example, Jonathan Sarna (1978) shows how immigrant groups with varying national identities (such as Jews who are German, Polish, Portuguese, or English) or regional identities (Ge-noese and Sicilians) became unified ethnics (Jews or Italians) in America. Kathleen Conzen and her colleagues also maintain that ethnic traditions were invented to "unify the group despite such differences" (1990, 38). The "umbrella" of ethnic culture had to be large enough and flexible enough to provide solidarity, smooth over differences, and mobilize diverse factions. Victor Greene (1975) referred to this as the process of "ethnicization"—the unification of fragmented immigrant groups around shared cultural symbols such as language and religion.

In the 1980s, Chicago Polonia was in the process of reinventing the umbrella of Polish identity. The momentous events in the homeland and the large number of new Polish immigrants led to a resurgence and reexamination of the meaning of Polish traditions, symbols, and group identity. Polish immigrants and Polish American ethnics perceived themselves to be members of different cultural and social groups. As one new immigrant said:

> I think that there is a big difference between the East and the West, and many times I can't communicate with Americans. They just don't understand. I don't think it's because of my language skills but something else. And the same is for the Poles. I don't have any problems being understood by Poles who were born in Poland, but I have the same problem with American-born Poles as I do with Americans. *There is still a language problem, even when I am speaking Polish with them.* (Emphasis mine)

The old Polish American ethnic identity no longer worked to unite the community in the 1980s. This identity, invented at the turn of the twentieth century, modified by the second generation in the 1920s and 1930s, transformed by the influx of World War II Polish émigrés, and revitalized by later generations in the era of cultural pluralism in the 1960s and 1970s did not fit the new Polish immigrants whose cultural identity was shaped by modern-day communist Poland, and whose social identity was linked to their immigrant status. As a result, the Polish immigrants rejected the old definitions and introduced new traditions and symbols. Nonetheless, the two groups shared a cultural history rooted in eighteenth- and nineteenth-century Poland, they shared social space in Chicago, and they shared a common goal of wanting to see Poland become an independent noncommunist nation-state. These common factors led to statements such as "We are all Poles," and were invoked to make demands on each other and to bring people together. The negation of that statement, "We are not all Poles," conversely kept the two groups apart and created territorial boundaries and struggles over who had the right to be called a Pole. Was a Polish immigrant from a communist system more communist than Polish? Was a third-generation Polish American more American than Polish? When the new immigrants arrived, fresh from the "front line of fighting communists," they claimed the right to be the political voice of Poland abroad. In doing so, they challenged rather than accepted the legitimacy of the established Polish American ethnic community.

The Polish community in America is not unique in its diversity. Today in the United States, new Chinese, Israeli, Haitian, Caribbean, and Mexican immigrants negotiate their identities within the context of the established identities of Asian, Jew, black, and Chicano. Shared ancestry, language similarity, and economic resources lead new immigrants to resettle in, demand resources from, and compete for power with the established ethnic community (Portes, McLeod, and Parker 1978; Luciuk 1986; Shokeid 1988; Schneider 1990; Portes and Rumbaut 1990; Hurtado, Gurin, and Peng 1994; Waters 1994; Erdmans 1995; Remy 1996). Still, the cultural meaning systems, political identity, and social and economic needs are different for the established ethnic and new immigrant groups. Social scientists know the importance of borders as sites of ethnic construction, but they have concentrated on identifying borders between rather than within groups. In contrast, this book examines the "in-house" cultural and social fault lines along which subgroups collide, differences appear, and identity emerges.

Borders Within Community

For most of this century, scholars defined ethnicity as a primordial identity connected to bloodlines and immutable characteristics, and ethnic ties as natural affinities (Geertz 1963; Shils 1957). Social scientists focused on the content of the identity rather than the process of identity formation. For example, Park and Miller's treatise *Old World Traits Transplanted* described immigrant groups according to social behavior types (for example, the Japanese were thrifty, clean, and eager to learn) (1921, 173–75). They created sociological taxonomies of the behaviors, customs, and norms of various ethnic groups in America. We continue to do this today when we define ethnicity by such things as mother tongue or culinary preference. This focus on content is captured in the conceptual cornerstones of ethnicity theory, assimilation and cultural persistence, which denote a tension between the parts of the content surrendered to the new country and the parts retained.

More recently, scholars have moved away from cataloging the content of ethnicity to focusing on how the identity is manufactured and what purpose it serves. A whole new set of words anchor the contemporary discussions. Historian Werner Sollors and his colleagues talk about "invented" ethnicity (1986; 1989); sociologists Mary Waters (1994) and Joanne Nagel (1994) refer to "constructed" ethnic identities. Reframing the concept of ethnicity necessitated the reformulation of research questions: Which historical contexts and belief systems shape the construction of ethnic identities? (Nagel 1994); how do ethnic identities become contested identities? (Chow 1993); which internal group differences and external group allegiances mold ethnic identity? (Miller 1985).

This constructionist model of ethnicity draws from the work of anthropologist Frederik Barth, who focused on "the ethnic *boundary* that defines the group, not the cultural stuff that it encloses" (1969, 15). While groups may internally disagree on the cultural content, they become unified and the identity becomes meaningful in the presence of and through interaction with the Other. Group identity is most visible and most important at the border because it orders relations with the Other; it signals such things as institutionalized behavior, stratification, value systems, interaction patterns, and group membership. The cultural content alone does not create or maintain ethnicity. It is the understanding of a "we" negotiated against a "them" that produces salient group identities. Edward Said's work on Orientalism (1978) is an excellent illustration of this point—the British and French construction of the Orient as dark, mysterious, and defeated allowed them to define Western culture as enlightened, rational, and powerful.

Borders change when groups move from one society to another, and along with it the identity of the group changes. Kirby Miller (1985; 1990) illustrates this in his work on the Irish. A good Irishman in Ireland was a nationalist, but a good Irishman in America was synonymous with being a good family man, a devout churchgoer, and a voting Democrat. In the United States, the Irish identity, like that of other minority identities, was constructed in relation to the dominant or majority group that has the power to distribute resources and define the situation. The dominant group has always been some variation of the "white" group (Anglo-Saxon Protestants, northern Europeans, Europeans), and this white majority serves as a yardstick for measuring the desirability, foreignness, and progress of minority groups. Studies of black-white relations emphatically demonstrate the hegemonic power of the white majority group to define and label the minority group (Giddings 1984; hooks 1992; Frankenburg 1993). Without a doubt, one of the central sites of identity construction is at the external border between groups, especially the border between majority and minority groups.[1]

In general, we perceive the distance between groups as being greater than the distance within groups (Zerubavel 1991). This epistemological tendency, however, causes us to overlook heterogeneity within groups and dismiss internal borders. The meaning and ownership of the identity is negotiated and contested as much within the group as it is defined from outside the group.

People share some cultural practices but not others, they interpret symbols differently, and they disagree about the obligations attached to and meaning of their identities. Political, cultural, and social differences undermine consensus on group identity, group membership, and group collective behavior. These differences become salient when groups try to engage in collective action. If group members do not agree on how to behave, whom to believe, and what to value, they have problems working together. The same things that hold people together (such as shared values, shared goals, and shared space) can become the points along which the identity becomes contested, wrested, and rent. These border disputes become expressly contentious when people debate the most essential question of group membership. Who is or is not Chinese, Native American, or Polish American depends on who benefits from inclusion or exclusion (Chow 1993; Nagel 1994). In many cases it is an in-house authority, not an external majority group, who defines the group's boundaries and cultural stuff within it.

In this book, identity and solidarity are variables influenced by borders created by migrational differences (the crossing of space) and generational differences (the passage of time). These internal borders signified the "us" and the "them" within Chicago Polonia. The first border was between migrant cohorts. Similar to Mannheim's concept of generation, a cohort is a group of people who experience similar events in similar social settings at

1. In addition to majority-minority group relations, researchers have also focused on borders between minority groups. For example, group differences, and thus identities, become meaningful when minority groups compete for resources (Hannan 1979; Bodnar, Simon, and Weber 1982; Olzak 1986; Pfeffer 1994).

similar points in their life cycles. A result of this common experience is a sharing of "social and intellectual currents" (Mannheim 1952, 304). Factors that influence the characteristic of the migrant cohort include the events that precipitated the migration (for example, political or economic turmoil, forced or voluntary migration), the characteristics of the migrants (class, education, skills, gender, political alignments, religious affiliation, regional/urban/rural background), and the migration process (legal or illegal entry into the host country).[2] While not dismissing the fact that there are differences within the cohort, these factors related to the home country, migrant group, and host country produce shared experiences among migrants. The political and economic situation in the home country influences the types of people who leave; the policy (influenced by the political and economic situation) in the host country influences the types of immigrants it receives. Because the societies of the home and host countries are different at different time periods, the migration cohorts are different. This is especially true for groups who migrated centuries apart. For example, Polish peasants who came to the United States in the 1890s intending to work for a few years and return home shared different experiences than Polish political refugees who arrived in the 1980s. Moreover, cultural identities continually change so that cohorts who migrate in different time periods bring with them different understandings of their cultural and national identity.

The second internal group difference was between generational cohorts. While migrational differences are created over space, by moving from one location to another, generational differences are created by the passage of time. In America, ethnic generations are often discussed in terms of their "staying power" and, as a result, theories on generations are intertwined with theories on assimilation. Assimilationist theories argue that each successive generation adopts more characteristics of the host culture, so that those generations farther away from the immigration generation reflect fewer ethnic differences (Sandberg 1974; Gans 1979; Waters 1990; Alba 1990).[3] Yet, there are differences in how the identity changes over

2. Numerous studies examine these variables. See, for example, Greene 1975; Portes and Manning 1976; Portes, McLeod, and Parker 1978; Padgett 1980; di Leonardo 1984; Miller 1985; Pedraza-Bailey 1985; Luciuk 1986; Miller 1987; Shokeid 1988; Margolis 1990; Erdmans 1992b, 1995; Ogbu 1992; Hurtado, Gurin, and Peng 1994; Kibria 1994; Nee, Sanders, and Sernau 1994; Espiritu 1996.

3. In contrast, Hansen's theory argues that, while the second generation tries to distance itself from their parent's ethnic identity, the third generation returns to its ancestral heritage

generations—in both the rate of change and the nature of the transformation. The identity of each generation is influenced by characteristics of the migrant group and the sociohistorical contexts of the home and host countries (Handlin 1966; Morawska 1985 and 1990; Bodnar, Simon, Weber 1982; Radzilowski 1986; Glazer 1959 and 1990; Waters, 1995). There are also differences within generations: some members of the group retain or transform their identity differently than other members depending on their social networks within America (Rumbaut 1994; Waters, 1994; Zhou and Bankston 1994). These variations aside, we still pretty much agree that the first-generation immigrants will have a different identity than their third-generation grandchildren.

Migrations and Generations in Chicago Polonia

The three main Polish cohorts in Chicago during the 1980s were: (1) Polish Americans, people born in America whose ancestors were born in Poland; (2) World War II émigrés; and (3) new Polish immigrants. The generative sources of the Polish identity in America were both Poland and the United States. Two main differences—the Poland from which they emigrated and the causes that gave rise to their emigration—created diverse migrant cohorts. The Poles who emigrated in the late nineteenth and early twentieth centuries were mostly peasants seeking material gains. They came from a Poland that did not exist on the map; it was partitioned by Russia, Prussia, and Austria. The regional identities of the early immigrants were unified on American soil under the umbrella of Polishness as a national and cultural identity. The identity of second-generation Polish Americans evolved in the 1920s and 1930s into a working class, white, ethnic identity. By mid-century, when the World War II émigrés arrived, Polonia was composed of mostly

---

(1990 [1937]). The principle of the third generation was also introduced by Margaret Mead (1942) who stated it more generally as the notion that all generations react to the generation preceding them. Scholars have debated the validity of Hansen's theory of the third-generation return (Kivisto and Blanck 1990). Some seriously doubt that all second-generation children try to forget and that the third-generation children really try to remember (Handlin 1966; Glazer 1990). Others argue that ethnicity is transformed—not lost and regained—across generations (Nahirny and Fishman 1965; Greene 1990). And still others question what it is that the third generation was able to remember if the second generation so effectively divorced themselves from their heritage (Gans 1994).

second- and third-generation Polish Americans whose Polishness was based more on a cultural attachment to an ancestral rural homeland than a political attachment to the Polish nation. The World War II émigrés, in contrast, raised in an independent Poland (1919–39), and exiled by the war and the new communist regime in Warsaw, were fiercely nationalistic and highly politicized. Members from the World War II cohort and the Polish American community formed a working solidarity around their mutual distrust and hatred of communism. The World War II émigrés helped "revive" Polish ethnicity in the United States, a revival supported by the mood of cultural pluralism in the 1960s and 1970s and legislation that distributed state resources along racial and ethnic lines. In reaction to the appearance of gains made by other minorities, Polish Americans lobbied for their own bigger "piece of the pie." The experiences of the Polish American and World War II émigré cohorts are discussed in Chapter 1, which describes the construction of the Polish American identity in the early and mid-twentieth century.

The third cohort, the newest Polish immigrants, arrived after 1960, and the majority came in the late 1970s and 1980s. These Poles, most of them highly educated with professional and technical skills, emigrated from communist Poland for economic and political reasons. Chapter 2 explains the events surrounding the formation and subsequent repression of the Solidarity opposition movement in Poland and other factors that precipitated the newest emigration. It also describes the members of this newest cohort, focusing on the heterogeneity within it. Three types of newcomers arrived: permanent immigrants admitted under numerical limitations, political refugees, and temporary migrants working illegally in the United States on tourist visas (referred to in Chicago Polonia as *wakacjusze*, which means vacationers). These newcomers had different routes of incorporation into American and Polish American communities (explained in part by their legal status at entry), and different patterns of collective action for the homeland (conditioned by premigration biographies).

The two most distinct groups in Polonia in the 1980s were the later-generation Polish Americans and the newest Polish immigrants. They differed along four dimensions: culture, networks, power, and national loyalty. First, while both groups claimed possession of a name ("Polish"), the meaning of this identity differed. Chapter 3 examines the cultural differences that resulted from having been raised in communist Poland versus having been raised in the strong anticommunist climate that characterized American society from 1950 to 1990. Experiences stemming from communist and capitalist-democratic social systems shaped the frames through which each group interpreted each other's behavior. For example, Polish immigrants, having left a highly centralized state bureaucracy defined the Polish American Congress as "autocratic," while for Polish Americans, the structure of this organization presented no problem. Furthermore, as Americans, many Polish Americans revered self-reliance and thereby defined state resources such as welfare as a public and private ill. New Polish immigrants had a different understanding of the relationship between the state and its citizens, one that did not define state support as dependency. Because their symbolic meaning systems did not always overlap, the two groups had problems working together and new immigrants created their own organizations instead of joining the established ethnic organizations.

A second difference between later-generation Polish Americans and new Polish immigrants was related to the fact that the former were ethnics and as such were established members of American society, while the latter were immigrants and, therefore, newcomers. Each group had different needs, resources, and networks. Comparatively, the immigrants had weaker ties in America and the ethnics had weaker connections to Poland. The needs of each group were related to their desire to strengthen these weak attachments. The immigrants needed networks that gave them information about American housing, schools, jobs, and city bus routes. In contrast, ethnic needs were linked to their generational distance from the ancestral homeland. Ethnics worked to maintain a positive attachment to their ancestry through cultural programs that promoted the continuance of traditions, and political agendas that advanced the status of the ethnic group in America. The interests of the immigrant and ethnic were at times contradictory. For example, the immigrant needed to learn English; the ethnic tried to learn Polish. This was another reason the two groups had problems coexisting in the same organizations. Chapter 3 shows that immigrants were not attracted to Polish American organizations that were set up to satisfy ethnic, rather than immigrant, needs. Immigrants wanted the Polonian organizations to help them find jobs; the ethnic organizations more often spent their moneys on folkdance groups and antidefamation programs.

The immigrant-ethnic distinction was also important because it influenced networks and resources. The immigrants had stronger ties—concrete and personal—to Poland; conversely, the ethnics had stronger connections to American institutions. This difference was not always problematic; in fact, it facilitated cooperative relations when immigrants and ethnics were working together for Poland's independence. For example, the immigrants' informal networks helped to smuggle money to the underground opposition in Poland, while the ethnics' institutional ties were more useful for lobbying activities in the United States. Chapter 4 shows how the two groups were able to work together precisely because they had different networks that gave them different resources to share. Each cohort had different types of information, membership bases, and legitimacy created by their generational and migrational locations. Ethnics used preexisting formal organizations and established ties to the ethnic community in America, the Roman Catholic Church, and the national Solidarity union in Poland. In contrast, new immigrants had informal networks to regional and local opposition circles in Poland, and they relied on personal ties for getting money and supplies into Poland. The new immigrants were also more closely tied to the new immigrant community in Chicago than were the Polish Americans.

The third difference between the two groups was that the established group had more power than the newcomer group. The incorporation of new immigrants into America was influenced by the presence of this established ethnic group. The ethnic group that already existed claimed "ownership" of the ethnicity. "Fighting for independence" describes the community's collective efforts on behalf of Poland as well as the new immigrants' fight to negotiate their own space and position in Chicago Polonia. This drive for independence was at times troublesome. Chapter 5 describes the rancorous power struggles that ensued when the new immigrants challenged the representational authority of the Polish American leaders. This challenge was present when the immigrants engaged in independent lobbying activities advocating policies that contradicted those of the established lobby, when they publicly criticized the Polonian leaders for being inept, and when they engaged in protest behaviors in the Chicago arena that the established ethnics did not sanction.

Finally, the two groups differed in terms of national loyalty, with each group favoring its country of birth. In Chapter 6 this difference is analyzed with data from the June 1989 Polish election in Chicago. This election, the first partially free election since World War II, allowed Poles abroad to participate by absentee ballot. Voting abroad was an immigrant activity, not an ethnic activity. The Polish election excluded Polish Americans because they were American citizens. In this arena, the hybrid Polish American ethnic identity was not meaningful; when discussing national loyalty one was supposed to be either a Pole or an American. Public discussion focused on the meaning of these political identities to determine who was an

American and who could and should vote. Should naturalized U.S. citizens participate in another country's election or did this threaten their loyalty to America? The election was clearly an immigrant activity, so even though both established ethnics and new immigrants supported the social reforms in Poland, it was the new immigrants who mobilized the voters and attracted political and media attention. In contrast to other times when new immigrants vied for leadership positions, during the elections, the immigrants' positions of authority caused little conflict or competition between the two groups. This was because nativity separated the two groups during the election, whereas at other times the umbrella of ethnicity brought them together and increased the potential for competition.

Despite their differences in culture, networks, power and loyalty, the groups still tried to work together, and sometimes did so successfully. As shown in the Conclusion, working collective identities were formed along the lines of generations and migrations. First, there was solidarity across migrant cohorts. For example, the veterans from the World War II émigré cohort worked closely with the Solidarity activists in the newest migrant cohort. These two groups shared a history of political activism, the experience of migration, and the experience of entering an already established community. Second, there was solidarity through the generations. Third and fourth-generation Polish Americans were linked through memories to their grandparents. In this concluding chapter, I also argue that ethnicity is a behaviorally meaningful identity for later-generation "white ethnics." Participation in ethnic organizations and collective action for the homeland were indications that ethnicity still mattered; it structured social activities, networks, and political interests.

Methods and Setting

Data for this study were gathered through interviews, archival resources, participant observation, and surveys (see Appendix, Table A.1). Between 1987 and 1989, I interviewed fifty-nine people, forty-five of whom were Polish immigrants and Polish Americans from all three cohorts active in Polonian organizations in Chicago (the other fourteen interviewees were new immigrant activists in California, and Americans with no Polish descent involved in refugee resettlement organizations in Chicago). I also used archival information from the *Dziennik Związkowy* (the Chicago Polish daily newspaper), and the Connecticut Polish American Archive and Manuscript Collection located at Central Connecticut State University, as well as organizational newsletters, documents, annual statements, and letters. Finally, I was a participant observer in the community from 1986 through 1990. I attended demonstrations, weddings, political rallies, symposiums, conferences, planning meetings, public forums, balls, religious events, parades, and festivals. Sometimes I was simply an observer, at other times I was a participant. I taught English to Polish immigrants, carried money to underground Solidarity members, helped new immigrants recertify university degrees, wrote letters to politicians, and recorded minutes at organizational meetings. I also conducted four surveys in different arenas to collect data on new Polish immigrants. These surveys are discussed in detail in Chapter 2.

I report the names of my respondents when the information was in a public document, when the respondent's identity could be deduced from the context (such as the president of an organization in a particular year), or when the informants gave me permission to use their names. Most fieldwork conversations were not conducted with the explicit understanding that I would use their names (so I do not), and many formal interviews were conducted on the condition of anonymity. Some respondents even asked me to turn off the tape recorder at times when they wanted to say something particularly sensitive (for example, about how money was smuggled into Poland) or damning of another person. The leaders of Polish American organizations most often granted me open interviews, and because they were public leaders of these organizations I report their names. It would be my preference to use no personal names because, as a sociologist, I want to emphasize social categories (immigrant versus ethnic), cultural identities (Pole versus Polish American), and organizational positions (leader versus member). I do not believe that it mattered as much that Kazimierz Lukomski or Jaroslaw Cholodecki did or said something as much as it mattered that one was a World War II émigré and the other a Solidarity refugee. Yet, many leaders of organizations are well known in Polonia and therefore it made sense to use their names, especially because historians are more grateful to us sociologists when we do so.

During my fieldwork I had more daily contact with new immigrants than Polish Americans. I danced, demonstrated, and debated with the new immigrants. Because their organizations were newer and less formally organized, they had limited archival information and organizational documents. In contrast, the organizational documentation and historical information were more extensive for the established ethnic community, but I had fewer face-to-face interactions with Polish Americans, and those that I did have tended to be in formal interview settings. The formal interviews were all tape-recorded. I also took copious field notes and many of the informal conversations were recorded as direct quotations (rather than as reported speech). (I learned this method from Howard Becker who convinced me that I did have a tape recorder in my head.) Unless another reference is given, all quotes come from these interviews. Most of the interviews and conversations were in English. My Polish improved over the years, but I basically learned Polish *na ulicy* (on the streets), so I speak broken Polish. (I read much better than I can speak, and I understand a lot more than I can say.) Some of the conversations were in extremely poor broken English or in both English and Polish, and these are most often paraphrased in the text. When I use direct quotations of English conversations, I present them in the exact language spoken—which means they often contain grammatical mistakes or jumbled idioms (one immigrant spoke of being "pissed up" instead of "pissed off"). I debated about doing this because I thought that it unfairly and inaccurately presented these immigrants as being uneducated. It is I, however, who was intellectually deficient. If I had spoken Polish more fluently I could have interviewed them in Polish and they would have sounded as educated as they really are. I decided to reproduce the quotations as is because they appropriately illustrate one of my main theoretical points—that immigrants are newcomers to a society and this status is a handicap (in this case because they had

Table I.1 Polish population in Illinois, 1980 and 1990

Population	1980	1990
Total Polish ancestry in Illinois	892,009	962,827
Total Polish foreign-born in Illinois	64,293	80,594
Percent of total U.S. Polish ancestry in Illinois	10.8	10.3
Percent of total U.S. Polish foreign-born in Illinois	15.4	20.8

SOURCES: U.S. Census of the Population, 1980: Ancestry of the Population by State, 12, 17; U.S. Census of the Population, 1990: Detailed Ancestry Groups for States, 3, 15; U.S. Census of the Population, 1990: The Foreign-Born Population in the United States, 11; U.S. Census of the Population, 1980: Detailed Population Characteristics, 1–9; U.S. Census of the Population, 1990, Social and Economic Characteristics, Illinois, 102; U.S. Census of the Population, 1980, Characteristics of the Population, General Social and Economic Characteristics, Illinois, 15–88; U.S. Census of the Population and Housing, 1990, Summary Tape File 1A.

to negotiate social relations in a new language). Finally, while I use diacritical marks on words in Polish, they do not appear in the more frequently used Polish proper names or cities.

Chicago Polonia provided a rich arena for the study of relationships between immigrants and ethnics because it has a long history of Polish immigration and one of the largest concentrations of Polish Americans. According to the 1980 Census, almost 8.2 million people in America reported some Polish ancestry, and in the 1990 Census 9.3 million people did. Roughly 10 percent of this population lives in Illinois, mostly in the Chicago metropolitan area (see Table I.1). Since 1960, roughly 350,000 legal Polish immigrants and refugees have immigrated to America, and Chicago is still the principal city of attraction for these new arrivals. From 1960 to 1980 Chicago had the largest number of foreign-born Poles of any Standard Metropolitan Statistical Area (Kromkowski, 1990, 23). In 1987, 24 percent of all new Polish immigrants listed Chicago as their intended city of residency; the next highest was New York City with 13 percent (*Statistical Yearbook of the INS,* 1987, 38). By 1990, one-fifth of the Polish foreign-born population lived in Illinois (see Table I.1). Because of its dense established Polish community and the continued influx of newcomers, Chicago was a fertile context for this study of relations between established Polish American ethnics and new Polish immigrants.

Chicago Polonia was also the ideal setting for the study of Polonian organizations because many organizations have their headquarters in Chicago. Most of the important Polonian organizations working for Poland's independence were located in Chicago: the largest Polish fraternal organizations, the Polish American political lobby organization (the Polish American Congress), and several new immigrant organizations. Furthermore, there is a Polish consul general in Chicago that provided a setting to study political activity ranging from protest behavior to voting behavior. This study focused on political organizations working on Poland's behalf. Because I wanted to understand how voluntary groups *with common goals* worked together, the organizations selected for study all had the goal of "helping Poland" as one of their founding principles. Political action for Poland was one arena that brought new immigrants and established ethnics into contact with each other and made the internal borders visible and salient.

1

Polishness in Twentieth-Century America

Our duty as Americans, our duty to our forefathers, who helped build this wonderful country, is—as we helped America be America—to help Poland be Poland.
    —Aloysius Mazewski, president of Polish American Congress, 1988

We fall into the category of being white, but we don't reap the benefits of being white.
        —a third-generation Polish American

Poles have been immigrating to the United States for over one hundred years, and the characteristics of each migrant cohort have changed as a result of changes in Poland. Each new migrant cohort aged into an ethnic cohort whose identity was continually recast to fit the changing American context. When new Polish immigrants began arriving in the 1960s they met an established community of Polish American ethnics whose identity welcomed a sentimental attachment to an ancestral Poland, a social attachment to American institutions, and a political attachment to the United States. Before I begin the historical accounting of the construction of the Polish American identity in the twentieth century, I want to make two assumptions explicit: (1) ethnic identification is a process in which the individual participates, and (2) this process is embedded in and influenced by a sociohistorical context.

Kathleen Neils Conzen and her colleagues have noted:

> [E]thnicity is to be understood as a cultural construction accomplished over historical time. Ethnic groups in modern settings are

constantly recreating themselves, and ethnicity is constantly being reinvented in response to changing realities both within the group and the host society. Ethnic group boundaries for example must be repeatedly renegotiated, while expressive symbols of ethnicity (ethnic traditions) must be repeatedly reinterpreted. (Conzen et al. 1990, 38)

Yet, cultural identities and shared symbols alone are not sufficient to ensure the emergence of an ethnic group. Patterson argues that members of a cultural group can unconsciously share symbols (such as language or religious beliefs) without being or becoming an ethnic group; and individuals can perform culinary rituals and hold values similar to those the ethnic group cherishes without being or becoming a member of that group. Ethnic allegiance requires a conscious sense of belonging, it is a "condition wherein certain members of a society, in a given social context, choose to emphasize as their most meaningful basis of primary extrafamilial identity certain assumed cultural, national and somatic traits" (1975, 308). Simply possessing certain physical or cultural features is not sufficient; ethnicity must be claimed. The individual must, at minimum, choose to be a member of an ethnic group (Patterson 1975; Yancey, Eriksen, and Juliano 1976; Yinger 1994, 4–5). Often this choice is reflected in participation in shared activities such as the ethnic organizations described in this study.

People construct an ethnic identity within specific sociohistoric contexts. In America, ethnic identity emerges from the initial interaction between the immigrant homeland culture and American society, and later interactions between the ethnic subculture and the dominant society. These interactions are influenced by the receptivity of American society at the time of arrival and during maturation (including patterns of nativism or forced assimilation), the "foreignness" of the new arrivals (along with hostility from dominant or other minority groups and discriminatory practices), the size and rate of immigration flows, the economic and political conditions in the home country (which shape the demographics of the migrant cohort) and America (which affect occupational incorporation and state resources), the process of entering the United States (including immigration laws and policies), and migrant group networks (which determine the intramural resources available to new immigrants and are in part determined by the length of time the group has been in America).[1] Ethnic

---

1. Numerous scholars have analyzed these variables (Handlin 1966; Bonacich 1972; Higham 1973; Bodnar, Simon, and Weber 1982; di Leonardo 1984; Bukowczyk 1984; Padilla

identities are expressions of how the migrant group and its generations fit into American society. This fitting-in varies across ethnic groups and time periods. The theoretical literature itself reflects changes in the process over time. In early assimilation literature, the endpoint to the assimilation process was a nondistinguishable, unhyphenated American (Thomas and Znaniecki 1958 [1918]; Handlin 1952; Gordon 1964). This straight-line theory of assimilation was challenged during the period of cultural plural-ism (Glazer and Moynihan 1970; Novak 1971; Vecoli 1973; Gans 1979), and rejected after the arrival of the new post-1965 wave of immigrants from Asia and Latin America.[2] Social scientists now question whether ethnics fully abandoned or lost their distinctness; whether there was a consistent, identifiable, monolithic American identity; and, if there was such an identity, what were its components? (Kazal 1995).

The point is, on arrival in America immigrants are not yet ethnics. They bring with them a homeland culture that they use to construct an American ethnic identity within a changing sociohistoric context. The construction of the Polish American identity in the twentieth century was an agent-directed, socially bound process influenced by the characteristics of the migrant cohorts, the process of migration, and the social, economic, and political conditions in the United States.

From Regional to National Identity

During the largest wave of Polish emigration, from 1870 and 1914, Poland did not appear on the map as a distinct political entity. By 1795, Poland's neighbors had carved her into three parts: Prussia controlled the Western

---

1985; Pedraza-Bailey 1985; Portes and Bach 1985; Nagel 1986, 1994; Olzak 1986; Portes and Manning 1986; Massey 1987; Conzen et al. 1990; Morawska 1990; Baganha 1991; Hein 1993; Fernandez-Kelly and Schauffler 1994; Rumbaut 1994; Zhou and Bankston 1994; Waters 1995).

2. See work by Alejandro Portes and colleagues. They replaced the term "assimilation" with "incorporation" and showed that immigrants do not all follow the same route of incorporation into America. See, for example, Portes and Manning's concept of immigrant enclaves (1986), Bonacich's concept of middlemen minorities (1973), and the current concept of "segmented assimilation" in the winter 1994 issue of the *International Migration Review*, devoted to the second-generation Latino and Asian post-1965 immigration. Scholars have also looked at how identities were transformed (rather than "lost") into political identities (Portes and Rumbaut 1990, chap. 7; Nagel 1995) and pan-generic identities (Enloe 1981; Alba 1990).

regions and the Northern Baltic provinces, Austria ruled the Southeastern corner of Poland known as Galicia, and Empress Catherine of Russia seized the largest area, the Northeastern regions and the central basin of Poland, which included the Congress Kingdom (the ethnographic Poland of the Russian Partition).[3] Prior to World War I, an estimated 1.5 million Poles immigrated to America from these partitioned lands.[4] The largest number of Polish immigrants came from the Russian Partition, which encompassed over 85 percent of Poland's former lands and 59 percent of its population (Table 1.1). This migration was mostly the movement of labor—Poles left places with fewer jobs and moved to cities that had more jobs. Many were transoceanic migrant workers who came intending to work for a few years and then return home. Estimates are that one-half to one-third of the Poles who came to America between 1901 and 1914 returned to Poland (Brozek 1985, 234; Walaszek 1992; Pilch 1975).

During the second half of the 1800s, all three Partitions were undergoing transformation from feudalistic traditional societies to societies with modern, money-based economies. Land reform, emancipation, agricultural modernization, and industrialization influenced the supply of land, jobs, and labor. Emigration from the Prussian Partition began in the 1870s, but slowed down considerably by 1900 when the mining and industrial districts of Silesia and the Ruhr basin were sufficiently developed to absorb surplus peasant labor. The Poles from the Russian and Austrian regions began

3. The Congress Kingdom appeared in the Russian Partition between 1815 and 1864 as a semi-autonomous territory, yet it was still under Russian rule (Davies 1982, 81–111).

4. The exact number is difficult to determine because of Poland's partitioned status. Lopata (1976, 34–42) and Brozek (1985, 34–43) provide detailed analyses of the methods and problems of recording Polish immigration, with comparative estimates of the immigrant population from various sources; for example, church statistics, Polish authorities, and the U.S. Census Bureau (see also Pinkowski 1978; Zubrzycki 1953; Kantowicz 1977). Poland was first listed in a separate column in the U.S. Census in 1860, but it did not appear as a major country in the American Immigration Bureau's annual report until 1885. From 1825 to 1898 the U.S. Immigration Statistics registered persons from the former areas of Poland as Poles, but from 1898 to 1918 it registered them as coming from their country of partition (Zubrzycki 1953, 248–50). For these reasons, scholars believe that the statistics underrepresent the number of Poles in America (Zubrzycki 1953; Lopata 1976; Bobinska 1975). In contrast, Brozek argues that estimates often overrepresent the number of ethnic Poles who settled in America because they do not take into account other minorities from Poland or those Poles who returned to Poland. He argues that the total immigration from Poland was 1.9 million, of which only 1.5 million stayed, and of this 1.5 million, only one million were ethnic Poles (1985, 37). The largest groups of misclassified others were Ukrainians and Jews. The problems of inaccurate estimates have a compounding effect on the estimates of subsequent generations of Polish Americans, making these numbers dubious as well.

Table 1.1 Polish immigration to the United States by partition, 1891–1914

	Prussian	Russian	Austrian	Totals
1891–94	53,800	79,796	—	133,596
1895–99	12,571	36,517	44,484	93,572
1900–1904	16,133	149,959	143,261	309,353
1905–9	14,494	242,276	211,216	467,986
1910–14	21,711	332,696	226,881	581,288
Total number	118,709	841,244	625,842	1,585,795
Percentage	7.5	53	39.5	100
Percent ethnic Poles by partition*	8.9	58.9	32.2	100

*Refers to the distribution of ethnic Poles in each of the partitions according to an 1897 census (Pinkowski 1978, 310–11). Source of immigration statistics: Brozek 1985, 233.

emigrating *en masse* in the 1890s. The lack of industrial development in Galicia (the Austrian Partition) forced many peasants to look for work outside the region. The metal and textiles industries in the Congress Kingdom provided some employment until the Russo-Japan war and the 1905 Russian revolution interrupted industrial and economic development (Golab 1977, 98; Zubrzycki 1953, 252). Countries like the United States that industrialized more rapidly attracted cheap labor from countries that had proletarianized peasants faster than they could give them work. Poles came to America because of the abundance of jobs, the higher wages, and the receptive immigration laws.[5]

The overwhelming majority of Polish migrants came from rural areas and had been agricultural and low-skilled wage laborers.[6] They were often labeled "land-hungry" or *za chlebem* ("for bread") immigrants. Still, not all migrants were peasants seeking material gains; Poles also emigrated to escape religious, political, and cultural persecution. Emigration from Prus-

5. American industries offered higher wages, more than double what the peasant-worker could find for seasonal or migrant work in Eastern Europe (see Morawska [1985, 68] and the immigrants' letters in Thomas and Znaniecki [1958]). Even the declining economy in America in 1890 did not dissuade prospective immigrants, though it did increase reemigration back to Poland (Brozek 1985, 25).

6. Between 70 and 80 percent of Eastern Europeans emigrating between 1880 and 1914 were from rural areas (Morawska 1985, 72; Lopata 1964, 204). The occupational breakdown for Galicians from the Austrian Partition between 1902 and 1911 was 33 percent independent farmers (peasants), 43 percent agricultural day laborers, 17 percent servants, and 7 percent skilled workers (Bukowczyk 1987, 11 and 26). In 1908, two-thirds of all Poles leaving Galicia were agricultural workers or day-laborers; only 6.6 percent were trained craftsmen (Bodner 1982, 40).

sian Poland was influenced by the *Kulturkampf*, or Germanization program, introduced by Bismarck in the 1870s as an attack on Catholics and Poles. The *Kulturkampf* suppression of religious institutions encouraged Polish Catholics, especially clergy, to emigrate. In the Russian region, Polish revolutionaries, mostly gentry or intelligentsia, fled from the political persecution that followed the failed insurrections of 1830 and 1863, the Russification program that intensified after 1864, and the failed socialist revolution in 1905. (In contrast to the other two partitioning powers, Austria's Hapsburg regime imposed no culturalization programs and the migrants from this region came almost exclusively for economic reasons.) The *Kulturkampf* and Russification program served to strengthen Polish identity in those regions. Zubrzycki argues that the *Kulturkampf* encouraged Polish nationalism in Prussian Poland; therefore, the Poles who emigrated from this region were more nationalistic than the Poles from Galicia who "were simply land-hungry peasants fleeing from an overpopulated country" (1953, 254). Similarly, Matthew Frye Jacobson argues that the numerous rebellions and uprisings in the Russian region led to "a highly politicized view of Polish culture" and the tendency "to guard cultural *Polskość*, or Polishness, as a political treasure" (1995, 34–35).

Émigrés from the Prussian and Russian regions, especially the intelligentsia, revolutionaries, and clergy, built the institutional base of Polish communities in America; in particular, the Roman Catholic parishes and larger voluntary social organizations (Brozek 1985; Parot 1981).[7] They became Polonian leaders because they were the earliest group to arrive, they were educated and nationalistic, and they were more often permanent settlers rather than the peasant transoceanic migrant workers. Many of these Polonian leaders organized efforts to support Poland's struggle for independence. These efforts began in the émigré communities of Europe, but

---

7. Exiles from the 1830 revolution included Henryk Kalussowski, founder of the first political organization, the Society of Poles in America (1842), as well as two hundred émigrés who formed the Polish Committee (Pienkos 1984, 47). Exiles from the 1863 revolution included Reverend Vincent Barzynski, the informal leader of the Polish Roman Catholic Union; Erazm Jerzmanowski, founder of the National League; Jan Lipski, founding member of the Polish Commune and the Polish National Alliance (PNA); and Wladyslaw Dyniewicz, founder of the Polish Chicago newspaper *Gazeta Polska*. Two other exiles from the 1863 revolution, while not residing in America, played significant roles in the émigré community's fight for Polish independence: Agaton Giller who was known as the "spiritual founder" of the PNA (Parot 1981, 33); and Zygmunt Milkowski, the leader of the Polish League and founding member of the PNA's *Skarb Narodowy* (National Treasury). Finally, a host of socialist intellectuals held offices in several Polish fraternal organizations.

by the late 1870s émigrés were increasingly interested in the resources of the burgeoning American Polonia, which because of its size, wealth, and potential influence became known as the Fourth Partition (after the Austrian, Prussian, and Russian Partitions).

To better mobilize the large immigrant population, the Polonian leaders undertook efforts to nurture the peasants' embryonic national identity. The Polish peasant's geographical identity was centered in the local parish or region (*Galicja, Podhale, Masowsze*), rather than in the more abstract concept of a nation (Brozek 1985, 170–85; Bobinska 1975; Pula 1995, 22). When the peasants arrived at ports of entry they often answered the question about country of origination by naming their village, parish, or region; when pressed they gave the name of the partitioning power (for example, Russia or Austria); and even when the conversation was carried on in Polish they seldom said that they were Polish (Bobinska 1975). While the gentry and intelligentsia thought of themselves as members of the Polish nation, believing that Polishness was both a political and cultural identity, the peasants were more likely to define Polishness as a linguistic and religious (Roman Catholic) cultural identity (Thomas and Znaniecki 1958, 1432–43). The religious and cultural identity were tightly intertwined. Jacobson writes that in "the vernacular of the Polish peasant Catholicism was frequently referred to as 'the Polish faith' just as speaking the Polish language was speaking 'in Catholic' (*po katolicku*)" (1995, 68).

Political exiles working for Poland's independence believed that in order to mobilize the resources of the peasant masses abroad they had to first transform the peasants' local and cultural identity into a national identity based on a shared history and national rights, and focus vague sentiments for the homeland into clear feelings of obligation for a nation-state. This intention is illustrated in a letter written in 1879 by Agaton Giller, an exile from the 1863 uprising, from the headquarters of the Polish Government-in-Exile in Switzerland titled "Letter on the Organization of Poles in America" (reprinted in Park and Miller 1921, 135–37). Giller believed it was the responsibility of the intelligentsia in emigration to direct the peasant immigrant's national consciousness that "originates in him spontaneously in a foreign country in consequence of the feeling of the striking difference between his speech, his customs, his conceptions, from those of the people who surround him" and transform it into a national identity. The feeling of being a foreigner provoked in the immigrants an awareness of their own identity as Poles; that is, in the presence of the Other as non-Pole, the immigrant developed a sense of Self as Pole. Jacobson adds that immigrant nationalism developed out of the experience of "departure and absence" from the homeland (1995, 2). The nostalgic longing for green pastures, friendly faces, and familiar tongues transformed "homeland" into a larger, broader concept. The immigrant as Pole in contrast to non-Pole and the homeland as nation in contrast to region both nourished the emergence of a national consciousness.

The political exiles were interested in cultivating the seeds of this national identity in order to provide a more secure base for patriotic sentiment and action for the homeland. They also were aware that the majority of the immigrants were far more concerned with day-to-day survival than Poland's independence. Thomas and Znaniecki noted that, for the peasant immigrant, Poland "is mainly the object of an almost purely aesthetic interest whose motive power is very small as compared with the many and complex practical interests connected with the immediate social environment" (1958, 1582).[8] To satisfy both the abstract political goals and concrete immigrant needs, Giller suggested that Polonia create an organization that "while serving the purposes of the Polish cause, will be not only useful but indispensable for the private interests of every one of its members" (Park and Miller 1921, 136). Toward this end, Polish American leaders founded national fraternal benefit associations that provided incentives to join in the form of accident and life insurance, the premiums from which served to finance the political activities for the homeland. By the turn of the century there were fifteen fraternal organizations, and another seven were established in the first three decades of this century. The three largest were the Polish National Alliance (PNA), founded in 1880, the Polish Roman Catholic Union (PRCU), founded in 1873, and the Polish Falcons of America (Falcons), founded in 1894. Immigrants joined these fraternal benefit associations because they needed the insurance and they wanted to participate in the social life of local lodges.[9] The leaders,

8. Jacobson disagrees. He argues that nationalism was present in immigrant communities—in their presses, their religion, their theater, and their fairs and festivals. This pervasiveness, he offers, suggests that "the distinction between 'bread-and-butter' issues and 'ideological' issues is at best misleading; nationalism surfaced and resurfaced in a myriad of cultural forms, infusing a wide variety of social activities" (1995, 92).

9. Immigrants needed insurance. First, immigrants were usually hired to work on a weekly or part-time basis (Bodnar et al. 1982), thereby relieving owners of social responsibility to their employees. Second, immigrants worked in high-risk industries, such as steel mills, coal mines, oil refineries, textile and meat packing industries, that increased chances of illness and

however, used these organizations to unite the immigrant community, strengthen the Polish identity, and advance their collective goals.

Polonian leaders at that time were engaged in a spirited debate over the meaning of Polishness. Polish priests defined "Polishness" along religious lines, while political leaders defined it as a national identity. Victor Greene argues in *For God and Country* (1975) that the schism between the religionists and nationalists contributed to developing the awareness of Self as Pole. The conflict surrounding this struggle called attention to and created a discussion about Polishness and increased ethnic awareness. The intracommunity struggle over who owned the parish and its property, and the discussion over whether one was a Catholic Pole or a Polish Catholic contributed to their identification as Poles. Regional and parish identities began to weaken as the new ethnic identity took shape.

This split was illustrated in the two largest fraternal organizations. The Polish National Alliance (PNA) stressed the secular definition of Polishness, thereby accepting as members any immigrants from partitioned Poland—Polish Jews, schismatics, nonbelievers, socialists, Ruthenians, and Lithuanians (Thomas and Znaniecki 1958, 1632). It also initially adopted a "Romanticist" ideology that called for Poland's national liberation from Russia, by armed revolution if necessary (Jacobson 1995, 37). In contrast, the Polish Roman Catholic Union (PRCU) was heavily influenced by the Roman Catholic clergy and espoused a "Positivist" ideology that divorced statehood from nationhood, declaring that a nation of Poles existed wherever Poles maintained their linguistic and religious ties. Thomas and Znaniecki wrote that when this Positivist attitude was transferred to America it meant "the preservation of the cultural integrity of Polish-American colonies—language, religion, mores—but no participation at all in the political life of Poland" (1958, 1603). The Positivists believed a Polish nation would survive through the economic, educational, and social development of a Polish peoplehood. In other words, nationhood was not a political state, and thus Poland need not be militarily wrested from its aggressors (Jacobson 1995, 37). The clergy behind the PRCU wanted to unify Polonia under the banner of Polish culture (with a language and religious base), and for this reason the PRCU accepted only Roman

---

accidents (Bodnar 1981; Slayton 1986; Pula 1995, 46). Moreover, commercial insurance companies discriminated against Eastern and Southern European immigrants because they were in high-risk jobs (Erdmans 1997).

Catholics and ethnic Poles as members and objected to the PNA's "secular definition of Polishness" (Renkiewicz 1980, 119).[10]

This political versus cultural debate over the meaning of Polishness mirrored the divisions within the independence movement in the partitioned lands. The radical and conservative wings had different ideas of who was a Pole and what an independent Poland would look like. Roman Dmowski and the National Democrats (the conservative right) wanted to liberate Poland's Prussian and Austrian regions and reunite them with the Congress Kingdom. They opposed national independence, yet wanted a separate and autonomous ethnic Poland that excluded the eastern Russian-ruled territories of Lithuania and Byelorussia (Davies 1982, 52–53). For Dmowski, the main enemy was Germany but Russia was a potential ally. In contrast, the radical leftists, led by Jozef Pilsudski, wanted an independent Polish nation. For them, Russia was the main enemy. They believed that a free Poland would include everyone (not just ethnic Poles). Polishness would be a nationality, not just an ethnicity, and the geopolitical borders of the independent state would constitute the boundaries of the Polish national identity.

American Polonia was initially split along the Pilsudski-Dmowski divide. Between 1895–1904, the PNA donated $24,000 to the Dmowski-backed Government-in-Exile. After the failed 1905 Russian revolution, an increased number of socialist exiles (who were often Pilsudski supporters) joined the PNA. With the tension surrounding the Balkan War in 1912, leaders from both the Falcons and the PNA formed the pro-Pilsudski National Defense Committee, and the more conservative Polonian leaders formed the pro-Dmowski Polish National Council. At the 1913 convention, the PNA decided to give all the money in the National Council treasury ($40,000) to the Pilsudski-led Provisional Committee of Confederated Parties for Polish Independence (Pienkos 1984, 84–85). In that same year, Ignacy Paderewski, a renowned Polish pianist, composer, and statesman toured American Polonia as a spokesman for Dmowski. During World War I, American

---

10. Thomas and Znaniecki argued that both the political and religious leaders were primarily motivated by self-interest. Both groups wanted to unify Polonia to build their own power base in America. The PNA was more nationalistic and believed an independent Poland would give the Polish community in America more clout; the PRCU wanted the community unified to strengthen the Polish parish. As events in Eastern Europe heated up in the beginning of the century and a Polish national identity became more visible, the PRCU could not ignore the immigrants' interest in the fate of the Polish nation and eventually engaged in its own patriotic actions for the homeland (1958, 1593–1609).

leaders in Washington, D.C., embraced both Paderewski and Dmowski. Subsequently, PNA and Falcon leaders withdrew support for the Pilsudski Provisional Committee and joined the pro-Dmowski National Council. At the time that World War I broke out, the Dmowski National Council, the PNA, the PRCU, and the Falcons all supported the Allies and sought Polish nationhood through diplomacy rather than military intervention. Only the socialists were left in the Pilsudski Committee, and they supported the Central Powers. Polonia's switch from Pilsudski to Dmowski was influenced by American politics. Russia and America were allies, and Germany was their common enemy. Once America entered the war, Polonia aligned itself with American policy.

In the first decade of the twentieth century, Polonia was still an immigrant community. It was composed primarily of peasants with a few aristocrats, some intelligentsia but mostly illiterates, bands of socialists, and hordes of Catholics. The heterogeneity within the community reflected the heterogeneity in Poland. Most of its members were foreign-born and maintained a loyalty to the homeland (either as sentimental ties or political obligations). The organizations served political homeland needs as well as material and social immigrant needs. Polish was the primary language for the media, theater, organizations, churches, and schools. This immigrant community slowly changed after World War I. Just as the Dmowski-Pilsudski debate was decided by American foreign interests, as American Polonia matured into an ethnic community, its identity was increasingly defined by an American, rather than a homeland, orientation.

From Immigrant to Ethnic Community

The immigrants, especially the temporary migrant workers and political émigrés, faced homeward. In contrast, the ethnic community was oriented more toward America. The transition from immigrant to ethnic involved both detaching themselves from the homeland and reconstructing a place for themselves in the new land. The process of detachment was buttressed by Poland's newly established statehood, pressures from American reformers, legislators, and educators, and the maturation of the second generation. The Polish Americans carved out a place for themselves in the United States as white, hard-working, religious, and disciplined people who celebrated a folk-based cultural attachment to their ancestors, but who maintained a political loyalty to America. It was from the more secure status as white American citizens that Polish Americans became ethnics.

Poland was granted statehood in 1919 at the Paris Peace Conference that formally ended World War I. Thereafter, Polonia became less involved in Poland's affairs. It became more difficult for Polonian organizations to claim any sort of role in Polish affairs once an independent government had been established in Warsaw (Brozek 1985, 184–92). Moreover, Poland as a political entity complicated matters for Poles trying to construct an American identity (advocates of Americanization discouraged allegiances to a foreign power). The National Department, a Polonian organization created in 1916 to assist Poland during the war, sent this recommendation to the 5th Emigration Congress in Detroit in 1925.

> The sphere of our affairs in this country must not have its center of gravity in Poland, precisely because Poland has gained her independence. We must readjust our attachment to Poland in such a way as to not lose our Polishness and preserve it for the future generations, but, on the other hand, to avoid the charge that we are not loyal citizens of the United States. (Quoted in Brozek 1985, 186)

As American citizens, they had more difficulty supporting Poland once it became a nation with politically defined borders.

Poland's statehood also took away much of the raison d'être for activism and ideology around which Polonia coalesced. Thaddeus Radzilowski comments:

> The birth of a new Poland ended the communal myth that they were Poles in America. As long as there had been no Poland it was possible to maintain the notion of the American Polonia as the fourth partition. Afterwards, it was impossible. Those coming to adulthood after World War I had to define themselves without reference to the struggle for Polish Independence which had so strongly shaped the ideology and outlook of their parents. (1986, 9)

Poland's independence cut Polonia adrift. Polonia could no longer rely on nationalist sentiment and political activity for the homeland to help forge a "we-ness."

Polonia turned its attention away from Poland for other reasons as well. Some Polonia leaders did not approve of the fact that Pilsudski's coalition governed the new nation. Pilsudski was a constituent player in the new nation-state and eventually seized power by a coup d'etat in 1926, and held it until his death in 1935. Other Polonians turned away from Poland because they were upset with how their countrymen treated them. Lopata's status perspective argues that Polonian leaders felt used by those delegates from Poland who only came to America looking for money. This request for money but not leadership "took prestige away from the local leaders by emphasizing their inadequacies" (1964, 219). Poland also rebuked any efforts by Polonia to direct internal Polish affairs, describing them as interference (Pula 1995). One Polish American priest expressed the opinion that Polonia had done enough for Poland, perhaps too much: "There is no reason why we scattered here over the United States should help save Poland for those who never showed us any consideration and even made fun of us" (quoted in Wytrwal 1961, 240). Finally, many Poles abroad had lost large sums of money investing in Poland (Lopata 1964; Pula 1995). Taken together, these actions estranged an increasing number of Polonians from Poland.

Negative sentiments against new immigrants fueled by World War I, the nativist movement, and eugenic theories also motivated Polonians to loosen (and even deny) their allegiance to Poland. America's need for national loyalty during World War I and the nativist "100 percent American" movement pressured immigrants and their descendants to surrender their foreign allegiances and become Americans. For the nativists, the American identity did not include ancestral cultural baggage. "The 100 percenters belligerently demanded universal conformity" as opposed to hyphenated Americans with dual loyalties (Higham 1973, 212). Nativists blamed the social ills in America on the arrival of large numbers of new southern and eastern European immigrants. The new immigrants, they claimed, were not fitting into America very well—they were too foreign, too dirty, too Catholic (or Jewish), and generally racially inferior to the descendants of the older northern and western European immigrants. At that time, the prevailing sociobiological paradigm explained differences between groups as immutable racial distinctions. Biological differences between groups supposedly generated difference in skills, aptitudes, personalities, and even hygiene. For example, David Roediger cites sociologist E. A. Ross, who wrote in 1914 that "the Slavs are immune to certain kinds of dirt. They can stand what would kill a white man" (1994, 191). Madison Grant's widely cited *The Passing of the Great Race* (1916) presented a scathing thesis maligning these new immigrants.

> The transportation lines advertised America as a land flowing with milk and honey, and the European governments took the opportunity to unload upon careless, wealthy, and hospitable America the sweepings of their jails and asylums. The result is that the new immigration, while it still included many strong elements from the north of Europe, contained a large and increasing number of the weak, the broken, and the mentally crippled of all races drawn from the lowest stratum of the Mediterranean basin and the Balkans, together with the hordes of the wretched, submerged populations of the Polish Ghettos. (Grant 1916, 80)

The belief in the racial inferiority of the new eastern and southern European immigrants was bolstered by intelligence testing and surveys. The intelligence tests developed in the beginning of the twentieth century by eugenicists Madison Grant, Charles B. Davenport, and others were designed to provide evidence that new immigrants were racially inferior. A series of tests and surveys conducted by the U.S. Immigration Commission (1907–10), the psychology tests of the U.S. Army, and surveys of school children whose parents were immigrants were designed to measure and document racial differences. Today it is widely recognized that these tests were based on fallacious premises, implemented with sloppy methodology, analyzed poorly, and conducted to support the thesis of racial differences rather than to test the thesis (Sacks 1994; Pula 1995, 1996; Carter, Green, and Halpern 1996). Still, in the early part of this century, the findings were readily accepted by nativists as proof of immigrant racial inferiority, especially intellectual inferiority. Many Americans doubted whether the nation could assimilate such peoples. After the war, attempts to limit immigration included legislation such as the Literacy Act, passed in 1917, which made literacy (a supposed measure of intelligence) a "useful means of distinguishing between foreigners likely to adapt to 'American ways' and those unable to break their bonds with native cultures" (Carter, Green, Halpern 1996, 141).[11]

Scholars, legislators, and civic reformers "racialized" the eastern and southern European immigrants. They were successful. The idea that being "white" made an immigrant more assimilable created a context within

11. However, the literacy laws were frequently used against labor organizers; a large number of those deported under literacy laws were industrial union organizers and other labor activists (Sacks 1994; Carter, Green, and Halpern 1996).

which it was possible to legitimately restrict the number of immigrants from so-called racially inferior groups (Carter, Green, Halpern 1996). Historically, racial classifications often have been used in this nation to determine citizenship rights (for example, the right to vote, the right to own property) as well as the right to become a citizen (Roediger 1994). Rights and privileges were attached to a "white" status, a slippery, shifting, and expanding category in American history (Sanjek 1994). In 1751, Benjamin Franklin referred to the Swedes as "swarthy," questioning their whiteness and hence desirability (Bell 1992, 29). At the beginning of the twentieth century it was the Poles, Italians, and Jews whose whiteness was shady.

Immigration legislation passed in the 1920s was a culmination of this xenophobia. It precipitously restricted the number of new southern and eastern European immigrants. The National Origins Act of 1924 (which was not fully implemented until 1929) set an annual ceiling at 150,000 immigrants and distributed quotas according to each national group's percentage of the white population in 1920 (Higham 1963, 324).[12] This quota system was intended to preserve America's racial status quo, that is, to ensure the numerical dominance of American descendants from northern and western European countries. While this act restricted all immigration, the restrictions drastically slashed the number of eastern and southern European immigrants whose rates had been highest in the preceding decades. Prior to World War I, annual immigration from the partitioned regions of Poland at times topped 100,000 per year, but beginning in 1930 Poles were allotted just 6,524 slots annually (Brozek 1977, 33; Pula 1995, 65). This policy remained in place until the Immigration and Nationality Act of 1952; and the national origins quota system was not abolished until the Immigration and Nationality Act was amended in 1965.

The early, large wave of Polish immigration slowed to a trickle after the

12. Each group was given a quota determined by a percentage of their population in America based on a certain year. The first law, the Dillingham Bill, was introduced in 1921 and set quotas by determining the number of foreign-born of each population based on the 1910 Census. In 1924, the Johnson-Reed Bill (known as the National Origins Act) used the national origins calculated for the entire white U.S. population (as opposed to only the foreign-born segment of the population). Until this law went into effect in the late 1920s, however, an even more restrictive measure to determine quotas was used, one based on 2 percent of the foreign-born population based on the 1890 Census (Higham 1963, 308–24). The Poles were especially hard hit because census calculations of Poles were inaccurate (Easterlin et al. 1982). The Polish quota for 1921 was initially 25,827, but after a dispute over borders it was raised to 31,146 (Brozek 1985, 33). For the few years after 1924, Poland's quota was reduced to 5,982 (Pula 1980).

implementation of the National Origins Act and as a result of improvements in Poland during its period of independence. Moreover, an increasing number of Poles in America chose to return to Poland (Walaszek 1992).
With fewer new immigrants in the community, the community changed
from a predominantly foreign-born to a predominantly native-born community. By 1920 in Polonia, the number of American-born second-generation
ethnics exceeded the number of foreign-born; 56 percent of the foreign
stock had been born in America, and by 1930 this increased to 62 percent
(Table 1.2). The percent of the population that was native-born was even
higher when the third and subsequent generations were counted (which
the census did not do). Between 1931 and 1940, only 17,026 Poles arrived
in the United States (*Statistical Yearbook of the INS*, 1990, 49). With fewer
immigrants around, the second-generation Poles who chose to be ethnics
assumed leadership positions, set organizational agendas, and determined
collective goals according to the needs of the native-born population.

Other second-generation Polish Americans chose not to become ethnics.
They either forgot or denied their parents' heritage, and there were strong
motivations to do so. Poles were branded an inferior race. The creation of

Table 1.2 Polish population in the United States and Chicago, 1910–1960

	United States		City of Chicago	
Year	Total foreign stock*	Percent foreign-born	Total foreign stock**	Percent foreign-born
1910	1,684,108	56	230,132	55
1920	2,436,895	44	318,338	44
1930	3,342,198	38	401,316	37
1940	2,905,859	34	297,300	36
1950	2,774,035	31	315,504	30
1960	2,780,026	27	258,657	36

*"Foreign stock" includes foreign-born Poles and native-born Poles of foreign or mixed
parentage (second-generation). For 1910 and 1920 the numbers refer to the "mother
tongue," and for the remaining decades they refer to the country of origin.

**Refers to total Polish population residing within the Chicago city limits. For the decades
1910, 1920, and 1940, the numbers refer to mother tongue, and for the other decades
they refer to country of origin.

Sources: *Statistical Abstracts of the United States*, 1925, 33; 1950, 17; U.S. Census of the Population,
1950, Subject Reports: Nativity and Parentage, 4:3A–85; U.S. Census of the Population, 1960,
Subject Reports: Nativity and Parentage, 2:1A–27; *Local Community Fact Book*, Chicago
Metropolitan Area, 1960, 291, 293; *The People of Chicago*, 1976, 33, 40, 62, 64, 68.

the "dumb Polak" stereotype at beginning of this century was grounded in anti-immigration sentiment, erroneous eugenics research, and the belief in the superiority of the western European race (Pula 1995 and 1996).[13] This negative identity led many to reject their Polish heritage and disavow affiliation in order to avoid the stigma of being an ethnic "Polak" (Lopata 1976, 72; Bukowczyk 1987, 67; Roediger 1994, 191). When the cost of the identity outweighed the benefit, some Polish Americans attempted to "pass" by changing their names. For example, the surnames Pawlowski became Paul, Chalwinski became Hall, Matecki became Mates, and Grazinski became Grayson.[14] Not all immigrants became ethnics. Those who opted out no longer used Polishness as a primary identity or the ethnic community as a primary network to friends, social activities, or jobs.

For those who did become ethnics, the shift away from a homeland to an American-orientation was accompanied by a transformation of the meaning of this identity. Polishness was no longer defined by patriotic acts for Poland, and the aggressors against whom Polonians struggled were no longer Germany and Russia but American nativists who defined Polish Americans as stupid, dirty, uncouth, and perhaps even un-American.

The construction of an American-based ethnic identity depended on how "American" was defined. Conzen and her colleagues argue that ethnic identities were compatible with being American; the negotiation of an American identity and an ethnic identity occurred simultaneously (Conzen et al. 1990). Roediger, however, argues that they were counterpoised, that becoming white was different from becoming ethnic so that "racial identity (whiteness) and ethnic identity are distinct" (1994, 182), and at times "a strong sense of ethnic identity could cut against the development of a white identity" (186). Both are right, but it was a stepwise process. Poles first became white and then became ethnic. Being white gave them a position of power (albeit small) relative to the earlier status of being racially inferior. And it was from a more secure position as "white" that the cultural ethnic identity emerged.

Matthew Frye Jacobson states that "for Celtic, Slavic, and Hebrew immigrants, 'becoming American' depended upon 'becoming Caucasian'" (1995, 182). Roediger also maintains that as "groups made the transition from Irish in America or Poles in America to Irish Americans or Polish Americans, they also became white Americans" (1994, 187). The more

---

13. Variations of this term are "Pollack" and "Polack."
14. I would like to thank Angela Helen Erdmans for these examples.

white they became the less ethnic they became, and he argues that their preference was "to be accepted as white rather than as Irish or Polish" (188). Immigrants sought to define the category "American" along the lines of whiteness rather than along the lines of ethnicity or nativity because they had a better chance of becoming American if American was defined as "white" than if it was defined as Anglo-Saxon. Jacobson argues that Poles resisted the definition of America as an Anglo-America, preferring instead to see a chasm between England and America, and America as a country of diversity (1995, 202–3). While Slavs were not Anglo-Saxons, "they were considered (and considered themselves) to be white" because they were allowed to become naturalized citizens, and American law "limited natural- ized citizenship to free 'white' immigrants" (184). While naturalization was denied to other groups, Asian Indians for example, it was granted to Poles (Roediger 1994). Yet this does not mean that Slavs had the privilege and status of the dominant Anglo-Saxon white group. As shown, Poles were considered racially inferior during the first two decades of the twentieth century. Compared to Anglo-Saxons, Slavs were a low-grade white, but their status whitened when compared to the darker and more foreign Asians and blacks. While the Irish became white in the middle of the nineteenth century (Roediger 1991; Allen 1994; Ignatiev 1995), it was not until after World War I that Slavic immigrants began to lighten their swarthy status. Jacobson argues that during the Spanish American War, Slavs proclaimed their racially superior position in relation to Filipinos. "In a context where white supremacy and European centrality were the founding assumptions" the immigrants were conscious of a racial boundary between Europeans and Filipinos (1995, 180). The real whitening, however, came about in the 1920s and 1930s with the increased presence of blacks in the northern urban neighborhoods. The presence of blacks increased contact and conflict between blacks and Polish Americans in neighborhoods, work sites, and public spaces (Wilson 1978; Pula 1995; Pacyga 1996; McGreevy 1996). To outsiders, the black-white division was most visible. While Polish Americans already saw themselves as white, the presence of blacks shaped the dominant Anglo-Saxon perception of Poles as white. John McGreevy argues that the immigrants "became 'Catholic whites' only in the context of African Americans moving in large numbers to a particular area. Ethnicity was flattened into race" (1996, 36).

As white, Polish Americans had more freedom to express, celebrate, and advocate for their ethnic group; but, there were limits. The ethnic identity they molded was more likely to survive if it did not threaten the majority identity. Conzen and her colleagues (1990) argue that intense nativism pressured immigrant groups to remake themselves into something that was both acceptable to the dominant society and the subordinate minority society. Ethnicity was constructed as a benign identity that would allow people an attachment to a subculture without challenging their loyalty to America. Loyalty to America was expressed as a political and national identity (American), while loyalty to the ancestral homeland was a cultural identity (Polish American), and this cultural identity did not interfere with the process of becoming American. The cultural behavior passed down to the next generation—culinary preferences, religious celebrations, cultural dances—did not threaten or eclipse an American identity. No aspect of the Polish American identity challenged capitalism, democracy, religious freedom, or the values of independence, individualism, and hard work. For example, Polish Americans appear to have collectively forgotten the socialists, who were very much present in the early immigrant community. Some socialist traditions survived as a working-class ideology, and the Polish Socialist Alliance itself was active into the 1960s (Gross 1976, 160). Yet socialism is almost never considered to be a component of Polish American identity. Historians continue to record only those values that did not contradict American values. For example, Bukowczyk argues that immigrant values that survived in the second generation were the peasant values of self-reliance, thrift, and hard work (1982, 76). Pula (1995) defines Polish values as respect for home ownership, community, and country.

The Polish American identity is solidly associated with its working-class character. Higham argues that the labor class movements during the 1930s gave previously excluded immigrant groups a way to feel included in America (1990, 33). Polish Americans were a strong component of the labor movement and their working-class identity became intricately interwoven with their ethnic identity (Pacyga 1991; Radzilowski 1990; Bodnar, Simon, and Weber 1982, 228; Bukowczyk 1987; Pula 1995). While the early Polish immigrant communities had diverse class structures, the vast majority of immigrants who arrived between 1870 and 1914 came from rural peasant backgrounds (though with differing relations to the agricultural economy in Poland), and in America most of them joined the proletarianized industrial labor force (Pinkowski 1978; Bukowczyk 1984; Morawska 1985; Pula 1995). The early immigrants settled in the large industrial cities in the eastern, mid-Atlantic and midwestern states. Their communities often abutted the work site, evident in the coal mining towns in Pennsylvania and the Back of the Yards adjacent to the meatpacking industries in Chicago. Throughout the twentieth century, many of the descendants of this early cohort were still concentrated in the northern industrial states and continued to be laborers in the manufacturing industries or lower-level clerical and managerial workers.

The transition from immigrant to ethnic community is reflected in Polonia's organizational agendas and community activities, which began to focus on domestic rather than homeland issues. The key issues at the 4th Emigration Congress in Cleveland in 1923 were Polish language maintenance, discrimination, Americanization campaigns, and organizational membership (Galush 1974, 217). In 1934, Polish Americans refused to join the World Union of Poles from Abroad (*Światpol*), an organization created in Warsaw. Their refusal was written in a document Reverend Jozef Swastek later called the "Polish American Declaration of Independence," which stated that the "delegates from Polish organizations in the United States, *composed of American citizens*" saw themselves as an "inseparable component of the great American nation" and would work with Poland in cultural exchanges only, pledging full solidarity and loyalty to America first (quoted in Brozek 1985, 190, emphasis mine). Polish organizations in America began to follow the slogan "*Wychodźstwo dla wychodźstwa*" (Emigrants for emigrants). Concern for their own affairs included the "survival" of their cultural practices in the American-born generation (Lopata 1964; Symmons-Symonolewicz 1966; Blejwas 1981). Toward this end, Polish American organizations sponsored Polish folk dances, choral groups, and Polish language classes. The Polish Highlanders Alliance in America (*Związek Podhalan w Ameryce*) was founded in 1928 to preserve the *góral* folk culture of people from the southeastern mountain regions of Poland (Zachariasiewicz 1978, 661). As more children entered public schools during the Depression, the number of Saturday schools teaching Polish language and culture increased. It was also during this period that monuments and streets were renamed for Polish heroes (in particular Casimir Pulaski, whose herodom is attached more to American soil), and the first Pulaski Day parade in New York was in 1937. The fraternal organizations addressed domestic needs when they began to offer home mortgage loans to its members in the 1930s (Erdmans 1997). The community and its organizations also supported domestic labor movement activities (Radzilowski 1990; Bukowczyk 1987, 80).

An assortment of new organizations were founded during this period.

Some of them were dedicated to the preservation of Polish culture: the Polish Arts Club in Chicago (1926), the Joseph Conrad Literary Club in Buffalo (which used English as their official language), and the Polish Museum of America in Chicago (1935), which "focused on collecting materials relevant to the Polish experience in America" (Pula 1995, 74). Others demonstrated the community's concern for domestic issues: new professional organizations (the Polish Lawyer's Association in 1931, the National Medical and Dental Association in 1928, and the Federated Merchant's Organization of America in 1936) reflected changing occupational needs, and social service organizations (the Polish League of Social Activities in the United States in 1937) helped alleviate the problems caused by the economic depression (Bukowczyk 1987, 78; Zachariasiewicz 1978).

New organizations helped and encouraged Poles to become naturalized citizens (Januszewski 1985). While there were no new political organizations formed on Poland's behalf, there were numerous new Polish American Democratic and Republican clubs and Polish American citizen clubs (Kantowicz 1975; Slayton 1986, 163–71). Edward Kantowicz argues that prior to World War I, the community was defined as "Poles in America" and "took no part in American politics," but after the war naturalization "proceeded rapidly, Polonia's participation in politics increased, and the term 'Polish-American' replaced 'Poles in America'" (1975, 163). Polish Americans became involved in American politics. They urged members of the community to become naturalized so that they could vote, supported the New Deal practices and liberalism, and became a part of the national Democrat Party alliance (Bukowczyk 1987, 70–81). The ethnic political agenda focused on influencing American state and local arenas rather than Poland's political scene.

These activities—cultural maintenance, professional organizations, social services, home ownership, labor movement support, and political activity show a community working to improve its situation here in America. The Central Council of Polish Organizations, created in 1935, listed their goals as:

1. Education, in particular getting Polish taught in the schools;
2. Nationality interests, celebrating Polish holidays;
3. Citizenship, helping people become American citizens;
4. Social service, especially concerns of juvenile delinquency. (Bodnar, Simon, and Weber 1982, 202)

These goals reflected ethnic needs; they show a community of people negotiating an American political identity (citizenship) alongside a cultural identity (holidays and language) and addressing domestic problems, such as juvenile delinquency. For Polish Americans, home was America. Poland was an ancestral source of culture, not a political or national identity. Bukowczyk argues that by the 1930s Polish American families "were no longer *Polish* or *peasant* families as the immigrant families of a decade ago had been" (1987, 82). The ethnic patterns of life were "made in America" through a synthesis of old world values ("thrift, hard work, and family cohesiveness") within the new world context of baseball, Democrats, and Polonized English (83).

World War II and Polonia

On September 1, 1939, Germany invaded Poland from the north, west, and south; seventeen days later the Soviets invaded Poland from the east. The Germans and the Soviets divided Poland along the Vistula and San rivers, according to a secret protocol of the Nazi-Soviet Non-Aggression Pact signed on August 23, 1939. After the Germans invaded the Soviet Union in June 1941, the Soviets became allies of the Western powers, and the Polish Government-in-Exile, with some nudging, shook hands in peace with the Soviets.[15] The Soviet presence in Poland influenced its postwar borders and government. The Roosevelt administration, aware that the Polish borders were an important issue among Polish Americans and that the Polish American constituency had voted for Roosevelt in his first three elections, worked to keep the border issue out of the public eye (Lukas 1978, 85–89). As the 1944 elections drew near, Roosevelt adopted an attitude of neutrality and silence on this sensitive issue (Lukas 1978, 32; Harriman and Able 1976, 360; Ciechanowski 1946, 294). The minutes of his meeting with Jozef Stalin in Teheran on December 1, 1943, read:

> [Roosevelt] said that we had an election in 1944. . . . He added
> that there were in the United States from six to seven million

15. The Polish Government-In-Exile, created in France in November 1939 and relocated to London in November 1940, was recognized by the Western powers as the legal government of Poland until 1945.

Americans of Polish extraction, and as a practical man, he did not wish to lose their vote. . . . [He said he] would like to see the Eastern border [of Poland] moved further to the West. . . . He hoped, however, that the Marshal [Stalin] would understand that for the political reasons outlined above, he could not participate in any decision here in Teheran or even next winter on this subject and that he could not publicly take part in any such arrangement at the present time. (*Foreign Relations of the United States*, 1943, 594, recorded by Charles Bohlen, chief of the Division of Eastern European Affairs, U.S. Department of the State)

Poland's borders were moved: it lost its eastern territories in Lithuania and the Ukraine and gained the German lands of East Prussia and Silesia. As a result, in Norman Davies figurative phraseology, after the war Poland was "bodily moved 150 miles to the West" (1986, 81).

In addition to the border changes, the Soviet presence also altered Poland's postwar government. The composition of Poland's government was vaguely defined at the Crimean Conference at Yalta as one that should include "democratic leaders" (it never did) and be decided by free elections (it never was). The stipulation for free elections was included in the Yalta Treaty, Roosevelt said, because it was important "that some recognition of the Polish-Americans' desire for free elections be in the final agreement" (Johnson 1950, 190). Soviet intervention in Poland's government, however, insured that there never were free elections (Lane 1948, 276–88). The Polish government was controlled by communists tolerant of the Soviet presence, and neither the Polish Government-in-Exile nor the Polonian leaders in America ever recognized the Warsaw regime as legitimate.

When World War II started, Polonia was composed mostly of Americans of Polish descent. In 1940, 66 percent of the Polish "foreign stock" were born in American (see Table 1.2). This ethnic Polonia was less active in the cause of Poland during World War II than the immigrant Polonia had been during World War I. Wytrwal commented that "poor response to recruitment campaigns, lack of central Polish associations, and concern with American war problems had indicated beyond a doubt that Polonia's attention was no longer concentrated on Poland" (1961, 261). Polonians were mostly sympathetic Americans of Polish descent with sentimental ties to an ancestral Poland, not nationalistic Poles living abroad politically committed to their homeland. This does not deny the presence of a strong nationalist sector in Polonia during and after the war, but suggests that most Polish Americans saw themselves as Americans first. As Americans, they did not enlist in the Polish army but fought in the American army; and their aid to Poland during the war was primarily limited to humanitarian assistance.[16] In 1941, the Polish fraternal leaders created the Polish American Council (*Rada Polonii Amerykańskiej*) to coordinate Polonia's relief efforts. The fraternal members bought nearly $25 million worth of U.S. war bonds, and Polonia raised nearly $30 million for humanitarian aid through national fundraising drives (such as the Ten Million Dollar Fund for Poland), local fundraising efforts, and taxing fraternal members five cents a month (Haiman 1946; Wytrwal 1961, 202–3, 262; Lukas 1978, 4–5, 108–9).

Polish émigrés who arrived during the war were upset by the political inactivity of Polonia, which they insisted "still had political obligations to Poland" (Blejwas 1981, 63). In 1942, a group of Polish Americans and new Polish émigrés created the National Committee of Americans of Polish Descent (known as KNAPP from the acronym of its Polish name *Komitet Narodowy Amerykanów Pochodzenia Polskiego*) to serve as the political wing of Polonia. KNAPP represented the more extreme, anti-Soviet, pro-Pilsudski faction in Polonia. Most Polish Americans, however, belonged to the moderate faction (fraternals, Polish parishes, and the Polish American Council) that was aligned with American policies and the Polish Government-in-Exile in Britain. Most Polish Americans were aware of the strong pro-Soviet sentiments during the war, and respected the U.S.-Soviet alliance (Lukas 1978, 86–106). Polish Americans were, after all, Americans; their ethnic identity was a cultural identity that was not supposed to challenge American foreign policy.[17]

---

16. During World War II American citizens were allowed to serve in another Allied army as long as they did not swear allegiance to the Allied country. In April 1941, General Wladyslaw Sikorski, leader of the Polish Government-in-Exile procured American lend-lease aid to equip and supply a Polish army trained in Canada, but within a year the project was canceled because there were too few enlistments (Lukas 1978, 5). In response to Sikorski's accusations that Polonia did not care about Poland, Polonian leaders wrote: "We have our own problems" (quoted in Wytrwal 1961, 261). In contrast, during World War I, 26,000 Poles living in America joined the Polish Army in France (Pienkos 1984, 111–13).

17. Ignacy Matuszewski, a 1940 émigré and one of the most controversial writers for the KNAPP publication *Biuletyn Organizacyjny*, pointed out that, because the Soviet Union got 4 percent of the lend-lease funds, Polish Americans in factories were working in fact to help the regime that imprisoned their families. Matuszewski irritated the Polonian moderates, and the liberal pro-Soviet American press and administration. The PNA claimed it did not need leaders like Matuszewski. One Polish American organization called for his arrest, while an American editor even blamed him for the dissolution of Soviet-Polish diplomatic ties. The

The moderates, however, became more openly anti-Soviet after the 1943 discovery of the grave of fifteen thousand Polish officers who had been shot and buried in the Katyn Forest in the Soviet Union. The moderates were also irritated by pro-Soviet Polish American groups, such as the American Slavic Congress and the Polish American Labor Council, that supported Roosevelt's wartime alliance with Stalin. While the moderates were unwilling to become radical anti-Soviets, neither did they want their community represented by pro-Soviets. Polish Americans were outraged when Reverend Stanislaw Orlemanski and Oscar Lange, both Polish Americans sympathetic to communism, were received in the USSR as informal representatives of American Polonia (Lukas 1978, 53–56). By 1943–44, as Soviet aggression toward Poland became more apparent, Polish American organizations more strongly embraced an anti-Soviet stance.

During the spring of 1944, Washington expressed concern about Polonia's growing anti-Soviet sentiment. The Foreign Nationalities branch in the U.S. government sent a memo to the director of strategic services that read:

> Concrete manifestations of a new movement taking form, which after the mammoth meeting in Buffalo next month may become seriously disturbing in American politics, include a shoving aside of the moderate leadership in the Polish-American fraternals and the alignment of these powerful organizations with the ultra-nationalist, openly anti-Russian leadership of the numerically small National Committee of Americans of Polish Descent (KNAPP). (quoted in Lukas 1978, 117)

The U.S. government's fears were unjustified. The "mammoth meeting" in Buffalo was the inaugural meeting of the Polish American Congress (PAC), founded on May 5, 1944, as an umbrella organization composed of national fraternals and their local lodges, as well as religious, cultural, educational, media, business, and political organizations in Polonia. While the PAC included members from the extreme anti-Soviet faction (several KNAPP officials even became members of the PAC executive committee), the

---

American administration, unsure of the loyalty of hyphenated Americans, and afraid of what information was being passed along in the ethnic presses, became particularly interested in the writings of Matuszewski and forced him to register under the Foreign Agents Registration Act (Lukas 1978, 109–14).

planks of the PAC platform had a moderate tone of cooperation with the United States in its war efforts, and support for a just program of peace within the framework of the Atlantic Charter. The Polish Americans took care to demonstrate their loyalty to America. The PAC declaration began "we solemnly pledge our unqualified service, love, and affection to our country, the United States" (quoted in Wytrwal 1961, 263). Lukas believes the Polish American Congress did not hyphenate its name because it was sensitive to claims that it was un-American, and for the same reason its leaders released a statement that read, " 'We maintain [that] our filial love for Poland does not in any way alter our loyalty to the United States. We are Americans first and last' " (1978, 119).

From its inception in 1944 until the fraudulent elections in Poland in 1947, the PAC fought determinately to prevent the imposition of a communist government in Poland. After the rigged 1947 election, Arthur Bliss Lane resigned his post as U.S. ambassador to Poland, and together with Charles Rozmarek, the PAC president, formed the Committee to Stop World Communism. Rozmarek and other PAC leaders took a hostile stance toward the Soviets; they were distrustful of and uncooperative with the Soviets, and even suggested a military liberation of Poland. By the 1950s, being anti-Soviet was not an "un-American" position but instead aligned them with the most American of Americans in the "hunt for Reds" during the height of the Cold War.

The PAC's strong anticommunist stance continued into the 1960s and was endorsed enthusiastically by the new World War II émigrés. However, by the mid-1960s, the United States was trying to build bridges with the Soviet Union and Eastern Europe, and U.S. foreign relations officials saw Polonia's insistence on Polish independence as antagonistic and unproductive (Pienkos 1984, 181). Eventually, the PAC began to bend, especially after Aloysius Mazewski became president of the PAC in 1968. While it never relinquished its goal of ousting the communist regime, the PAC did begin rebuilding its cultural and educational linkages with Poland. During the 1970s, the PAC encouraged U.S. economic assistance to Poland but at the same time promoted psychological resistance to communism through support of Radio Free Europe (Pienkos 1984, 340–43). In 1975, PAC leaders voiced their objections to Poland's proposed constitutional changes that would have strengthened the role of the Soviet Union in Poland. For the most part, however, even though PAC leaders disagreed with Washington's policy of containment in the era of détente, they did not lobby strenuously against it (Pienkos 1991, 167–69). They never accepted the communist government but they stopped insisting on liberation.

The World War II Cohort

Over 200,000 Poles arrived in America during and after World War II and most were refugees of the war. Many of them came in through the Displaced Persons Act of 1948, which admitted over 120,000 ethnic Poles (*Statistical Yearbook of the INS*, 1978, table 6E).[18] In addition, this cohort included roughly 18,000 soldiers who had served in the Allied armies in Europe (for which reason some refer to this group as the soldiers emigration). Members of this cohort were pushed out of their homeland by war, border changes, and the repressive postwar communist regime. They defined themselves as political emigrants to distinguish themselves from the earlier economic immigrants. Calling oneself an emigrant puts the emphasize on leaving; whereas immigrant places the accent of arriving. On numerous occasions, the World War II émigrés stated explicitly, "We are émigrés, not immigrants." For this reason, I refer to members of this cohort as World War II émigrés.

This cohort of involuntary exiles differed from the earlier cohort of voluntary *za chlebem* ("for bread") immigrants. These émigrés, who grew up during the interwar years in an independent Poland (1919–39), had different experiences in Poland than those Poles who lived in Poland during the partition years (1795–1918). Between the wars, Poland was in the process of rebuilding itself politically, economically, and culturally as an independent nation-state. The creation of the Polish nation elevated nationalistic feelings as did the experiences of World War II. Having first rebuilt the Polish nation, and then having fought in the war to save it, having experienced the death of family members and friends, and having witnessed the physical destruction of their cities, the war émigrés were highly politicized, extremely anticommunist, and very bitter about what they perceived to be the Western powers' "betrayal" of Poland at Yalta (Gross 1976; Lopata 1976; Lukas 1978).

The migration process by which most World War II émigrés came to

---

18. The term "ethnic Poles" excludes Lithuanians, Ukrainians, and Jews living within the boundaries of the nation-state.

America also bolstered feelings of patriotism and nationalism for Poland. The early immigrants chose to leave Poland in search of work. In contrast, the World War II émigrés chose not to return to Poland. Most of the émigrés were outside of Poland when the war ended: they had been taken to Germany during the war as prisoners, concentration camp inmates, or forced laborers; they had fled Poland for fear of persecution; they were members of the Polish forces serving with the British Army; or they were part of a displaced population uprooted from towns in Poland's eastern territories that became part of the Soviet Union after the war. Of those admitted into the United States between 1946 and 1954, on the average only 3 percent listed Poland as their last country of permanent residence (*Annual Report of the INS*, 1947–55, tables 6 and 6A). Members of this cohort explained their decision not to return as an act of patriotism. One man said, "I was patriotic, believing I was living for Poland free, not under the communists. Our stay [in America] we consider as a protest." Another veteran said, "It's very important from our point of view, that 20,000 soldiers—privates, officers, politically involved, not involved— decided in protest to stay overseas. We are not accepting conditions in Poland." In Danuta Mostwin's study of 2,049 war émigrés, 62.5 percent said they left Poland for primarily political reasons (1971, 146). The process of forced migration separated this cohort from the earlier cohort. One war veteran wrote that when he came to America he found he had nothing in common with the earlier immigrants who had "chosen" to leave their homeland. In his view, members of his cohort were "political victims of the conditions created by Yalta" (Carrer 1970, 195).

Members of the World War II cohort defined Polishness as a political identity that entailed certain obligations to the homeland. This is shown in a political cartoon that first appeared in 1951 in the publication *Zgoda* (Unity) in Chicago. A large bell sits on a hill with "*Zgoda*" written on its base and "Political emigration from Poland" on its side. A woman ringing the bell has written across her back "Polish Affairs as a Forum for the World." A man walking away from the bell carries a sack over his shoulders with the words "self ambition." Another man calls to him, "Leave that and come with us." This cartoon typifies the feelings of moral obligation and duty toward the homeland characteristic of this cohort. The émigrés felt that this component of the Polish identity was weak or missing in the Polish American community. One veteran émigré said, "The old Polonia, the people who immigrated before World War I, was a commercial immigration. These people have their sentiments to the old country but they don't see things politically."

Another difference was the class composition of the cohorts. The early cohort was composed mostly of uneducated peasants. Members of the World War II cohort were generally better educated, more urbanized, and of a higher social class than the peasants in the early cohort (however, many farmers also came in through the Displaced Persons Act from the eastern territories) (Janowska 1975; Mostwin 1971; Lopata 1976). In Mostwin's sample, 47.7 percent had at least some college education, and roughly 38 percent had been professionals or higher executives in Poland (1971, 151–52). According to immigration statistics, 40 percent of the Poles admitted into the United States between 1947 and 1954 had had skilled or professional occupations in Poland (*Annual Report of the INS*, 1947–54, table 8). Their higher occupational and educational levels, coupled with the fact that most considered their stay in America to be permanent (or at least lengthy), resulted in faster rates of occupational mobility than the earlier transient peasant migrants. The cohort differences in class origin produced different expressions of Polishness. Stanislaus Blejwas reports that when Polish Americans spoke Polish, they usually did so with a rural dialect, while the World War II émigrés spoke "the literary tongue" of the urban centers (Blejwas 1981, 79). The new émigrés criticized Polonia for having too few educated priests, proficient Polish speakers, and fine arts institutions as well as its inability to raise large sums of money and influence American foreign policy. Although not all members of the early cohort were uneducated peasants, the war émigrés characterized them as such. One World War II émigré said, "Now, most of the people, those immigrants who arrived here before the First World War, I know they were like my uncles and so on. They came from villages, from poor families, they hardly know how to read and write." Polish Americans naturally recoiled from this negative characterization. Blejwas reports that Polish Americans resented the émigrés' arrogance and referred to them as "ingrates and show-offs" (1981, 76).

In addition to the differences between the migration process and the characteristics of the migrants, the other main difference between the two groups was that one was an immigrant group and the other was an ethnic group. Polonia in the mid-twentieth century was a Polish American ethnic community. The ethnic identity, constructed in the image of America, in many ways did not resemble the Polishness to which the immigrants subscribed. Lopata wrote that the World War II émigrés viewed Polonia "as a limited community with little remaining Polishness" (1976, 29). This Americanized ethnic group contrasted sharply with the émigrés. "The presence of the fresh arrivals seemed to have increased the Americanization of the original Polonia residents by showing them how non-Polish they had become" (Lopata 1964, 213). Some new émigrés refused to recognize the Polishness of most Polish Americans. One new émigré believed that, in the 1950s, "among the 600,000 people in Chicago Polonia there are about 5,000 Poles" (quoted in Blejwas 1981, 79). The sense of "otherness" or difference was felt within the community—not between Poles and Americans but between Polish émigrés and Polish American ethnics.

These differences produced two distinct migrational and generational cohorts. The differences led to parallel rather than integrated organizations and communities, which Blejwas refers to as the "dualism of immigrant groups" (1981, 80). I argue instead that an immigrant community took root alongside the ethnic community. The newcomers formed scientific and cultural organizations that reflected their orientation toward Poland and their cosmopolitan definitions of Polish culture. The World War II émigrés established scholarly organizations that dealt with Polish affairs and promoted contemporary Polish writers and artists. The Alfred Jurzykowski Foundation, founded in 1956, built a research library, a Polish historical archive, and gave financial support to scholars from Poland. The Polish Institute of Arts and Sciences, established in 1942 by Polish scholars in America initially waiting out the war, did not become receptive to Polish American scholars until the late 1950s (Best 1982, 157–59). The World War II émigrés also tended to buy homes outside of the Polish neighborhoods; only 20 percent of the World War II émigrés in Mostwin's sample lived in Polish neighborhoods (1971, 251); and only 40 percent of this cohort attended church in a Polish parish (Blejwas 1981, 75). Lopata said the émigrés "preferred to develop their own subcommunities or to turn instead to the American sources to meet education, occupation, and housing needs" (1976, 104).

The new émigrés also challenged the established ethnic leaders. The new émigrés felt that they had a right to be the representatives of Poland in America because most of the Polish Americans had little attachment to or knowledge about Poland (Blejwas 1981, 68). This attitude placed them in competition with the Polish American ethnic leaders. Blejwas writes that the dualism in veterans' organizations was "provoked by the fears of the old Polish American veterans that the 'new arrivals' would seize control of their group, and, indeed, by the desire of some former Polish politicians and soldiers to do just that and establish themselves as commanders of Polonia" (71). Polish American organizations such as the PAC and the Society of Veterans of the Polish Army safeguarded the positions of their Polish American leaders by passing bylaws that stated that organizational officers had to be American citizens. New arrivals must be in America at least five years before they can become citizens, and many World War II émigrés, because of their patriotism to Poland, did not want to become American citizens. As a result, these by-laws initially kept most émigrés out of these offices.

Even though, as one war émigré explained, members of the PAC treated them as "outsiders" and "foreigners with wild ideas," the newcomers eventually found a place for themselves in established Polonia. Symmons-Symonolewicz noted about the World War II émigrés that "some fusion of these elements, especially when isolated, with the Polish-American elite does occasionally occur" (1966, 3). Lopata also found that there was cooperation between the two groups "on occupational and educational levels which cut across 'degree of Americanization lines'" (1964, 213). The elite World War II émigrés and the Polish Americans who had formed the cultural and educational organizations between the wars were most willing to work with each other. As a result of this union, the World War II émigrés reintroduced Polish Americans to their national culture and stimulated Polonian interest in the political fate of their homeland. Ultimately, this activity helped to revive an increasingly Americanized ethnic group. Lopata writes that World War II émigrés were more "conscious" and "proud" of their Polish culture while Polish Americans were "frequently ashamed" of their heritage (1964, 213). The World War II émigrés, through their cultural programs, media participation, and higher levels of self-esteem, helped to erode the negative "Polak" stereotype.

> The intelligentsia of the new emigration, shocked at the lack of knowledge of the Polish national culture, began a process of "educating" Polonia through the development of new activities and through the press. Although the new emigration created conflict and competition within Polonia, it influenced the orientation and continued interest in Poland, laying foundations for current attitudes. (Lopata 1976, 27)

By 1960, the World War II émigrés dominated the PAC national and state committees focused on issues relating to Poland.

The new émigrés, new organizations, and new members in old organizations served to reorient the ethnic community and strengthen its
commitment to Poland. The new émigrés also brought with them new
interpretations of Polishness. Their presence expanded and made more
complex the notion of Polishness. Polishness now included more recognition for scholarly accomplishments and high culture artistic achievements.
The new émigrés and the new political situation in Poland also added a new
component to the Polish identity: a strong anticommunist ideology. Both
migrations and generations coalesced around this ideology. In the 1950s,
most Polish Americans were anticommunist (as were most Americans).
Their anticommunism was engendered by sentiments for their ancestral
homeland and supported by the opinions of the Church and both major
political parties in the United States. This anticommunist ideology was a
new component of the Polish American identity; it was very compatible with
the American culture; and it resonated with and was strongly supported by
the World War II émigrés. This new component expanded the umbrella of
Polishness to cover both the new migrant cohort and the older ethnic
generation. The two groups worked together mostly in those organizations
working for Poland's independence, where the anticommunist conviction
was most relevant.

Ethnic Survival

There was an increase in ethnic activism among descendants of European
immigrant groups (that is, "white ethnics") in the 1960s and 1970s. Assimilation was no longer a forced necessity, instead the democratic base of
American society was considered strong enough to support a profusion of
cultures. In the climate of cultural pluralism, ethnic identities became a
source of pride as well as a base for claiming state resources. Some scholars
argue the ethnics had never melted to begin with, and the "ethnic revival"
was really a new understanding of something already there (Glazer and
Moynihan 1970; Novak 1971). Others explain the revival as the powerless,
white ethnic groups' reaction to the gains of other ethnic and racial
minorities (Greeley 1974). Both explanations are somewhat correct. Ethnic
activism in the Polish American community during this period was influenced by a combination of three factors: Polish Americans defined themselves as a discriminated group deserving of a larger piece of the American

pie; Polish Americans wanted to disengage themselves from the negative "white ethnic" label that had become synonymous with racism; and economic restructuring and desegregation threatened urban working-class communities and made Polish Americans defensive under the guise of ethnic identity.

First, distributing state resources on the basis of ethnic heritage created an incentive to claim ethnic affiliation. Before the individual could receive benefits, however, the group had to be defined as a minority, that is deserving of state resources on the basis of past or present discrimination. Polish Americans argued that they had experienced discrimination for centuries—persecution for being Polish in the former partitioned lands in the nineteenth century induced their ancestors to emigrate, then they were discriminated against in America during its strong Americanization campaign that forced immigrants to "melt" into American culture (Pula 1995). Moreover, they claimed they were still being discriminated against in contemporary society. In 1969, in Illinois, a state that had at least a quarter of a million Poles, of twenty-four governmental departments only one was headed by a Polish American, and of forty-five boards created to assist the Illinois Government, none were headed by Polish Americans and only five Polish Americans served as members on these boards (*PAC Newsletter*, July 1970). In 1972, PAC officials complained there was "lack of proper and just representation of Americans of Polish origin in elective and appointive positions" (*PAC Newsletter*, September 1972, 1). Polish Americans were also underrepresented in the federal administration, according to a survey done by the PAC in 1977. Fewer than 1 percent of the federal administrators in the State Department, Department of Commerce, Environmental Protection Agency, and the Department of Health, Education and Welfare, were Polish Americans (*PAC Newsletter*, April 1977).[19]

Polish Americans felt betrayed in the political climate of the 1960s (Pacyga 1987). Not only did the affirmative action programs ignore Polish American's history of discrimination, they also felt these programs created an additional discrimination, a "reverse discrimination" because Polish Americans were lumped with the privileged white majority and thus became ineligible for retribution programs. On several occasions Polish

19. Polish American historians continue to argue and document their minority status into the 1980s. Using indicators of representativeness, they show that the number of Polish Americans appointed to be federal judges, elected as local, state, and national officials, heads of corporations and city commissions are still not reflective of the populations of the city, nation, or state (Kromkowski 1986; Pula 1992).

Americans sued on the grounds of ethnic discrimination, but their cases were dismissed because the discrimination was not based on "race" (Pula 1996, 84). This judgment denied Polish Americans and other white ethnics the right to sue for discrimination. They fought against affirmative action policies on the grounds that they did not distribute resources fairly to all groups. A PAC director, Leonard Walentynowicz, prepared amicus curiae briefs for the 1976 *Bakke* case in California and the 1979 *United Steelworkers of America v. Weber* case. These briefs criticized the implementation and principles of affirmative action. For the Bakke case, Walentynowicz argued against affirmative action programs by asking whether these programs had become "vehicles by which some disadvantaged and discriminated groups and individuals secure benefits and special privileges while other disadvantaged and discriminated groups and individuals are still denied the promise of America?" (quoted in Pienkos 1991, 160). In PAC's brief for the *Weber* case, Walentynowicz argued, "We are disappointed that the drive for equality and opportunity for everyone that began with the Civil Rights movement of the 1950s and 1960s is turning into a battle for preference and privilege where groups and the individual who are perceived to be politically weaker are disregarded" (160). Linking state resources and privileges to ethnic and racial identities encouraged Polish Americans to emphasize both their ethnic identity and their rights to these resources.

While political resources were being distributed to nonwhites, the whites were attributed the blame—but not all whites shared the blame equally. "White" was redefined by the (mostly nonethnic) middle class to mean "white ethnic," and this phrase was used to insinuate "racism." Herbert Gans argues that in the 1970s "ethnicity" had become a "code word for anti-black feelings" (1974, xi). It was the working-class white ethnics who were most often cast in the role of the bigot. The Polish American community took efforts to underscore their unique Polish American identity to separate themselves from the stigmatized "white ethnic" label. By emphasizing their individual ethnicity rather than their collective race, Polish Americans attempted to distance themselves from some of the blame and to procure some of the benefits of multiculturalism.

Furthermore, beginning in the 1950s, many Polish Americans witnessed the ruination of their communities as a result of economic restructuring, industrial relocation to the suburbs, urban renewal and gentrification, and new expressways that cut through the heart of several Polish American communities (Pacyga 1987; Pula 1992). In addition, the influx of non-Polish groups into their neighborhoods destabilized the communities.

While most people focus on the black-Polish conflict, Paul Wrobel's ethnography of a Detroit parish shows that Polish Americans felt threatened by Albanians and Yugoslavians as well as blacks (1979, 140). It was the non-Polish nature of the incoming group rather than the race that was troublesome. The real estate agents took advantage of these fears, and using scare tactics and illegal methods to get Polish Americans to sell their homes for low prices, they incited the rapid out-migration of the established residents (130–35).[20] James Pula argues that property ownership was a cherished value in Polish American communities and Polish Americans only felt "secure from overt discrimination" in their own neighborhoods (1992, 14). The resurgence of activism under the banner of ethnicity was a reaction to the perceived destruction of these safe havens.

Competition and insecurity also occurred in the job market (Pula 1992 and 1995). Because of the restructuring of the economy, white working-class ethnics were finding it difficult to get and maintain stable working-class positions in the inner city. Economic restructuring increased competition for jobs near the old inner-city communities. Dominic Pacyga argues that in Chicago, Polish Americans "felt that blacks might leap over them into a higher status position" (1987, 51).

Many Polish Americans felt their jobs, their communities, and their way of life were threatened by the changes taking place in the 1960s and 1970s. Reactionary ethnicity, employed as a defense mechanism, took the form of community action to save parishes and neighborhoods and harassment of non-Polish newcomers to the community. Most notably, Polish Americans worked to prevent the integration of blacks into their communities by implementing rigid housing segregation (Parot 1975, 32).

During this period, Polish Americans also moved away from their urban neighborhoods because, like other middle-class Americans, they wanted to and they could (Gross 1976). Economic mobility, job relocation, and marriage outside the ethnic group all pulled Polish Americans out into the suburbs and away from the ethnic neighborhoods. This voluntary movement away from the old neighborhood weakened ethnic bonds. In contrast,

20. Paul Wrobel (1979) provides an excellent illustration of this in his ethnography of a Polish American community in Detroit in the 1970s. The real estate agents created a panic by manipulating residents to believe that the presence of one or two Others would automatically lead to the complete changing over of their neighborhood. The fact that communities changed so quickly during the 1960s and 1970s attests to the effective strategies of these agents. He argues that the suggestion that it "would" turn over led to a self-fulfilling prophecy as white flight created space for newcomers.

reactionary ethnicity, which came about when Poles perceived that they were being forced out of their neighborhoods or jobs, strengthened ethnic identification.

This resurgence of ethnicity is reflected in the activities of Polonian organizations that centered on issues of defamation and discrimination. Polish Americans began a significant drive to stop the "Polish joke" that generally equates Polishness with stupidity. Polish Americans were increasingly irritated by the prominence of the Polish joke, especially in the period of cultural pluralism when racial slurs were becoming taboo. Wrobel argues that the Polish joke allowed people to claim they were not prejudiced by substituting Pole for black in a demeaning joke (1979). In the late 1970s Charles Keil wrote, "Poles are still, among all of America's ethnics, the easiest group to pile abuse upon, the group that one can have the most racist feelings about while having the least guilt feelings, the group you can call stupid and dirty without feeling the unpleasant surprise of suddenly feeling a little stupid and dirty yourself" (1979, 39). The Polish joke is a vestige of the racist eugenic theories of the early twentieth century and symbolizes the negative connotations associated with the Polish American ethnic identity: stupidity, vulgarity, racism, anti-Semitism, illiteracy, and filth (Kuniczak 1968; Lopata 1976, 77; Sandberg 1974, 74; Kleeman 1985, 13; Pula 1996). In 1969, the Polish American Advocates Society initiated a PAC advertisement campaign in the English-language press promoting the self-defense of Polish names (*PAC Newsletter*, September 1969). Later that year, the PAC formed a Civic Alertness Commission to serve as a public relations program and watchdog for libel and slander suits. The PAC president intervened with the publication of "The Official Polish Joke Book" and had it removed from several stores (*PAC Newsletter*, July 1970). And in 1972, the PAC published "A Guide to Anti-Defamation Activities."[21] Polonia's struggles were directed toward recasting the image of Polish Americans in a more positive light.

21. The PAC also supported House Congressional Resolution No. 308, which dealt with films and broadcasts defaming racial and ethnic groups, as well as Congressman Heltstoski's Anti-Slur Bill. By 1978, the Michigan Sentinel Committee was the "antidefamation arm" of the PAC, and the PAC was pushing to have sentinel committees in every state division. Polish American organizations protested against CBS, Hallmark Cards, Burt Reynolds, and Joan Rivers for their derogatory statements against Polish Americans (Pula 1995, 133). In 1984, a PAC leader stated that "discrimination remains our most important domestic problem" because it leads to defamation, denial of upward mobility, lack of federal funds, and fewer educational opportunities (*PAC Newsletter*, August 1984, 2).

As mentioned, the PAC also became active in fighting affirmative action legislation and proving that Polish Americans still suffered from discrimination. They created a Commission on Civic and Political Activities in the summer of 1969 to document the lack of Polish representation in governmental posts and to search for qualified Polish Americans willing to fill these posts. In 1975, the PAC Illinois Division created the Action Program with the purpose of securing increased representation for Polish Americans on the boards of Chicago's education, ecumenical, and governmental bodies. The Action Program was a direct reaction to the racial affirmative action programs and quotas taking form in the 1970s. The PAC, concerned about the low number of Polish Americans in American political life, mobilized to secure their share of governmental resources and political positions. It also funded projects that assessed the upward social mobility of Polish Americans (such as the presence of Polish Americans in professional medical schools) (Pacyga 1987, 47–48).

A second focus during this period of ethnic revival was on the celebration of cultural heritage and the creation of educational programs. In the 1970s, there was a "renaissance in ethnic interest" as scholars studied Polish Americans, families reintroduced Polish customs, and cities funded ethnic festivals (Pula 1995, 122). By 1974, there were over one hundred Polonia ethnic publications; a little less than half were in Polish, another third were bilingual (143). In 1970, PAC president Aloysius Mazewski introduced an Advisory Council on Cultural and Educational Affairs. The PAC also supported the Ethnic Heritage Studies Act (proposed by Chicago Alderman Roman Pucinski, a state director of the PAC) that created resources for the scholarly study of ethnic and immigrant issues.

According to its charter, the PAC had a dual agenda of working for the betterment of Poland and Polonia. Charles Rozmarek, leader of the PAC from its inception in 1944 until 1968, made Poland's liberation PAC's primary purpose. While the World War II émigrés supported this orientation, most American-born members of the ethnic community were more concerned with the domestic agenda of Polonia. When Aloysius Mazewski beat Rozmarek in a tough campaign for president in the late 1960s, he ran on the platform *Wychodźstwo dla wychodźstwa* (Emigrants for emigrants), the same rallying cry heard in the 1930s that urged the PAC to expend more resources to help Polish Americans. PAC editors wrote, "For the first time in its 26 years of history, the PAC . . . paid particular attention to what might be described as 'internal affairs' of American Polonia" (*PAC Newsletter*, July 1970, 3). Throughout the 1970s, the PAC concentrated mostly on the domestic issues of defamation, discrimination, cultural maintenance, and social mobility. Polonian historian Donald Pienkos even goes so far as to say that the concern for Poland was a "special interest" of the PAC (1984, 460). The interests of the PAC reflected the interests of the majority of Polonians. The ethnics were concerned with their own issues. "Although the young sympathize with the sufferings of the postwar Polish émigrés, they do not share any preoccupation with Polonia's relationship towards Poland. They want instead that greater emphasis be given to the fulfillment of their own well-being and their advance in the country" (Zachariasiewicz 1976, 665). In contrast to Polish Americans, the World War II émigrés felt that fighting for Poland's independence was the PAC's primary purpose rather than a special interest. As a result, PAC's work for Poland was done almost exclusively by World War II émigrés—they dominated the committees on Polish affairs, wrote the memoranda and statements, and crafted PAC's political stance on U.S.-Poland relations.

In the late 1970s, the PAC began to take a renewed interest in the homeland as the opposition in Poland became more visible, active, and formalized. In addition, the pontification of the Polish Cardinal Karol Wojtyla as Pope John Paul II in 1978 led to a resurgence of ethnic pride within the strong Roman Catholic Polish American community. PAC president Aloysius Mazewski said, in regards to the revitalization of Polish American ethnicity:

> Solidarity or the Polish Pope, that had a big effect, too. See this brings pride. I had one man, after many years I knew him, he finally admitted his wife was Polish, but he did it because the Pope. I had ambassadors that I was with that never told me they were Polish till later on they said, "You know, we're Polish." I said, "What the hell's the matter with you. I wear mine." You see, but that's the difference. It's the pride that has developed. The Polish pride that has been developed, [and] the elevation of the Pope has lot to do with Polish pride since the late seventies.

The excitement, hope, and publicity generated by the new Polish pope and the Solidarity movement captivated the attention of the PAC and many Polish Americans. Polish Americans were openly proud to be Polish and their organizations became more involved with Polish homeland affairs.

Conclusion

At the beginning of the twentieth century, Polonia was an immigrant community concerned with newcomer needs and its members had a strong attachment to the homeland. Community leaders struggled to define the nature of Polishness, broadening the regional cultural identity to include a national political component. The original diversity within the turn-of-the-century immigrant community was reflective of the diversity in the homeland, which included peasants and intelligentsia as well as socialists and nationalists. The ethnic group that emerged from this immigrant community, however, stressed only those features that complimented American mainstream values. In a reversal of Edward Said's concept of the construction of the Other in opposition to the Self, in the United States, ethnic identities (the Other) were constructed to compliment the American identity (the Self) by affirming and reflecting its values. The socialist wing of Polonia is seldom mentioned beyond the immigrant generation in the various tomes of Polish American history (Lopata 1976; Brozek 1985; Pula 1995). The anti-Russian and anti-Soviet sentiments in the community were also modified at various times to reflect the policies of Washington, D.C. Whenever Russia or the Soviet Union was an ally of the United States, Polonia's established leaders held their tongues. Even the reconstruction of the ethnic community as a "white ethnic" group in the 1960s served the needs of American society looking for a scapegoat for racism.

In the second generation the community shifted toward an American orientation. Fighting against the racist eugenic theories of the time, the community claimed a white identity and from this more secure position they constructed an ethnic identity based on the folk culture of their ancestors. The concerns for Poland during World War II and the arrival of the new émigré cohort restored some of Polonia's interest in Poland. The arrival of the educated cosmopolitan World War II émigrés, however, also emphasized just how much the Polish identity had changed. Two distinct groups existed in Polonia—the new émigré cohort and the established ethnic generations. The émigrés and ethnics found a collective identity under the banner of anticommunism and concern for Poland. The survival of Polishness into the third and fourth generation, however, was connected to domestic concerns in America. The social movements of the 1960s and the climate of cultural pluralism created a desire and opportunity to act together as an ethnic community. Polishness was uncoupled from the negatively defined white ethnic identity, and was used as a base for demonstrating structural and symbolic discrimination. While Polish American ethnic activism in the last three decades was associated with the issues of defamation and discrimination, the ethnic identity was also linked to cultural practices and a sense of peoplehood manifest in shared rituals and symbols such as the Christmas Eve supper (*Wigilia*) and the blessing of the Easter baskets (Sandberg 1974; Obidinski and Zand 1987). Parot (1975) shows that as late as the 1960s, at least thirteen communities in Chicago qualified as "Polish" based on population (at least a quarter of the population was Polish foreign-born or had at least one Polish foreign-born parent) and the presence of Polish institutions (churches, cultural, and social groups).

When the new Polish cohort arrived in the 1970s and 1980s, Polonia was composed of these World War II émigrés and their second-generation children, as well as the second-, third, fourth-, and fifth-generations of Polish Americans who were descendants of the early migrant cohort. In 1980, only 5 percent of the over 8 million Polish Americans in the United States had been born in Poland (U.S. Census, 1980: Detailed Population Characteristics, 1–9; Ancestry of the Population by State, 12). The overwhelming majority of Polonians were Americans of Polish heritage. Many of them were no longer active ethnics—they had no interest in Polish or Polonian affairs and did not define themselves by their ethnicity. For others, however, ethnicity was a salient identity as indicated by their continued participation in Polish American organizations.

In the 1980s, more than a hundred years after the onset of the early peasant migration, Polonia had not perished. Transformed, yes, but it was still an active community, and members of this community still participated in its organizations, celebrated its heritage, and identified themselves as Polish.

2

Immigrants, *Wakacjusze,* and Refugees

I simply thought there was no hope. I am not a hero. I am not a martyr.
—a Solidarity refugee

In the early 1960s, the Warsaw regime, under the leadership of Wladyslaw Gomulka, a "Polish" communist, allowed the Roman Catholic Church greater freedoms, returned social sciences to academic curriculums, expanded intellectual and artistic cultures, and relaxed censorship. Reformers (known as revisionists) were still active in the Communist Party, hoping "to give Polish Marxism a human face" (Davies 1982, 552). The Polish state and society were, however, still dominated by the Communist Party. Those who rejected communism were still dissatisfied, and when they publicly expressed this dissatisfaction they were often times persecuted. One man who emigrated during the 1960s said, "There was an awful hardship at home. My father was always kind of punished at work because he didn't want to join the Communist Party. He was suspended from being a sailor." Others emigrated because the communist economic system was unable to satisfy their material wants. Even so, living conditions in Poland were not unbearable, and in the 1960s there was no large scale emigration from Poland.

During this time, ceilings placed on immigration limited the number of Poles admitted to the United States. In the first half of the 1960s, roughly 7,000 Poles were admitted annually under the numerical limitations of the national origins quota system established in 1924 and modified in 1952. After the 1965 amendments to the Immigration and Nationality Act even fewer Poles were admitted. The 1965 act maintained a national ceiling (290,000 for all immigrants) but eliminated national origin, race, or ancestry as a qualification for entry. It opened America's border to immigrants from all continents, and as a result the percentage of slots allocated to immigrants from Europe dropped sharply. After this act took effect, the majority of new immigrants came from Asian and Latin American countries. In 1968, the number of Poles admitted under numerical limitations dropped to around 4,500, and averaged about 3,000 annually for the next twenty years (Table 2.1).[1] The 1965 act gave first preference to relatives of U.S. citizens and permanent residents for the purpose of family reunification, and second to immigrants with professions of exceptional ability and skilled or unskilled labor that were in short supply in the United States. More than three-quarters of all Poles admitted under numerical limitations came in under family preferences rather than occupation preferences.[2]

In the late 1960s, political, economic, and cultural conditions in Poland deteriorated. In 1968, unrest in the universities, initiated by intellectuals but manipulated by factions within the Polish Communist Party, ended any serious attempts to reform the Communist Party. Most revisionists, who emerged in 1956 as a group of intellectual party members strongly socialistic but disillusioned with Stalinism, were expelled from the Party by 1968. A wave of strikes in 1970, precipitated by price increases in basic foodstuffs and marked by state violence against the workers, led to a reshuffling of communist leaders. With the opening up of relations with the West beginning in the 1970s (Nixon traveled to Poland in 1972), Edward Gierek, the new First Party secretary, initiated a series of economic programs oriented toward increasing exports, improving agriculture, and raising the standard of living (Davies 1982, 626–29). For the first years of this new regime the mood was optimistic—there were more goods on the shelves, real wages

---

1. For most immigration scholars, the "new immigration" begins with the 1965 Immigration and Nationality Act because it drastically changed the composition of the immigration flow by admitting more Asians and Latinos (roughly 80 percent of new immigrants admitted after 1968 were from these two regions of the world). The 1965 act, however, had a reverse effect on European immigrants, restricting rather than expanding the numbers admitted. It therefore does not make as much sense to use the 1965 act as a beginning date for the new Polish immigration. Instead, I mark the beginning of the new Polish cohort with the year 1960, even though most of the newcomers arrived in the 1970s and 1980s. A beginning point is necessary in order to separate the new cohort from the World War II cohort. By 1960, most new arrivals to the United States had lived in communist Poland for at least fifteen years, and the majority of arrivals listed Poland as their last country of residence. Both of these factors separate them from the World War II émigrés who had little or no experience living in a communist regime and who often arrived from a third country such as England or Germany.

2. Eighty percent of the visas for all immigrant groups were distributed under the four family preference categories (*Statistical Yearbook of the INS*, 1990, A.2–7).

Table 2.1 Polish Immigrants and Nonimmigrants Admitted into the United States, 1960–1993

Years	Polish immigrants admitted*			Polish nonimmigrants admitted**		
	Total number	Number admitted under numerical cap	Percent admitted under numerical cap	Total number	Number admitted as visitors for pleasure	Percent admitted as visitors for pleasure
1960–69	77,650	61,604	79.3	166,815	121,390	72.7
1970–79	42,378	31,940	75.4	352,269	239,619	68.1
1980–89	81,578	28,996	35.5	449,235	356,266	79.3
1990–93	93,086	51,747	55.5	262,861	184,663	70.3
Totals	294,692	174,287	59.1	1,213,180	901,938	73.3

*Total immigrants include both new arrivals and those who adjusted their status to permanent resident. Immigrants not subject to numerical limitations include refugees and asylees, as well as immediate relatives of adult U.S. citizens (parents, spouses, and children) until 1993. Beginning in 1993, immediate relatives were included under the numerical cap as were "diversity immigrants." As a result in 1993, 96.8 percent of all the new Polish immigrants were under the numerical limitation, compared to only 38 percent for 1990–91. In 1992, 9,383 Poles were admitted as "diversity transition" immigrants; in 1993, another 14,806 were admitted.

**Other nonimmigrants include: temporary visitors for business, treaty traders and investors, intracompany transferees, returning resident aliens, transit aliens, parolees, students, temporary workers and trainees, exchange visitors, foreign government officials, international representatives, NATO officials, representatives of foreign information media, spouses and children of students, temporary workers, exchange visitors, intracompany transferees, and fiancees of U.S. citizens and their children.

Sources: Columns 2–4: Immigrants admitted by selected class of admission and region and selected country of birth, *Annual Report of the Immigration and Naturalization Service*, 1965–78; *Statistical Yearbook of the Immigration and Naturalization Service*, 1979–93. Columns 5–7: Nonimmigrants admitted by class of admission and region and selected country of birth, *Annual Report of the Immigration and Naturalization Service*, 1965–78; *Statistical Yearbook of the Immigration and Naturalization Service*, 1979–93, Washington, D.C.: GPO.

rose, and job opportunities expanded. A Pole who did not emigrate until the 1980s said: "You see, in Poland it was not always bad. In the seventies it was really nice. We go to school and we could read and have our little apartment. The economy was not bad."

Loans, however, needed to be repaid. The influx of Western dollars had not altered what Miaria Los termed the "dogma of the total subjugation of production to the party" and the inevitable production inefficiencies and generally poor management practices that were a part of that subjugation. The result was predictable. Los concludes: "The initial improvements in the artificially revitalized economy proved to be short-lived and the increased expectations of consumers were left unmet" (1988, 34). In addition to this, Poland was acutely crippled by the oil crisis and international recession in the mid-1970s. The oil crisis hindered Poland's industrial production and the international recession contracted their export market; as exports decreased, imports decreased and the consumer market dwindled. In 1975, debts exceeded exports and Poland began to incur new debts to repay old debts. In June 1976, the government tried to solve this debt problem by raising food prices by 60 percent. This led to work stoppages and riots. Price increases were rescinded and, with extensive government subsidies, the prices stayed at the 1975 levels for the next four years. The next attempt to raise them in 1980 sparked the wave of strikes that led to the formation of Solidarity.

Immigration to the United States rose steadily throughout the 1970s. Although not reflected in the numbers of Polish immigrants admitted under numerical limitations (which remained constant throughout the 1970s because of the ceilings imposed by the United States), the growing dissatisfaction with the Polish economy was reflected in the escalating number of temporary visitors. Temporary visitors are officially classified as nonimmigrants when they enter the United States. They do not have permanent resident status, they are allowed to stay in the United States for only a limited time period, and most do not have permission to work in the United States (the exception are those on special work visas). This group includes tourists, business people, students, and government officials. The largest group of Polish nonimmigrants are those who enter as tourists (officially classified as "temporary visitors for pleasure"), usually on visas valid for six months. They are known in Chicago Polonia as *wakacjusze* (vacationers). Many *wakacjusze* violate the restrictions of their visa by working in the United States and overstaying their time restrictions. These *wakacjusze* represent the Polish version of illegal migrant workers. On average, twelve thousand temporary visitors entered annually in the 1960s and this number doubled to almost twenty-four thousand as an annual average in the 1970s (see Table 2.1).

For the temporary migrant worker as well as the permanent immigrant, the money earned abroad often supported families back in Poland. Working abroad was both a tradition and a necessity in Poland. Lech Walesa, the leader of the Solidarity movement, wrote about his parents going to America in 1973: "They didn't go there out of a sense of adventure. The decision to go was dictated by common sense and tradition: in our family there had always been someone on the other side of the ocean. It was in our blood: one or another went over there so that the rest of the family could count on some security and a chance of financial help" (1987, 33). The exchange rate was extremely favorable when Poland was a communist country—a week's salary at minimum wage in the United States was close to a year's salary in Poland. One *wakacjusze* said, "I arrived on Sunday [to Chicago] with a job waiting for me, and by noon on Monday I had earned a month's salary."

For others, the economic freedom in America's open market was a reason for coming and staying. One vexing source of frustration in communist Poland was the restricted consumer market (which is why Gierek's strategy of using Western loans to stock the shelves was so popular). Access to telephones, houses, and, as one man said, "brown rice" attracted Poles to the United States. One woman who emigrated in the late 1970s said, "Most people come because they don't have to wait in line for toilet paper." Several Poles had come to the United States for a visit and, as one said, after "seeing the life in the West, the material stuff, and the way people could express themselves" later returned as permanent immigrants.[3] While some who emigrated in the 1970s pointed out the "feeling of being a free person" as a primary motivation for coming to the United States, the desire for increased political and civic freedoms was stated more often as a reason for emigrating by Poles who arrived in the 1980s. In the 1970s, most emigrated for economic reasons.

A manifest opposition coalesced in Poland in the late 1970s and early

---

3. In addition to political and economic conditions, people also emigrated to change their private situation. Some women emigrated to escape abusive husbands, parents emigrated to be with their children, and spouses emigrated as an alternative to divorce (Mostwin 1991, 15). Massey et al. (1987) also note that in mature emigration waves, economic conditions explain less than they do in young emigration waves. By the 1970s, emigration from Poland to the United States had been a tradition for over a century.

1980s. The first open and legal opposition organization was the Workers' Defense Committee (KOR, after its Polish name *Komitet Obrony Robotników*), formed to defend workers who had been fired and imprisoned after the 1976 strikes in Radom and Ursus.[4] Following KOR there was an explosion of organized opposition activity: the Flying University (formally called the Association for Academic Courses, which offered classes in such taboo topics as "real" Polish history), the Farmer's Self-Defense Committee and other human rights groups, critical discussion groups, independent publishing houses, art showings, and critical theater. Between 1976 and 1980 there were at least one thousand strikes in Poland (Staniszkis 1984, 185).

The most dramatic and momentous of these was the August 1980 Gdansk shipyard strike, which led to the formation of the trade union *Niezależny Samorządny Związek Zawodowy* (Independent Self-Governing Trades Union), known in Poland as *Solidarność* (Solidarity). Solidarity became the organizational vehicle for both the trade union and the democratic opposition movement in Poland. The strikes in the summer of 1980 were once again a reaction to an increase in prices and a failing economic system. In addition, the previous opposition activities had awakened public sentiment and helped mobilize collective action. The numerous underground publishing houses were printing details of Poland's desperate economic and environmental conditions; the Flying University provided uncensored courses in Polish history. The pontification of Jan Pawel II (John Paul II) in 1978, and his visit to Poland in June 1979, instilled national pride and gave Poles the assurance that they were capable of organizing and policing large manifestations. Solidarity encompassed every part of Polish society: intellectuals, religious leaders, workers, professionals, and Communist Party members. At its peak, 80 percent of the industrial work force in Poland (50 percent of its total work force) were Solidarity union members. All together, roughly ten million Poles were allied with Solidarity, almost one-third of the nation's population. While Solidarity was officially a labor union, its broad-based reform goals and wide-spread support justified its title as a social movement.[5] It sufficiently threatened the Polish and Soviet regimes, and on December 13, 1981, General Jaruzelski imposed martial law. Roughly ten

    4. In 1977 this organization renamed itself the Committee for Social Self-Defense (*Komitet Samoobrony Społecznej* or KSS) and is often referred to as KSS-KOR. I will simply use KOR.
    5. The twenty-one demands presented by the Inter-enterprise Strike Committee in August of 1980 included four democratic demands, such as the right to strike and the appointment of management by merit; three information demands, such as the right to publish their own news and access to truthful information; eight monetary demands, such as increased wages and

thousand national, regional, and local Solidarity leaders were imprisoned, and the opposition moved underground. In July 1983 martial law was lifted and a general amnesty was granted in July 1984. (The majority of political prisoners were held six months to one year.) Over 10,000 people spent time in interment and thousands of activists chose to emigrate once they were released (Amnesty International Reports, 1983).

The imposition of martial law in Poland and the enactment of the Refugee Act of 1980 in the United States resulted in a wave of new Polish refugees. Until 1980, the United States admitted refugees on an ad hoc basis of government acts and presidential directives. After 1965, refugees were admitted as a seventh preference of immigrants, and were given 6 percent of the total slots available to immigrants. The Refugee Act of 1980 eliminated this seventh preference category and began admitting refugees on a uniform basis according to the definition of a refugee as a person residing outside his or her country of nationality who is unwilling to return to that country because of a well-grounded fear of persecution based on race, religion, nationality, membership in a particular social group, or political opinion. In the 1980s, over thirty-three thousand Poles were admitted to the United States as refugees or asylees (Table 2.2).[6] Between 1983 and 1985, almost a thousand Polish refugees were resettled in Chicago, representing 8 percent of the Polish refugees in the United States during that period, and there was a significant (but uncounted) secondary migration of Polish refugees who moved from their original U.S. city of resettlement to Chicago (Cichon, Gozdziak, and Grover 1986, 5–9).

In addition to the refugees, a large number of *wakacjusze* arrived in the 1980s. In that decade, nearly 450,000 nonimmigrants arrived and almost 80 percent of those came as temporary visitors for pleasure (see Table 2.1). The director of the Polish Welfare Association in Chicago in 1988 estimated

pensions; and six social demands such as no-work Saturdays, day-care centers, and lower retirement age.

Those interested in the various revolts and opposition movements in Poland have several excellent sources available. See Bethell (1969) for a fuller discussion of the 1968 revolt. Staniszkis (1984) offers an insightful class analysis of the problems and revolts in the 1970s, while Goldfarb (1982) examines the political undertones of the cultural arts community in the 1970s. Kubik (1994) examines the symbolic struggles between the Church, state, and opposition during the 1970s. Lipski (1985) analyzes the formation and activities of KOR. In addition, Walesa (1987), Ash (1983), and Ascherson (1981) all present very readable descriptions of the events of 1980–81.

6. Asylees are similar to refugees except that at the time of their application they are already residing in the United States or are at a port of entry.

Table 2.2 Polish refugees and asylees granted permanent resident status, 1961–1992

Years	Number	Percent
1961–70	3,197	6.6
1971–80	5,882	12.1
1981–90	33,889	69.6
1991–92	5,717	11.7
Totals	48,685	100.0

SOURCE: *Statistical Yearbook of the Immigration and Naturalization Service*, 1990 (table 34), 1993 (table 33). Washington, D.C.: GPO.

that approximately one-third of the *wakacjusze* overstay their visa limitations, so that the number of *wakacjusze* in the United States in any given year is far greater than the annual number admitted. Using this one-third estimate, by 1991 there were about a quarter of a million *wakacjusze* in the United States.[7] Polonian and social service leaders estimated that fifty thousand to one hundred thousand of them were living (and working) in Chicago.

The situation in Poland changed dramatically in 1989. Between 1986 and 1988, economic conditions in Poland continued to worsen and eventually led to an outbreak of strikes in May and June of 1988. In the climate of *glasnost* and *perestroika* introduced by Mikhail Gorbachev, which permitted discussions of political and social issues, government policies, and economic reform, the Polish government sat down with opposition leaders and charted out an initial course of action that included legalization of Solidarity and the promise of partially free elections. Elections were held in June 1989 for a two-house parliament. Solidarity candidates won all but one of the seats open to them. Solidarity candidate Tadeusz Mazowiecki became Poland's prime minister and the new Warsaw government began implementing economic, social, and cultural reforms. In the eyes of Western politicians and entrepreneurs, Poland was no longer a communist country.

7. This estimate may be high given the low number of Polish immigrants who applied for amnesty following the Immigration Reform and Control Act (IRCA) in 1986. This legislation offered permanent residency to illegal immigrants who could prove they had been in the country since 1982. As of 1991, only 17,014 Poles filed amnesty applications, compared to 1.2 million filed by Mexicans (*Statistical Yearbook of the INS*, 1990, 91). Many illegal Polish immigrants were ineligible for the program, others were afraid to come forward, and some had not decided whether they would stay in America.

The dismantling of the communist regime and the rebuilding of Poland in the image of Western capitalist democracies affected migration in several ways. First, Poles lost their raison d'être for being political refugees. Refugees admitted in the early 1990s represented processing backlogs. The number of *wakacjusze*, however, grew steadily. On the average, roughly forty-six thousand temporary visitors for pleasure arrived annually between 1990 and 1993, compared to an average of thirty-five thousand annually in the 1980s (see Table 2.1). The number of immigrants admitted under numerical limitations also swelled as a result of changes in U.S. policy. The Immigration Act of 1990 raised the ceiling for all immigrants (to seven hundred thousand for the years 1992–94). Included under that cap were slots for fifty-five thousand "diversity immigrants," defined as aliens from countries that were adversely affected by the 1965 Immigration Act. These slots were primarily reserved for European immigrants, who received three-quarters of the visas, with Polish and Irish immigrants as the largest recipients. Between 1990 and 1993, 93,086 Poles were admitted under numerical limitations, while in the three previous decades combined only 201,606 were admitted.

To summarize, between 1960 and 1993, almost three hundred thousand Polish immigrants were admitted, and about 60 percent of them fell under numerical limitations. In addition, over 1.2 million Poles arrived in the United States on temporary visas, and 73 percent of them were *wakacjusze* on "temporary visas for pleasure" (see Table 2.1). And, finally, nearly forty-nine thousand Polish refugees were admitted into the United States, and almost 70 percent of those were admitted during the 1980s (see Table 2.2).

Betrayal, Hopelessness, and Frustration

The reasons for emigration in the 1980s were both political and economic. Those who faced prosecution in Poland as a result of their oppositional activities emigrated to escape imprisonment, police surveillance and harassment, and job blacklisting—basically the inability to move around freely in their home country. One immigrant said, "Every person has a right to live in freedom, to live without the secret police knocking on the door." One man left because he could not face going to prison a second time: "My colleagues told me the first time was much easier than the second time." Another emigrated because he considered his other two options to be: "Stay in the underground or go to prison." At least sixty activists had been killed in the year following martial law, and the use of terror and intimidation by the state militia continued into the mid-1980s (Los 1988, 35–51).

The communist regime encouraged political prisoners to emigrate (Amnesty International Reports, 1983). Prime Minister General Jaruzelski announced that interned opposition activists would be released from prison and permitted to travel to the United States (Department of State Bulletin, December 1982, 58). One émigré described the atmosphere in a jail in Nysa, Poland, after this announcement.

> There started to be a tremendous discussion in jail. . . . Some people had a really hard time in jail. And for them, this notion that they could change their position, they are now in jail, but it depends only on their simple decision, and they can go to somewhere like California, and lying underneath a palm and drinking American beer. . . . [If you decided to emigrate] immediately you were released from jail, you were released from this oppression, and for us, it was a matter of pride not to compromise ourselves to this extent. Because at this moment it was not our decision.

Some men did leave at this time, but most did not emigrate until 1983, after they had been out of prison for over a year. It was generally frowned upon to exchange a political prison sentence for life abroad. Opposition leader Adam Michnik wrote that the "interned Solidarity activists who choose exile are committing an act that is both a capitulation and a desertion" because their escape will cause the nation to lose confidence in the opposition (Michnik 1985, 23). He argued that for Solidarity activists, emigration was no longer a personal decision but a public issue, and that the activists were obligated to consider how emigration would affect their compatriots. Politics in Poland, he wrote, "is inseparably linked with morality" (1983, 23). As I have written elsewhere, during this period and especially for the political activists, emigration was constructed as a moral issue (Erdmans 1992a). Helena Flam also found that issues of honor and obligation, accompanied by feelings of abandonment and desertion, marked discussions regarding emigration. One activist she interviewed said:

> The most painful issue was the decision to emigrate, with which I struggled terribly long. The decision was intertwined with the prestige issue. Here I circumvent its extreme formulation articulated by Michnik in one of his letters, probably prison letters, to the effect

that "saving my neck I do not want to lose my face." . . . It was a macabre, tragic decision. In the airplane I broke down into tears from shame. (1996, 112)

Polish refugees were painfully aware of the fact that emigration was defined as desertion. One night a refugee helped me translate an article, written by the Polish episcopate, urging Poles to stay home and help rebuild the nation instead of emigrating. One sentence read, "Emigration is escaping from our fraction of responsibility to the nation." At that point the refugee put the paper down and said, "Mary, I can't do this any more. This is me. I escaped. Don't press me to do this, it's self-annihilation." He stopped translating.

Within this context of emigration as betrayal, some refugees retained their honor by explaining the situation in Poland as hopeless and beyond repair. They felt the ship was sinking fast and they would have drowned had they not abandoned it. The mood of optimism and hope during the heady 1980–81 years, and even during the time of martial law when many were imprisoned, vanished in the face of the harsh realities of a bankrupt economy and oppressive military regime. After their release from prison, activists returned home to communities that were scared, impoverished, and simply tired of fighting. This was the point when many activists decided to emigrate. One activist stated: "One year before exile, when I start to think about emigration I thought that everything gone, that this is finish of Solidarity. . . . I decided to leave when I got out of prison and talked to people." Another said that when he returned from prison, "There was only a small group of people willing to fight. Most of the population didn't believe in anything, they didn't believe the communists, they didn't believe Solidarity." Some were empathetic to the desperate plight of people. One refugee said, "People have to stand a couple of hours in line for food, they have no time to think about politics." But others expressed anger and frustration toward their communities' unwillingness to organize. One man was upset that people opted to work instead of strike. He said: "I really pissed up. I wanted them to turn off the machines and stuff. And this is the first time I started to think, 'I can't stay here. I can't just stay and not support but be like vegetable.' And I say, 'I gotta do something, I gotta go somewhere.'" Flam also noted that opposition members pointed out the "gray" mid-1980s as a period when "activists were confronted with mass indifference and so with the issue of the futility of their own actions" (1996, 107).

Refugees in their late twenties and thirties believed there was no longer any chance of changing the ruling regime, that no real change could come from working within the system, and that their futures would be wasted if they remained in Poland. One refugee said, "I became dissatisfied and I couldn't resolve the structural problems. I felt wasted. I was working without satisfaction." A thirty-year-old refugee who had been a regional union leader in Silesia described his feelings of despair and futility as connected to his inability to see any results from his actions.

> At a certain period of time I realized I was wasting my time. One year after I left jail and I had made a hundred attempts to do something, I realized that the hundred-and-first attempt would be as good as the ninety-ninth. It means that it's hopeless. I didn't have any independent position in society and I didn't have anything to give my family. . . . I realized that my skills are wasted. In this area I was spending my time undercover, hiding myself. I'm not helping people. I was handicapped. . . . I wanted to use my life in a very egoistic sense. To take advantage of my age. To do something else, because I realized in Poland there is a limit to my ability to do something.

Asked whether he thought that things would have gotten better in three or five years, he responded: "Maybe I did think of that, but five years is a very long time, and I realized that my skills would be wasted, simply wasted, because I couldn't improve my ability to be a leader even. It was a very, very, for me, disappointing situation . . . my friends gave me money to survive, I didn't have any work, and this gave me shame." Frustrated in their attempts to bring about change in the public sphere, they chose instead to change their private situation. Social change writ small. They chose emigration as their last act of defiance, their last statement against the regime. Social protest writ small.

Another reason for emigrating in the 1980s was the disastrous economic situation—power shortages were more frequent, there were problems getting gasoline, lines were longer at the store, nonnecessities could only be bought on the black market, and basic foodstuffs were becoming scarce.[8]

---

8. Even though I separate economic from political factors, no sharp division necessarily exists. As Norman Davies states:

> All political exiles are affected by the material circumstances of their departure, just as every economic migrant adds to the political and cultural consequences of mass

The economic problems of the 1970s became magnified in the 1980s. People could not support themselves and their families. One man said, "The six-person family would be no problem in the United States but it was in Poland." Poles came abroad (temporarily or permanently depending on which visas they could get) because they could not support themselves in the lifestyle they preferred on only Polish wages.

Poles also emigrated because of the limited occupational opportunities in Poland. First, party control over state institutions limited opportunities for upward mobility to members of the Communist Party, and second, more generally, as the economy lagged, occupational mobility dragged. Jadwiga Staniszkis notes that in the 1970s upward mobility had slowed down; economic stagnation and a glut of university graduates left few open spaces for advancement. By the mid-1970s, every eighth employee was a manager (1984, 109). During this period, Solidarity had offered an alternative status structure. Staniszkis writes, "More people with personal status problems became members of regional authorities of Solidarity. Many dislocated, marginal, white-collar workers, their upward mobility blocked, were elected" (115). When the union was disbanded, this alternative status structure collapsed and activists emigrated. Moreover, as the economy worsened in the 1980s, many professionals found it difficult to advance in their careers. One immigrant said, "I was a photographer and studied law and philosophy. I couldn't do anything with these interests and I became dissatisfied. I felt I was wasted and I was only thirty years old." A *wakacjusze* who was a physicist in Poland came because he could not do research with the poor technical equipment he had in Poland.

In addition to political, economic, and occupational reasons for emigrating, Poles were also psychologically motivated. The contradictions in the communist system became glaringly ridiculous and for some, unbearable. Marcin Kula argues that emigration from communist Poland "often meant departure from the world of the absurd" and draws from the memoirs of one émigré who wrote:

---

movements of people. . . . The starving migrant who blames his poverty on the neglect or mismanagement of the ruling government is making a political comment no less than an economic decision. (1986, 254–55)

In reference specifically to the new emigration from Poland, Marcin Kula (1996) argues that because of the intertwined nature of the economy and polity in communist Poland, it is difficult to separate political and economic motives of emigration.

> Doublefacedness and hypocrisy have become the standard of social adaptation, which resulted in social, economic, and political absurdity. . . . The most discreditable was the permanent lack of articles used for personal hygiene as well as footwear and clothing. There were also shocking shortages of food, medicines, books, schools, hospitals and flats. But there was plenty of policemen, soldiers, tanks, armoured transporters, tear gas, and cells in prison. (1996, 51–52)

Asked whether he would return to Poland, one immigrant responded excitedly, "Didn't you see what it is like!! The whole system is irrational. How can any sane man live there?" An article written by the Polish episcopate, published in Chicago in 1988, entitled "The Emigration of Young Poles," pointed out that young people were emigrating because they did not find the collective ideology of communism attractive and that living in a dual economic system where even everyday foodstuffs had to be bought on the black market was psychologically frustrating (*Prymasowska Rada Społeczna*, 1985). Another author wrote:

> There are those who can not emotionally handle living in the homeland, and even though they would probably be alright financially, they emigrate looking for a more just—in their eyes—life. Not everyone has the strength to stand up to unwritten laws, informal "deals" and so-called "arrangements" which have shaped the present day reality in Poland. (Sieradzki 1989, 3)

In the late 1980s, graffiti on the walls of Polish cities read "*Emigruj albo strzelaj*" (Emigrate or shoot) reflecting the hopelessness and frustration of the youth in Poland (Bukowski 1989, 4).

Jan Kubik (1994) provides a meticulous account of the Polish communist regime's double-speak, its manipulation of national Polish symbols, and distortion of Polish history—all of which the Polish people saw through. The regime, he argues, tried to legitimate itself by co-opting parts of the existing national culture, but failed miserably. While most Poles had never fully recognized the Warsaw regime's right to govern them, the discourse of the opposition further discredited the state. After 1981, the state's repressive actions against the opposition destroyed its last vestige of legitimacy for many people. One man, who emigrated in his early twenties in 1987, said he had decided to leave when he was sixteen years old and read about the massacre at the coal mines in Katowice during martial law: "I remember

I was crying when I heard that I think nine people died. And I told my parents, 'I don't know when I'm going to leave, all I know is I'm going to leave this country.' " At the university, he consciously chose a course of study that would help him achieve his goals—he majored in English and emigrated shortly after he graduated. In one poll in the late 1980s, three-quarters of the Polish youth expressed a desire to emigrate (Bukowski 1989).

To summarize, in the 1980s, Poland's failing economic system, political repression, restricted civil liberties, and saturated job market influenced Poles' decisions to seek a better life abroad. These economic, political, and psychological conditions were experienced, in varying degrees, by all Poles. Thus, the conditions that gave rise to their departures were quite similar— Poles could not find a place for themselves in their home society. The routes by which they entered the United States, however, were different, and reflected variations in personal biography that gave them access to different resources in America. Those who had family abroad could apply for immigration visas; those who had been very active in the Solidarity movement could apply for refugee status. The rest applied for tourist visas.

Description of the Survey and Interview Samples

The following (and preceding) sections rely on data I collected during my fieldwork and through formal interviews with and surveys of Polish newcomers. I formally interviewed 31 new refugees in Chicago ($N = 21$) and California ($N = 10$). I also conducted several surveys. The first was a survey of Poles who voted by absentee ballot in the June 1989 Polish elections (the sample included 457 Poles who had arrived after 1960). The second was a survey of members of the Polish-American Economic Forum, an organization formed in 1989 to promote business linkages between Americans and Poles and encourage the growth of Poland's new market system. Of the 109 members surveyed (roughly one-fourth of the membership), 92 were members of the new migrant cohort. Third, I distributed questionnaires to Poles attending the English As a Second Language (ESL) classes I taught at the Polish University Abroad (PUNO) in Chicago between 1988 and 1990. Fourth, in 1989, I completed a survey of 183 businesses in the Polish immigrant community in Chicago known as *Jackowo.* Fifth, in 1992, I interviewed 35 Polish immigrants working as home health care workers for the elderly in Chicago, most of whom were working illegally. (See Appendix, Table A.1, for a summary of the data sources; and Table A.2, for descriptive statistics of these samples.) Taken together, these samples represent data on 685 Polish newcomers and 183 businesses. They provide information on the three different newcomer groups. Information about refugees comes primarily from the interviews and fieldwork. The survey of voters provides comparative data on permanent immigrants (53 percent of the sample) versus temporary migrants/*wakacjusze* (42 percent); the Forum sample includes mostly permanent residents (86 percent); and the sample of home health care workers represents the *wakacjusze*. The ESL students were the most diverse group and included *wakacjusze*, immigrants newly legalized under the Immigration Reform and Control Act of 1986, permanent residents, and even a few refugees.

Poles in these samples were fairly recent newcomers; a great majority arrived in the United States in the 1980s (see Table A.2). They were a little "newer" than the national population of Polish newcomers; 60 percent of all Poles who arrived after 1960 came between 1980 and 1993 (see Table 2.1). More than half of the newcomers in these samples emigrated when they were in their twenties and thirties, and in three of the samples a large majority were men (see Table A.2).[9] The newcomers were mostly from urban areas; no more than 16 percent from any sample came from villages.[10] Many newcomers arrived from the established sending regions of Poland (such as the southeastern region Galicia and northeastern region Masuria).[11] The refugees all came from urban areas, especially those cities

9. This sample is a bit younger and has a higher proportion of men than the national immigrant population. Between 1980 and 1993, only 49 percent of Polish immigrants were twenty to thirty-nine years old, and roughly half were men (*Statistical Yearbook of the INS*, 1980–91, Table: Immigrants Admitted by Selected Country of Birth, Age, Sex). Whereas my samples include quota immigrants, refugees, and temporary visitors, the national figures pertain only to immigrants admitted under numerical limitations.

10. Poles in emigration appear to be more cosmopolitan than Poles in Poland. In Poland, 38.8 percent of the population lived in rural villages in 1988 (*Rocznik Statystyczny*, 1989, 50). The sample of ESL students had the lowest percent living in large cities but the sample also had a majority (52 percent) from the southeastern provinces, a mostly rural region.

11. In the sample of 457 voters, thirty-nine of the forty-nine provinces in Poland were represented. The largest numbers of voters came from the provinces of Warsaw ($N = 62$), Krakow ($N = 58$), Tarnow ($N = 53$), and Nowy Sadz ($N = 36$). All six provinces that make up the southeastern region were represented in the sample, and together they made up 40 percent of the voter sample.

that had strong opposition organizations (Gdansk, Szczecin, Wroclaw, Warsaw, for example).

Emigracja to deklasacja

This is an educated, skilled, and professional migrant cohort. Most of the newcomers had some postsecondary education. More than 90 percent of the refugees had university education or technical degrees in such fields as journalism, economics, chemistry, and engineering. The immigrants who were admitted under numerical limitations (hereafter referred to as "quota" immigrants) were also well educated, many with Master of Arts degrees, and all with high school or vocational school educations.[12] The *wakacjusze* were the most diverse. Many were educated professionals, but this group also included migrants from rural farming and mountain regions with only vocational or high school educations. Still, in the sample of voters, 43 percent of those with temporary visas (the *wakacjusze*) had some postsecondary education, and over 90 percent of the *wakacjusze* working as home health care providers had some postsecondary education.[13]

Most immigrants were unable to find positions in the United States commensurate with their education or occupations in Poland. For them, migration represented a decline in occupational status, expressed in the oft heard phrase *emigracja to deklasacja*, which translates unpoetically as "emigration is downward class mobility." This was most true for those who came from the middle or professional classes in Poland. Medical doctors became nursing home attendants; engineers became drafters; and school teachers became maids and child care workers. The decline in status was most apparent among *wakacjusze* because they did not have valid work permits.

12. Another study of Polish refugees in Chicago in 1983 by the Catholic Social Services also found that Polish refugees had more education than other refugee groups (11.3 years, but this included children), and they had had professional occupations (25 percent) or skilled and semiskilled occupations (53 percent) in Poland (Templeton 1984, 27–28). In Mostwin's survey of 552 Polish immigrants who arrived between 1974 and 1984, she found that 29 percent had university degrees, and only 8 percent had less than a high school education (1991, 100).

13. The *wakacjusze* represented in the sample of home health care workers were employed in one of the best jobs available to illegal workers, taking care of rich elderly clients. Most had medical backgrounds that gave them access to these positions. See Erdmans 1996a and 1996b for a more extensive discussion of this sample.

An article published in *Tygodnik Podhalański* in Poland described the work situation in America in the following humorous expose:

> Certainly, we can only be proud, when we hear the conversation on the porch during lunch time, when the docent [associate professor] of the cultural history department discusses with the gynecology graduate about the best wax to use and the appropriate thickness of the layers of the wax; the graduate from the Polytechnic [Technical University] in Warsaw argues with the dentist about the effectiveness of the mops made from artificial materials feathers for gathering dust; the chemist, who was an assistant at Jagiellonian University, at that moment is divided about the best way to sanitize the office bureau that he cleans. (Tyszkiewicz 1993, 7–8)

The two most common occupations for the *wakacjusze* in Chicago were construction for men (especially tuck-pointing and roofing), and domestic services for women (housekeeping, child care, and elder care). Newcomers with and without working papers (such as a permanent visa or "green card") often found jobs within a few days of arrival. Employment agencies, newspaper advertisements, and word of mouth provided information about where to find jobs and how to circumvent the legal system (for example, how to get an illegal Social Security card). In Chicago, employment broker agencies helped even undocumented workers find positions (Erdmans 1996a and 1996b). These agencies were listed in the phone book, and their offices were in high visibility areas; they were not clandestine, backroom operations.

Newcomers who were permanent residents were less likely to work in the same labor sectors as the *wakacjusze*, and when they did they were able to negotiate better working conditions (better salaries, hours, and benefits). For example, one woman who was an elder care worker for several years at the standard salary of $50–$60 for a 24-hour day, upgraded her position after she got her work documentation to a wage of $12 an hour and worked only in the afternoons. Permanent immigrants were also more likely to be foremen and contractors at construction sites. Because quota immigrants and refugees had work authorization, and because their stay in the United States was more likely to be permanent, they had more opportunity and incentive to improve their job situation. Permanent residents were more likely to return to school to recertify their degrees or learn new skills. Still, even for those who stayed permanently, it was very difficult to overcome the negative effects of migration (such as language barriers and circumscribed networks) to get a position at the same level they held in Poland (Erdmans 1995). For example, a chemistry professor in Poland held a series of research assistantships at several prestigious universities in the Chicago area, but was never able to regain his former position as an associate professor. One man, a successful journalist in Poland, told me, "I can not gain anything in this country in a professional sense." Another said, "In Poland we were members of the elite, but not here."[14] Despite the high educational levels of the refugee and permanent resident samples (for example, the interview and Forum samples), less than half of them had professional occupations in the United States.

Refugees and quota immigrants were similar in that they were both in the United States permanently, which set them apart from the *wakacjusze*. Still the two permanent groups differed in the types of support they received. Refugees were eligible for government assistance upon arrival. The Refugee Act of 1980 established a program for the resettlement of refugees that included state and federal support for language and job retraining, as well as housing allowance and food stamps. In the mid-1980s, a refugee could receive assistance for up to thirty-six months after arrival. The refugees often stayed out of the job market for a few months or years to improve their language skills or upgrade their education so that they could get a better job (Cichon et al. 1986, 14). Unlike the refugees, quota immigrants could not apply for government support until they became permanent residents (a process that took at least one year), and even then they were not eligible for as much support as refugees. As permanent residents they were eligible for the same types of government assistance available to all American citizens. Quota immigrants who had family in the United States might rely on them for support and stay out of the labor market for a few months until they learned the language. More often than not, however, they were encouraged by their families (if not actively forced) to find a job within a few weeks after arrival.

In summary, there was little difference among the newcomers in terms of education and occupation in Poland. They were mostly educated, working-

---

14. One study of Polish refugees found that the majority of the sample had completed college and over half had masters' degrees; however, the refugees initial jobs were entry level positions including housekeeping, landscaping, waiting tables, building maintenance, construction, and clerical (Cichon, Gozdziak, and Grover 1986). The study also found that almost all of the refugees improved their positions within a few months as soon as they learned English; however, they never found jobs equivalent to the positions they had in Poland.

and middle-class people with skilled, technical, and professional occupations. Nonetheless, they had different routes of incorporation into the U.S. labor markets. The *wakacjusze* were more likely to be found in secondary labor market positions characterized by low pay, low benefits, and low prestige. The permanent immigrants (refugees and quota immigrants) eventually found employment as skilled laborers, technicians, low-level management, and a few fortunate ones even became professionals.

To Stay or Not to Stay

The incorporation of newcomers into American institutions and Polonian communities was influenced by their degree of permanency. Their occupations, residence, and organizational activity were conditioned by whether they intended to stay in the United States for a temporary period of time or whether they were here for the "long haul."

Permanency of stay is related in part to legal status at entry. Those who entered as refugees or quota immigrants had permanent residency status that gave them the legal right to stay. Many migrants who entered on temporary visas, however, became permanent residents by changing their visas. In the Forum sample, 51 percent of the respondents entered the United States as temporary immigrants, yet by 1990 only 16 percent of the same sample had temporary visas. They became permanent residents through political asylum, marriage to American citizens, amnesty under the 1986 Immigration Reform and Control Act, or an employer who procured a work visa for them.

While legal status influences a newcomer's choice, it does not determine entirely who will stay. Permanency of stay is more than a legal status, it is also a state of mind. Those who want to stay look for ways to get permanent visas, and those with permanent visas do not always intend to stay. As long as newcomers plan to return to Poland, they continue to think of Poland as their "home" and the United States as simply a place of employment.

In the sample of voters, legal status only slightly influenced the likelihood of wanting to return to Poland: Almost half of those with permanent resident status planned to return to Poland, but more than 80 percent of the temporary residents said they would return. In samples of permanent migrants (the interviews and Forum sample), less than a quarter said they would return to Poland. Many, however, were uncertain about whether to stay or not—more than 30 percent of the respondents in all of the samples except the home care workers did not know whether they would return to Poland or not (of all the samples, the home care workers were the most definite about returning home). This uncertainty calls into question the newcomers' commitment to resettling in the United States. The less sure they were about staying in the United States, the less interest they had in taking measures to improve their position in America. One indicator of desire to stay was their effort to learn the host country language. Of all the samples, the ESL students had the largest percentage of respondents who said they definitively did not intend to return (56 percent), and the lowest number who said they did plan to return (12 percent). The refugees in the interview sample had the next highest percentage of respondents who said they did not intend to return to Poland (50 percent). In contrast, only 4 percent of the voters in the election sample were committed to staying in the United States.

Most *wakacjusze* came with the intention of returning to Poland, and the limitations of their visa reinforced this intention. They were more likely to say they would return and more likely to actually return. In contrast, refugees usually left Poland with the intention of never returning. Most refugees had disposed of their material possessions in Poland and oftentimes there was some departure ceremony marking the closure of their relations with family and friends. Some refugees escaped from Poland, and this illegal departure reinforced the idea that they could not return there. Quota immigrants were between refugees and *wakacjusze* with respect to intention to return. Since they exited Poland and entered the United States legally, they had the option of staying or returning. Still, some quota immigrants had been involved in opposition activity in Poland, which led them to fear that they would be persecuted if they returned to Poland. Several of the Poles active in political Polonian organizations in Chicago who arrived in the 1970s feared that, if they did return, they or their families would be persecuted—not because they had been involved in any antistate activities in Poland, but because of their political activities in Chicago.[15] In

---

15. On March 4, 1985, the Prosecutor General's Office in Warsaw issued a statement that referred to Pomost (a political organization in Chicago created by new Polish immigrants) as an organization with a "terrorist bias . . . whose activities damage the interests of the Polish People's Republic." It further stated that "cooperation with foreign enemy institutions is a criminal act and is punishable under Polish law" and that "these acts will be severally punished." Statements like this made some immigrant activists afraid to return to Poland (quoted in the *Index on Censorship*, March 1985, 4).

the 1990s, after the changes were initiated in Poland, some refugees and immigrants did return home, but very few.[16]

Jackowo: The Polish Immigrant Community

The geographic center of the new Polish community in Chicago is located in a neighborhood known as *Jackowo*, which refers to the Roman Catholic church in the community. (The name represents the locative case of the word *Jacek*, the name for the church that Americans call St. Hyacinth.) In 1987, Father Rog, pastor of St. Hyacinth church, stated that more than half of the parish of almost four thousand families was Polish, mostly immigrant Poles, and most of the immigrants had arrived within the last ten years. Three of the six priests at this parish were from Poland, and five of their nine weekend masses were said in Polish.

Jackowo is the Polish ghetto of Chicago. The businesses are owned and operated by Poles (mostly immigrants who arrived in the 1960s and 1970s), and their workers and customers are mostly new Polish immigrants. In 1989, I surveyed the 183 businesses located on Milwaukee Avenue between Belmont and Diversey, the business center of *Jackowo*. Many of the businesses were fairly new: 21 percent had been operating at that location for less than a year; 29 percent had been there between two and nine years; and 19 percent had been there for five to nine years. Almost 40 percent of the owners were Polish immigrants and another 22 percent were Polish Americans. More than 50 percent of the workers were new Polish immigrants and another 24 percent were Polish Americans; and more than 90 percent of the customers were Polish immigrants or Polish Americans (the majority being new immigrants). *Jackowo* is more of an "immigrant" community than an "ethnic" community, and this is reflected in the type of businesses found in the community: overseas shipping and money transit services, passport and visa offices, and employment agencies for immigrants without "green

16. By 1990, most of them had been in the United States close to a decade or longer. Many with children, especially teenagers, did not want to uproot them once again. Moreover, Poland was and still is in a transition period. Not all things are better in Poland even though it is no longer officially communist. One indication of this is the long lines of Poles applying for visas. While in the 1990s we have record high numbers of nonimmigrants and immigrants admitted under numerical limitations, U.S. embassies in Poland were rejecting 60 percent of the applicants (*Gazeta International*, 1990, 2).

cards" (Erdmans 1995). A wide array of Polish-speaking professionals (lawyers, doctors, dentists, and morticians) also had their practices in this community. The immigrant community was spatially defined by this dense cluster of Polish businesses. In contrast, the ethnic Polish American community in the 1980s was a dispersed network of organizations. No large Polish American organization was headquartered in *Jackowo*—none of the large fraternal organizations, not the Polish American Congress, nor the wide variety of cultural organizations.

While all three types of new immigrants frequented *Jackowo*, the Poles living in the neighborhood were mostly *wakacjusze.* None of the refugees in my study lived in the *Jackowo* region. The quota immigrants generally did not live in *Jackowo* proper, but many lived in adjoining neighborhoods; 38 percent of the sample of voters and 25 percent of the Forum sample lived in the four–zip-code areas that overlap with *Jackowo.* In the sample of voters, only 27 percent of the permanent residents lived in this four–zip-code area, but 50 percent of the temporary migrants with invalid visas lived there.[17] The first step a migrant makes is out of the Polish ghetto. Yet, most newcomers stay within the city limits, especially the most recent ones: 77 percent of the voters, 74 percent of the PUNO students, and 57 percent of the members of the Forum sample lived within the city limits. Most immigrants living in the city lived in Polish neighborhoods on the Northwest and Southwest Sides (Jefferson Park, Belmont-Cragin, Portage Park, Archer Heights) but not necessarily in the Polish ghetto. Most refugees lived in the suburbs and other non-Polish areas of the city.

Collective Action for Poland

While the *wakacjusze* were more visible on the streets of *Jackowo*, the refugees were more visible at the organizational level, especially political organizations working on behalf of Poland. While it may seem that Poles who expected to return to Poland would have more incentive to be involved in action to improve the economic and political state of Poland, the *wakacjusze* were not proportionally represented in either the established

17. Not all who reported these zip codes lived in *Jackowo* proper. The *Jackowo* area—about eight blocks long (Belmont to Diversey) and twelve blocks wide (Kedzie to Kostner)—is part of four zip code regions.

ethnic or the new immigrant organizations. Voting in Poland's national election through absentee ballot was the most significant action under-taken by the *wakacjusze*. It was not expectations of returning that best predicted who would be involved in collective action for the homeland, but premigration activity. Basically, those who had been active in Poland were more likely to be active in the United States. In the Forum sample, those who had been involved in political action in Poland were more likely to be involved in political action (on behalf of Poland) in the United States.[18] It is not surprising, then, that the political refugees who represented less than 10 percent of the new cohort disproportionately took leadership positions and were disproportionately represented in the new political organizations working for Poland's liberation.

Several factors explain why Solidarity refugees were more likely to be active than *wakacjusze* or quota immigrants. First, past involvement in the opposition was likely to engender feelings of moral obligation to the political fate of their homeland. If people felt apathetic to the cause while in Poland, they were likely to feel even more apathetic to the cause when they were out of Poland. This is not to say that all Poles active in America had been active in Poland. Most of the Poles who left Poland before the opposition was institutionalized as Solidarity had not been involved in opposition activity, mostly because the opposition was less tenable. But it was those who had been active in Solidarity who used expressions like "duty" or "obligation" to the homeland, thereby displaying a moral incentive for their involvement (Erdmans 1992a). One refugee said that after he arrived here and realized, "I am more free here" than his compatriots back in Poland, he asked himself: "Why I come here? There's only one way, I must help the people in Poland now because I got out. Now I stay here, I gotta money, house, wife, everything, family, everything. I think to myself, I must help the people now. . . . I hate the communists, that's why I'm helping the people that fight the communists." Another interviewee said, "I feel it is the responsibility of those who left to help those who stayed behind." No Polish Americans, or Poles who arrived between 1960 and 1979 (that is, those from the new cohort who came before Solidarity), voiced any similar sentiment of devotion, duty, or obligation. Only refugees who were involved in Solidarity expressed the feeling that

18. In the Forum sample, 86 percent of those active in Poland were also active in the United States, compared to only 69 percent of those who were not active in Poland. This difference was significant at the .05 level using chi squared statistics.

they "betrayed" the revolution by emigrating, and used political activity in the United States to, as one refugee said, "erase this shame we brought with us when we left Poland at a time when our friends were fighting."

The second reason refugees were more politically active for Poland was because their past affiliation with the opposition created premigration networks. Quota immigrants, who had come primarily as family reunification cases, had ties to family members in the United States. In contrast, the refugees often had no family in the United States. Many refugees, however, quickly developed ties to other refugees. While some had known each other from prison or regional opposition activity, most of the refugees had not known each other in Poland. Still, their affiliation with Solidarity tied them to each other. Refugees already living in the States sought out new refugee arrivals and introduced them to the political landscape in Polonia. One refugee was picked up at the airport by two refugees and the next evening he was introduced to several other refugees in Chicago. Participation in Solidarity created a premigration network that tied the new refugees together. Similar to the way that the veterans in the World War II cohort had premigration ties through their military units (such as the First Airborne Division or Third Panzer Division) or felt a common affinity from having fought together at Monte Casino, Poles who were active Solidarity union organizers or who were imprisoned during martial law shared an identity, had common experiences, and were linked to the opposition networks.[19] These premigration ties separated the Solidarity refugees from the quota immigrants and *wakacjusze*.

Third, their previous experience with Solidarity meant that refugees had some concrete connections to the opposition in Poland. Opposition members still active in the underground often communicated with the refugees, informing them of the situation in Poland, and more important, informing the refugees about what types of assistance the opposition needed. These ties to the opposition inflamed the feelings of obligation, provided strategic directions to the refugees about how to help the opposition, and gave refugees a conduit through which resources could flow back into Poland. In sum, political refugees were more involved in collective action than non-refugees and temporary migrant workers because they had better networks

---

19. Mostwin also found that there were strong loyalties among Solidarity refugees that created effective organizational networks they used to support each other. She also found this group to be similar in this way to the soldiers emigration (the veterans in the World War II cohort) (1991, 156–58).

to political organizations in the home country, more contact with other Solidarity refugees, and stronger feelings of moral obligation.

Conclusion

Poles emigrated from communist Poland for both economic and political reasons. Many new immigrants, discouraged by Poland's failing economy came to America seeking economic gain; others, especially those involved in the opposition movement, were escaping political repression. All came because they thought America offered them a better chance to do something with their lives. The immigrants were similar in age, occupations in Poland, and education, but they differed in terms of their legal status in the United States and their premigration involvement with the opposition in Poland. Those with permanent resident status and ties to the opposition were more likely to be involved in collective action than temporary migrants and those without a history of activism.

In general, the temporary visa of the *wakacjusze* structured their choices in the United States. These migrants made less attempt to assimilate into America than the more permanent refugees and quota immigrants. As a result, this subgroup often remained more "visibly Polish." The *wakacjusze* lived in the Polish neighborhoods in Chicago, attended the Polish churches, and worked in the Polish enclaves of the construction and domestic service industries. Many of the opinions that both Polish Americans and non-Polish Americans had about newcomers stemmed from the characteristics of the *wakacjusze.* For example, Polish Americans criticized newcomers for not joining Polish organizations, not registering at the local Catholic church, or not learning to speak English. These things were more true of *wakacjusze* than the quota immigrants or refugees. The key determinant here was the temporariness of the newcomer's stay. In this case the refugees and other permanent immigrants acted very similarly—they arrived in America prepared to stay and began immediately to learn the language, upgrade their education if necessary, buy a house in the suburbs, and integrate themselves into American society. They did so by different means. Refugees usually had more government resources, but family-preference quota immigrants often had more family resources.

The presence of a new migrant cohort within Polonia was most evident in the 1980s, when refugees and an increased number of *wakacjusze* accompanied the steady inflow of quota immigrants. A "new group" was here, not just a few immigrants. On the radio, in the magazines, and from the pulpit there was continual discussion about the *nowi imigranci* (new immigrants). There were books, plays, and movies about these newcomers (for example, Janusz Glowacki's play *Hunting Cockroaches* and the semi-autobiographical fiction series by Zofia Mierzynska, titled "*Wakacjuszka*"). The presence of a "new immigration" was also pronounced because of the proliferation of magazines, quarterlies, radio stations, and eventually Polish television stations created by new immigrants for new immigrants. Eight new monthly magazines were published in Chicago in the late 1980s (*Relax, Alfa, Rewia, Panarama* among them), two Polish-language television appeared (Polvision was the main Polish channel and other Polish programs aired on the Ethnic Broadcasting Television channel), and six new radio programs. Most notably recognized were the politically active Solidarity refugees and the large population of *wakacjusze*, each visible in the community but for different reasons—the latter because they resisted assimilation and the former because of their involvement in collective action for Poland. Throughout the remainder of this book, I use the terms quota immigrant, refugee, and *wakacjusze* when differences between these newcomers are salient; for the most part, however, I refer to the entire cohort as the new immigration, and the newcomers in general as immigrants.

3

Culture and the Discourse of Communism

April 5, 1988

Dear Mr. Mazewski,
Whatever the merits — or confusion and unnecessary recriminations — in the recent radio discussion series of refugees' complaints, I believe that the problem merits consideration. Polonia has adopted a "hands-off" attitude towards the refugees leaving the matter to the Immigration Committee [PAIRC], which I don't think is handling the problem satisfactorily, appearing to regard the refugees as a troublesome burden. . . . The question thus is: does Polonia continue its disinterested attitude, or consider extending to them a helping hand? I am well aware of the justified complaints against many newcomers. But surely, raw anger voiced by older immigrants, that the newcomers are communist agents, and if they don't like it here they should return to socialist Poland is inadmissible. Such people oversimplify the problem. It hurt me to listen to mutual accusations, vociferous and angry, voiced by both the newcomers and older immigrants, as if they were adversaries, and not all of them Poles. . . .

Kazimierz Lukomski, a World War II émigré and vice-president of the Polish American Congress (PAC) wrote the above letter to Aloysius Mazewski, president of both the PAC and the Polish National Alliance (PNA). In a memo dated April 9, 1988, Mazewski wrote back, "I concur that the refugees need our help. To whom will they turn if not to us? We must forget their attitude, the experiences of ingratitude, the demands they make as if we were obliged to help them, etc. But not all are like that—so with the hope that they will change—we must continue to help them."

This exchange provides a glimpse into one of the main conflicts in Polonia during the 1980s. New immigrants wanted ethnic organizations to lend them a helping hand; ethnics interpreted this outstretched hand as dependency, a negative vestige of their communist upbringing. Both new immigrants' demands and Polish Americans' feelings of obligation were premised on the understanding that they were "all Poles," for "to whom would they turn if not to us." Yet this perceived affinity did not translate into strong and concrete attachments to each other. Their interactions were often better characterized as "mutual accusation" rather than helpful cooperation.

Polish Americans and Polish immigrants may have shared an historical identity but they did not share a contemporary identity. Polish Americans were ethnics not immigrants, and their identity was rooted in twentieth-century capitalist America. Polish American ethnics were established members of American society while Polish immigrants were newcomers. Moreover, Polish immigrants had been socialized in twentieth-century communist Poland. These different social identities (as ethnics and immigrants) and experiences (in capitalist America and communist Poland) created different lenses through which they perceived and interpreted the behavior of each other. In sum, they had different cultures. Culture is not a static identity, but it is socially constructed, shaped by place and time. Because they came from different cultures they interpreted behavior differently.

All groups—Americans, Polish Americans, World War II émigrés, and new Polish immigrants—used communism as a discourse for interpreting behavior. Ruth Frankenberg defines discourses as "historically constituted bodies of ideas providing conceptual frameworks for individuals" (1993, 265). Frameworks are schemata for interpreting behavior. Erving Goffman stated that a primary framework "allows its users to locate, perceive, identify, and label a seemingly infinite number of concrete occurrences defined in its terms" (1974, 21). The framework provides background information and helps to answer the question: What's going on here? Cross-cultural conflict can be understood as an issue of frame discordance that produces varying interpretations of behavior.[1] In Chicago Polonia, the new immigrants and Polish Americans were socialized in different social contexts, with different symbolic meaning systems (especially as they related to

---

1. Snow and Benford's application of frame analysis to social movement participation is useful here (1988). They argue that frames need to resonate in order to mobilize people to participate in collective action. Cross-cultural variations lead to different experiences, which explain, for example, why different frames were used to mobilize members of the peace movement in Europe and the United States.

communism); thus they had different frameworks for interpreting behavior.

When discussing the behavior of the new immigrants, every Polish American and World War II émigré I interviewed mentioned communism at least once, and some of them used the discourse of communism to explain numerous aspects of new immigrant behavior, such as work habits, attitudes toward government assistance, and unwillingness to join established Polish American organizations. In comparison, only a few new immigrants used the discourse of communism to explain new immigrant behavior; those that did were more likely to have arrived in the early 1960s as young adults and, as a result, had twenty-five to thirty years of socialization in American culture. New immigrants who arrived post-1980 seldom used the discourse of communism, and when they did, they used it to describe Polish American organizations (which they saw as resembling communist organizations).

The Evil Stench of Communism

Irene Claremont de Castillejo (1972), a Jungian analyst, argued that communism was America's national shadow. In Jungian analysis, we project upon a shadow all those qualities that we do not desire, but that most likely reside within ourselves.[2] America's abhorrence of communism was based on more than simply military fear; communism was positioned as antithetical to the basic American value of freedom. In other words, Americans cast communism as the Other. The Other, constructed in opposition to the Self, is invested with all the negative traits that the Self denies. The Other illuminates the Self in a value-oriented way so that the Self is of higher value than the Other (Said 1979; hooks 1992; Frankenberg 1993). Casting communism as the Other, then, helped define democracy and capitalism: Democracy was freedom, communism was slavery; democracy was partici-

---

2. Writing in the 1970s, Claremont de Castillejo stated:

> Today we spend a lot of energy rabidly hating the Russians or the Chinese for their disregard of individual life and individual liberty. . . . We see the tyrannies in Russia and China and hate them with our souls, but because we have not noticed that we are no longer free ourselves, we vent our hatred on the Chinese or Russians, instead of on the tyranny. (1972, 31)

patory decentralized government, communism was hierarchical centralized government; capitalism was private property, communism was state
ownership; capitalism rewarded ambition, hard work and self-reliance,
communism created disincentives to work and state-dependency.[3]

In American Polonia, this hatred of communism and communists, intensified by the presence of the communist regime in Warsaw, had been
nourished for decades. What, then, were Polish Americans and World War
II émigrés to make of these new immigrants who had been born in
communist hospitals, educated in communist schools, and employed by
communist bosses? Polonia was somewhat suspicious of these immigrants. A
Polish American working for Catholic Charities, an agency that helps
resettle refugees, said she had difficulty finding sponsors. "I called one
woman, a Polish American, and asked if she would help resettle this new
Polish immigrant and she refused because, she said, 'He's probably a
communist.' "

Because communism was seen as antithetical to capitalist democracy,
resettlement agencies assumed Polish immigrants would have a hard time
adjusting to life in the "land of the free." One document from World Relief,
a U.S. organization that helps resettle refugees, noted the following about
Polish immigrants:

> The Polish people are very independent-minded . . . [they] like to
> decide their own lives and work for their own goals. However, 30
> years of communist rule have not gone by without making an
> impression on the present generation of Poles. Even though most of
> the Polish refugees dislike their political system, they are a product
> of it and do not question many of its components. In fact, they are
> used to, and expect that many decisions are made for them, and that
> they will be taken care of by the state. When the state's control is
> removed upon coming to the United States, they may be unprepared
> to take full charge of all aspects of their lives in a free society. Polish
> people are not used to picking from a variety of choices. In Poland,
> you don't even need to make a decision of what to have for
> supper. . . . The most difficult adjustment the Polish refugee has

3. This argument does not suggest that there was no valid intellectual, military, or moral
objections to communism, but it does maintain that America's anxiety was at times akin to a
national phobia, which does imply that at times the threat was exaggerated and irrational. See
Crockatt (1995) for an analysis of the real military threats during the 1950s.

to make is adjusting to the freedom in American society, which means the freedom of choice, including the freedom to make profit, but also the freedom to be poor. (Li 1982, 5–7)

This pamphlet reflected the attitudes of people who had not lived in communist Poland. They expected immigrants to have a basic problem understanding "freedom" (for example, they won't even know how to decide what to have for dinner!). Although emigration represented a rejection of communism, they believed the refugees had nonetheless internalized its practices. Refugees were unwitting victims of communism.

Polish Americans and World War II émigrés did not blame the immigrants for being influenced by the communist system—they blamed the communist system. Yet, with heads nodding in measured sympathy, they often stated that the immigrants themselves were unaware of how extremely "indoctrinated" they were. The World War II émigrés repeatedly described communism as an inescapable dogma that contaminated the psyches of its citizens. One World War II émigré compared communism to smog, "You can't help breathing it, and those who breath it are polluted." Another World War II émigré said: "Forty years ago the system was introduced, so the generation that comes over here is already a result of the communist indoctrination. . . . [W]e have to understand that it will take time before they shake everything what we think the system has imposed on their minds." These émigrés frequently used the terms "indoctrination" and "brainwashed" to explain this socialization process. One World War II émigré said:

> They [the new immigrants] are not communists, they are against communists, which is a surprise to some degree because they were brainwashed from childhood—in schools, media, newspaper, radio, everything—they were brainwashed. . . . They were born there and educated there and worked there, from childhood until they left they were under constant influence. So I am surprised they are so anticommunist in spite of all this. . . . But at the same time they picked up a certain way of life, [hushed tones] way of thinking even, way of writing.

These quotes illustrate the sympathetic yet suspicious perceptions of Polonians toward the new immigrants. They constructed a reality whereby even though the immigrants engaged in anticommunist activities, even though some of them were imprisoned because of their antistate activities, and even though they chose to flee the communist system, still, these people carried the taint of communism with them to America. They believed the immigrants were politically against the communist state but socially and psychologically influenced by the communist system.

A few new immigrants also spoke of the ubiquitous nature of communism. One new immigrant who arrived in the late 1970s said:

> We were raised in communist system with quite different mentality, with quite different problems, work, everything. Because there's no doubt, I don't think that anybody could somehow avoid the influence of communist propaganda. There's no way, because they control your life from the very beginning. You were born in a government hospital, then you go to government pre-school, then you go to government elementary school, then government high school, then government university, and each step of the life is controlled by the government. The media is controlled by the government. Teachers have to follow very strict instructions from the government. Art is controlled by the government. So, there is very strong influence of the government philosophy on their individual lives. There is no way, you can't resist.

This man, however, when giving examples of how the system influenced him, spoke more about false information rather than about some deep psychological alteration that would incapacitate him in a democratic capitalist system. His "shock" when he left Poland was about the "lies" he had been told; he never spoke about not being able to adjust to life in a democratic society. He said:

> I know Polish literature, for example, very well. And I didn't realize when I escaped from Poland I went to Sweden, and I somehow met a guy who gots piles of books, published in the West, and most of them written by the writers in exile. You know, I was surprised, it was for me such an unbelievable shock, I realized that literature abroad is equally good and in some cases even better than that in Poland. And I considered myself as an educated man. And there was many more shocks like that. For example, my wife went to Sweden and

suddenly she was so surprised that the education in Sweden is free, even government provides papers, pencils for students. She was convinced, and she's not stupid, believe me, she was convinced that in capitalist country everybody has to pay for education.

This man did not convey the notion that communism seeped into his unconscious, but that he had been told stories that he later learned were false. Learning about the lies confirmed the negative feelings he already had toward the communist government in Poland.

Only three other new immigrants mentioned the indoctrination of the communist system, and they all had been in the United States for twenty to thirty years. They did not speak of this indoctrination as something that was causing them problems personally, but as something they saw in other immigrants—especially the newest immigrants. They used the language of "them" rather than "us" and talked about "those new immigrants" as a way of separating themselves from this indoctrination. One immigrant who arrived in the 1960s stated: "These Polish people there's a lot of misunderstanding. They don't understand. Because in Poland the government is manipulate people. . . . The party has complete control over radio, TV, and press. And so when these people come in here they don't understand." The only immigrant (1968 arrival) who referred to his own indoctrination also pointed out that he had changed. "You have to remember that every one of us, I am supposed to say myself, because I am quite a bit here, I change, for sure I am not the same person who came here. We have to realize that we are like a child of that system, too, I mean the communist system. They brainwash us that far that it's not like that [snaps fingers] to get rid of it."

The quotes chosen represent only a sample of the types of the statements I heard from Polish Americans and World War II émigrés. In contrast, they represent all of the discussion on this topic from new immigrants (and I interviewed and talked with more new immigrants than with members from either of the other two cohorts). The new immigrants simply did not trace their resettlement problems to the communist system. Immigrants related their problems to their newcomer status. As recent arrivals, they needed to learn a new language, find a job and a place to live, and learn how to maneuver through a new set of institutions. They did not say they had problems with too much freedom or that they were uncertain about what to have for dinner; they had problems learning English and finding good jobs.

Poor Work Ethics and Welfare Dependency

Another perception was that communism destroyed the Poles' work ethic and fostered an attitude of dependency on the state. An America director of the Polish Welfare Association (PWA), which employed Polish immigrants and also helped new immigrants find employment, was extremely critical of the work habits of new immigrants.

> You're dealing with people that lived under socialism, where people don't work hard . . . the old Polish work ethic is not there. This is something I see on my staff, there's not a lot of initiative. . . . Their expectations of the American work force are completely unrealistic. We have a lot of people being sent on jobs quitting the first day—it's too hard, they go to people and ask for more money the first week, right away, it's crazy, it really is.[4]

This director also thought that communism made people manipulative:

> I think that growing up in Poland under communism you get to be very manipulative. You learn how to manipulate the best you can. And if it means in Poland you bribe an official for a better house, you do. You learn how to manipulate the system in America. You work illegally, there are people who over-extend their visa, you are here illegally, or even if you are here on a six-month visa and when you don't have work authorization, again you're manipulating the system, you're doing something illegally.

These statements were contradictory. At one moment, Polish immigrants did not want to work because communism destroyed their work ethic; in the next moment, the immigrants were sneaking around trying to get jobs. This second behavior was also attributed to communism. In the hands of people socialized in capitalist democratic America, communism was a conceptual

4. It is important to note that only legal immigrants could use the Polish Welfare Association (PWA) to find employment. This means that those people seeking work were looking for permanent employment, for careers rather than short-term jobs. Also, many members of the new cohort had been educated professionals in Poland, and they wanted the PWA to help them find similar occupations in the United States. The PWA did not have strong networks into the professional communities. In fact, in the late 1980s the PWA advised Polish immigrants with professional credentials to go to Jewish Vocational Services.

tool used to invent explanations for a variety of behaviors. It became the catch-all term for explaining conflict and the scapegoat for undesirable behavior.

A few of the earlier arrivals in the new cohort expressed kindred viewpoints about the destruction of the work ethic. One man who arrived as a teen in the early 1960s stated: "In the first place there is the work ethic, which is basically missing, especially from the so-called intellectual elite." But other new immigrants, even ones who arrived in the 1960s, offered a more elaborate analysis of immigrant work habits. One new immigrant (1962 arrival) explained, "They have to work hard here. If in Poland they work hard there are no results, you don't see. Over here you can see results if you want. In Poland you don't, because all your efforts are destroyed by the Party, by the system." She noted that Poles were eager to work in a system that rewarded hard work, implying that people acted differently in America than in Poland. In effect, she was saying that behavior could be explained by systemic rather than psychological factors.

Immigrants who left Poland in their late teens and early twenties had less experience than someone who had actually worked in a communist system for several years. Immigrants who had more experience working in Poland were also very critical of the communist system, but they were not critical of Polish workers. One new immigrant vehemently countered this criticism of poor work ethics. He said:

> The people say, "Oh, you no like work over there because you nothing do." But this not true. The Polish people, I know, because I been in shipyards, in Szczecin, the people work very hard, very hard. . . . Like coal miners, he make big money in Poland, *ale* [but] he work seven days straight, Saturday and Sunday even, and very, very hard. . . . And why the Polish people come to America, because he been good worker. I no say everyone, but I am sure 80 percent of people who work in the United States and the factories, the owners been very happy for the work. He say the Polish worker he work very hard and very correct, he have no problem with these people. Why, because he learn in Poland. Because he work very hard for nothing in Poland. If he come here to America and he see the dollar and how much he make at the end of the week, how much he make for the month in Poland, he make here a lot more, so after that he very, very good worker. You no find better worker than Polish worker.

This statement represents the attitude most new immigrants had—that they preferred working in America because there was a positive relation between the number of hours worked and the size of the paycheck. Work habits were more related to the system within which one worked than the character of the worker.

In addition to the perception of poor work habits, members of established Polonia also believed that the immigrants had been socialized to depend more on the government. This was expressed by Americans, Polish Americans, and World War II émigrés, but no new immigrants (not even the early arrivals) expressed this belief. The perception was based on the understanding that communist governments provided their citizens with health care services, education, and jobs and therefore the immigrants arrived in the United States expecting the American government to do the same. The director of the Office of Refugee Resettlement in Chicago, an American, stated:

> Their homeland experiences precondition their expectations. The fact that Poles have immigrated from a communist country affects their behavior when they arrive here. This is true of Poles, Rumanians, Soviets, Czechs, Bulgarians and all those from communist countries. . . . They do have a certain inherent response to government programs, they feel that the government has a responsibility to them.

One Polish American said, "When they come here they have this Socialist mentality. They come here with there hands out." Another said, "They want everything done for free." A Polish American who worked for the PAC stated: "They have been indoctrinated in Poland for thirty years. The state gives you a job, the state gives you medical insurance, the state gives you free education. Then when they come to America they are lost." Another Polish American woman expressed the same idea:

> The Eastern Europeans have problems adjusting to the system in America. They come from a system where the state takes care of their education and all their medical problems. The state supports much more of the system there than it does here. They have problems because of that. . . . They can't understand that the state doesn't take care of their medical problems; see the health care is subsidized in Poland. Another example is the theater people who come over

here. See, the state also subsidizes the theater and the arts in Poland. If one is an actress or an artist then the state pays them a salary to do that. They are shocked when they find out that if they want to do theater work here they also have to work, that it's not government subsidized like it is in Poland.

Polish Americans and World War II émigrés framed their understanding within an American cultural system that venerates hard work and scorns state dependency, a system wherein capitalism was sacred and communism profane.

In addition to using American frames of discourse, Polish Americans also interpreted the immigrants' behavior from an ethnic framework. Polish Americans used their own constructed identity of Polishness (thrift, discipline, and hard work) and their parents' and grandparents' stories of immigrant struggles to explain why they were against state support for new immigrants. In ethnic folklore passed down through the generations, Polish Americans told how their parents, or grandparents, or the generic "early Polish immigrants" started at the bottom and nobody helped them, they had to make it on their own without expecting a handout (reminiscent of the "I walked ten miles to school in the snow uphill, without shoes" cant). An older second-generation Polish American said in reference to the new immigration: "It's the new thing. It isn't only the Polish. They just hold their hand out." And then, in reference to her parent's generation, she said: "None of them felt that this country owed them anything. They knew they had to work. They expected to work. You know, no work, no eat." The Polish Americans believed the new immigrants should "pull themselves up by their own bootstraps" as their ancestors did. One World War II émigré compared the behavior of new immigrants to older Polish Americans who had lived through the Depression and did not have enough Social Security in their later years.

> Then came those food stamps and we tried to convince them [older Polish Americans], but they don't want to go. They said, "I am not beggar." It was hard to convince them that this is nothing wrong, you deserve it, you should go and get them. Well, with this people coming now, it is just the reverse. They are looking what they can get for nothing, you see. I know many cases, for example, that they could get a job for four dollars an hour, well they don't want it. They figure out, I am on welfare, I get more than if I am working. And the

old-timer it was awfully hard to convince them even to get unemployment compensation because they say, "I am not beggar."

The equation here is that to receive state support implies that one is a beggar, and the suggestion is that new immigrants would rather go on public aid than get a job.

The World War II émigrés also had their own immigrant experiences to draw upon. Having arrived in the 1950s before the Great Society era, many pointed to their own hardships as immigrants and took pride in the fact that members of their generation resisted state support. One World War II émigré said: "When they were young, most of my friends, when we first came here, had at least one and a half jobs. In other words, one regular job and then at least a couple of evenings in some sort of money-making situation." Another World War II émigré made the following comparisons between his cohort and the new immigrants:

> This forty years or thirty years of the communist rule, going to communist school, they had to change little the psychology of the people. And their psychology was changed. For example, I give you the example of the difference. Let's say when our immigration was coming here to the United States we didn't expect somebody's going to welcome us with the red flowers, the red carpet at the airport or at the train station or on the boat in the seaport or anything like this. We just came, we just realized that we are coming here to make a living . . . that we practically have to start from the beginning. And we didn't look for someone to help us financially or give us money for start or things like this. Nothing like this happened. This people [new immigrants], in many cases, they think that somebody should await them with couple of few thousand dollars so they have a start, and they sort of holding the grief against us that we not doing this.

In contrast to the perception that new immigrants expected a handout, I found just the opposite to be true. Polish immigrants had low rates of welfare usage, underutilized state resources, often worked more than forty hours a week, and in fact were critical of Americans who did "go on welfare." A group of Polish immigrants who were students in an English language course I taught at the Polish University Abroad (*Polski Uniwersytet na Obczyźnie*) (PUNO) in Chicago, had the following conversation about American life. One student said:

> People [in America] are poor because they no want to work. . . .
> [P]eople from Poland taking this $3.75. That's normal pay for us.
> And they have family here. . . . Even with this money you can live,
> maybe not normal life, you have to be careful how you spending
> money. But if you using it right you not poor. I am not thinking I
> am poor and I making this $3.75. And there's enough to even save
> some.

This student (and others expressed similar attitudes) perceived the benefits
of the American system to be that they were given an opportunity to work,
not that they were given a handout. They defined "poorness" as a fault of
the individual in this "land of opportunity" and did not expect the state to
give them a job or a house (though they did think of education and health
care as a citizen right). In 1988, Lorrain Majka, who worked in refugee
services for the Jewish Federation of Metropolitan Chicago, said:

> The Poles are different because they hang onto jobs, they don't want
> to go on state welfare. They think there is some crime or shame. It is
> very difficult, for example with the PWA [the Polish Welfare Asso-
> ciation], they can't fill their quotas. A certain percentage of their
> clients have to be on public aid, and they just can't find that many
> Poles on public aid to help out. So they had to request less money for
> next year because they can't find enough people on public aid. They
> have a lot of clients, but most of them get a job and then hang on to
> their job.

Polish refugees in Chicago accessed fewer state resources than other
refugee groups. One study of non-Southeast Asian refugees found that
Polish refugees used assistance at half the rate than did other refugee
groups; in 1985 only 18 percent of Polish refugees in Cook County who had
been there three years or less were receiving public assistance, while 38
percent of all refugees in the county were receiving assistance (Cichon,
Gozdziak, and Grover 1986, 48). They also reported that Polish refugees
found jobs quickly and "underutilized" the employment services (14, 26).
In another study of refugees in Chicago by Catholic Charities, Anne
Templeton found that 84 percent of the Polish refugees were employed
within the first six months of arrival, compared to only 68 percent of the
Assyrian refugees (who were coming from a noncommunist country)
(1984, 27). Moreover, of the ten refugee groups included in the study, Poles

received the least amount of cash assistance averaging only $81 per capita compared to a rate of $659 for the Vietnamese. Templeton argued that this finding was "not unexpected" because the Polish refugees "found employment more quickly than any other nationality group" (1984, 37).

Taken together, these studies show that Polish refugees do not appear to be state-dependency slackers looking for a hand out and unwilling to take a job. It is important to remember that these studies were of refugees, newcomers who were eligible for the most state assistance. Other immigrants were not eligible for state resources until they had permanent residency status, and then they were only eligible for state and federal funds appropriated for all U.S. residents (such as Aid to Families with Dependent Children and food stamps). Temporary visitors with valid or invalid visas are by definition not permanent residents and thus not eligible for any assistance. If assistance usage rates were low for Polish refugees, we can assume that illegal immigrants and legal immigrants were even less "dependent" on the state.

In addition to these reports of low welfare usage, my ethnographic data indicate that new immigrants were more likely to be workhorses than freeloaders. Owners of construction and maid companies told me they considered Polish immigrants to be among the best laborers. Many immigrants worked two jobs and sixty hour weeks. No one I interviewed was receiving state assistance. Some refugees, however, did report that when they first arrived they stayed out of the labor market for a few months (seven- to eighteen-month range) to improve their language skills, recertify degrees, or seek additional training. This initial preference to accept state assistance rather than take a low-paying job may explain why Polish Americans had the perception that newcomers were looking for a handout. Polish refugees reported that "Polish American service providers accuse them of being lazy if they want to go to school and learn English" (Cichon, Gozdziak, and Grover 1986, 18). Still, state support was a luxury that only a small percentage of the new cohort could afford. Less than 10 percent of the newcomers were refugees; the other 90 percent of the newcomers were not eligible for these state assistance programs.

So why did the established Polonian community perceive the new immigrants as coming here "with their hands out" and wanting "everything for free?" First, as mentioned above, they interpreted the behavior of immigrants from communist Poland through a frame that assumed they would be state dependent. Second, while new immigrants did not rely much on the state, they did in fact expect Polonia to help them. At a community forum in February 1989, immigrants directed hostile questions at the speaker (an employee of one of the Polish American fraternals) concerning the lack of help given to immigrants. One man said, "The [fraternal] doesn't help us; they look pretty but they don't do anything. They have meetings and *Wigilia* [the Christmas Eve supper] but they don't help us." Another man bluntly asked the speaker, "Why don't you give us jobs?" One immigrant blamed the Polish American community for the large number of professional, well-educated Polish refugees who were forced into menial labor positions in Chicago. He expected the Polish American organizations to help new immigrants improve their occupational status in America. On a Polish-language radio talk show in Chicago in March 1988, two new refugees called to complain about the lack of support they were receiving from Polish American organizations. One said, "If you find a job or an apartment it's usually through friends, or a friend of a friend," that is, not through one of the ethnic organizations.[5] Ewa Betka, executive director of the PAC Illinois Division said that immigrants often called asking for help. She explained:

> They arrive in Chicago [and] they start calling the Polish organiza-
> tions. And they find out that I don't have an apartment to give them.
> I don't have a job to give them because I don't know of any today.
> The most I can do today is to make sure they get a basket of food. I
> can have the city put them up in one of those overnight shelters. And
> then the resentments start. "What, you're a Polish organization, what
> are you here for? You're supposed to be helping me." . . . They
> come in and they expect the Polish organization to be ready and
> waiting to give them a job, housing, clothing and school.

While the new immigrants often complained about lack of support, the two studies of Polish refugees in Chicago in the 1980s found that Polish refugees had more community and sponsorship support than other refugee communities (Templeton 1984, 22, 34–35), and the lower welfare usage among Polish refugees was partially attributed to this strong sponsorship and community support (Cichon, Gozdziak, and Grover 1986, 15). None-

5. The study of non-Southeast Asian refugees found that 75 percent of employed Polish refugees found jobs through informal referrals, another 21 percent through newspapers or professional journals, and only one person found a job through an organization (Cichon, Gozdziak, and Grover 1986, 59).

theless, this second study also noted, in several places, that the Polish refugees expressed strong dissatisfaction with and alienation from the established Polish American community (18–19, 27, 32).[6]

The new immigrants expected help from Polish Americans and criticized the organizations for not helping. The Polish Americans defended themselves by redefining the conflict as a negative consequence of communism. In many cases, it was during a conversation about conflicts in Polonia that Polish Americans and World War II émigrés brought up the topic of welfare dependency. The real problem, they said, was not that they were not helping the newcomers, but that communism had made the new immigrants expect too much.

The Non-Joining Behavior of Communist Immigrants

Leaders of Polish American organizations were particularly galled by the fact that the new immigrants would ask them for help but were unwilling to join their organizations. Helen Zielinska, president of the Polish Women's Alliance related the following story of a family involving wife abuse, visa problems, and financial need.

> I had a man call up yesterday and say, "I came from Poland, can you help me." And he had a problem and talked for half an hour and I said, "Sir, I can not give you any more time." I said, "because what you want I can not help. . . . You have a problem and I don't want to mix into it." . . . See those are the problems. Everyday I get calls from people to help. Yet they won't belong to a fraternal, yet they'll call us for help. . . . I said to the man "I can not help you." And he said, "But I come from Poland." And I said, "Well, if you had money to come here from Poland, you could have used that money and get help."

6. In Mostwin's survey of 552 Polish immigrants who arrived between 1974 and 1984, the respondents listed their three most important needs in order as work, learning English, and finding a place to live (1991, 78). They were also very critical of "*stara Polonia*" (old Polonia) precisely because they did not help them meet these needs. On man wrote, "It's not worth writing about old Polonia; they would rather take than help" (80).

The frustration Polish Americans felt toward immigrants asking for help but unwilling to help in return is expressed in the following comment:

> For the past twenty years or more the new immigrants that have come to America have shown themselves to be above our Polonia. They are not interested in joining organizations, fraternals, churches, or even help groups that work for the assistance to Poland or new immigrants coming to America. The Polish American organizations are criticizing us for catering to people who want our help but will rarely help the organization offering assistance.[7]

Not joining organizations was problematic because Polish American organizations needed new members. Many Polonian organizations formed in the first half of the twentieth century had a declining and aging membership in the 1980s. Fraternal organizations like the PNA peaked in terms of membership and lodges in the post–World War II era and total membership declined from 336,159 in 1960 to 294,761 in 1980 (Pienkos 1984, 329). Membership for all but one of the top five Polish American fraternals (the Polish Falcons was the exception) declined from 1970 to 1980 (323). Moreover, the organizations' remaining members were aging, which is fiscally problematic for fraternal organizations whose assets are built on life insurance policies. An aging membership is also dangerous for any volunteer organization. Without new and young members the organization faces the threat of dying with its members. One director of the Polish-American Women's Coalition said, "The problem is that it really needs some new blood. Most of the women are old and we were supposed to make an effort to recruit young women but we haven't been too successful." Helen Zielinska, the president of the Polish Women's Alliance said, "We are looking for a lot of young members to take our place. . . . To run a fraternal you have to have members, you have to have an increase in members, especially young members . . . I mean up to about 38 to 45, you know, that's young people, compared to us older people." Francis Rutkowski, who in 1986 served briefly as the president of the Polish Roman Catholic Union, said, "A lot of the members are old, they are dying . . . all

7. This statement came to me from Michael Blichasz, national chairman for the Polish American Heritage Month committee, sponsored by the PAC, who sent me information about the October 1988 activities in a letter dated February 2, 1989. He compiled a summary of the positive and negative comments he received about Heritage Month. These comments are not his own, but reflect a synthesis of the opinions of various members of Polonia.

fraternals are faced with the problem of fluctuating membership." Anthony Piwowarczyk, a vice-president of the PNA, stated that "in the PAC, there is a need of new blood. Absolutely." He also explained that the PNA is top-heavy, and as an insurance company it needs to bring in young members: "That's why we run the youth jamboree . . . this is the purpose, to get them involved in activities so that they go out and get in the organization. We have to propagate."

The organizations were unable to attract enough new members from the second-, third-, and fourth-generation ethnics. They hoped to enroll large numbers of new immigrants arriving in the 1970s and 1980s. Yet, no significant number of new immigrants joined the organizations in the 1980s. An administrative assistant for the PAC said, "No, they are not coming to the PNA. Even though there is a big campaign to get them, they are not joining. Even the Solidarity people, the intelligent, educated ones, they are sticking to themselves. It's the same thing with the artistic commu-nity. They gather in one place, and they include only this one group of people." For the most part, the new immigrants did not join the established Polish American organizations. Among those I interviewed in Chicago, the only organization the new immigrants joined was the Polish National Alliance (PNA) by forming new fraternal lodges, and a few were active in the Illinois division of the PAC. No one in the sample of home health care workers joined Polish American organizations, and less than 20 percent of the sample of the members of Forum and less than 10 percent of the sample of ESL students at PUNO belonged to any Polish American organization. And even though immigrants attended Polish churches, they were not as inclined to officially join the parish (Cichon, Gozdziak, and Grover 1986; Mostwin 1991; interviews with Polish priests).

To explain this nonjoiner behavior, the Polish Americans and World War II émigrés turned to their favorite whipping boy—communism. They believed that communism had destroyed the "natural instinct for group-ness." PAC members, especially World War II émigrés, explained the new immigrants' behavior as a rebellion against their earlier experience of being forced to join organizations in the communist system. One PAC director stated: "Any organization in Poland had to be regime sponsored. They grew up antiorganizational, and they still carry it to some extent." Another World War II émigré stated: "They stay away from others. They have this suspicion of organizations. They just want to be dispersed. Free. Not organized." The following quotes by World War II émigrés active in the PAC make evident this opinion.

These people were brought up in slavery and they have a different attitude. They will have some chips on their shoulders, maybe even some Sovietization. They don't know it, but there's terrific propaganda which comes from Moscow in the schools—false history, false literature, false information. And then they come over here hating these organizations because they were forced to join them in Poland.

Another said:

Our generation [World War II émigrés] could be described as very prone to organize itself. When you have the next generation, which comes now from Poland, they stay from organizing themselves, they stay away, because they were pushed by the communist government to organize. They attended these forced meetings so much that they hate even the word organization.

The leaders of these established ethnic organizations did not reflect on aspects about their organizations that may have made new immigrants unwilling to join. They started with the assumption that their organizations were good and necessary and if new immigrants were not joining there was something wrong with the new immigrants. The explanation was that the experiences in a communist society destroyed associational behavior.

A handful of new immigrants used this same explanation. Both of the following quotes are from immigrants who arrived in the United States in the late 1970s. Notice again that when discussing new immigrants they do not use the inclusive "we" pronoun but the otherized "they" pronoun. "The problem with the new immigrants is that they were raised in communist Poland. See, it is the natural desire of people to identify with some other group of people, to belong, feel they belong to a group. This desire was crushed by the communists. After forty years of communism they have destroyed this natural instinct for groupness." The other said, "These people who have arrived here from Poland, who have been forced for years to join the Party, to join this or to join that, they come here and they want to remain anonymous. They don't want to join organizations. Because they've been forced to do this, for years, and I think this is part of the problem."

It was true that Poles were "forced" to join organizations in communist Poland, and the organizations were created and controlled by the communist state. (KOR, formed in 1976, was one of the first autonomous and open organizations in communist Poland.) In interviews with Poles in Poland in 1987, many talked about this manipulation and forced participation. One Pole succinctly described such a situation:

> People were automatically signed into organizations like the ZMP [Youth Organization], it was mechanical. Most of us didn't know we were assigned, we didn't sign up. Our directors, principals in the *liceum* [high school] informed us one day, "Oh you are members of ZMP." One had to be really brave to stand up and say, "Director, I don't want to be member of this organization. Cross me out."

Nonetheless, this is the same country that gave birth to Solidarity, a union that at one point almost a third of the population joined voluntarily. The comments from the new immigrants above represent the ideas of those who left Poland before Solidarity. Only one post-1980 immigrant noted her reluctance to join organizations.

> Yes, I am a member of KIK [the Club of Catholic Intellectuals in Chicago]. It is the only organization I am really a member. It is my decision not to belong to any organization here. It was also my program in Poland since Stalinist period when I dropped Youth organization. I say, "Enough" any organizations, but, of course, later, I was a co-operator of KOR, I was co-founder of Solidarity in my factory and so on. But it wasn't, I *must* do it.

The interesting thing is that these three immigrants—and they were the only ones from the new cohort who made statements about communism spoiling their desire to join organizations—were, in fact, all members of organizations. This last women was also a member of KOR and a co-founder of the Solidarity union in her region. In America, however, they were members of small, informal new immigrant organizations rather than the larger, more formal Polish American organizations.

While established Polonia blamed communism for the new immigrants' nonjoining behavior, the new immigrants blamed the established ethnic organizations. Some newcomers stated that the reason they were reluctant to join established Polonian organizations was that they were too formal, autocratic, and centralized. When discussing their reasons for not joining, new immigrants used phrases from and analogies to the communist system to disparage the organizations. One immigrant said, "This organization [the PAC] is run like an oligarchy and we are very familiar with this system, we lived for a long time in totalitarian rule so we know how they are running things." Another immigrant said in reference to the PAC, "There is no opposition, there is only autocratic rule." Because of the older age of the average PAC members, another new immigrant likened them to the Central Committee of the Communist Party. When the twenty-year PAC president died in 1988, a new refugee compared the situation to the death of Stalin: "In communism, you have a specific dominant authoritarian leader like in [the PAC], where at the top you have only one leader. When this leader dies there is a gap, like when Stalin died." One refugee who worked for WPNA, the radio station owned by the PNA, said in reference to a directive telling announcers not to broadcast news about a demonstration in February 1989, "I obeyed the . . . official party line." Another new immigrant said, "New immigrants are pissed off because Moskal [the PAC president] took his guys, his *aparatczy* from his office to go with him" when he went to Poland. Another immigrant called one PAC board member "the main political member of the politburo." At a public meeting with a representative from the PNA, who was speaking to a room of mostly new immigrants, one immigrant who had come in the late 1970s said, in reference to the fact that Polish American organizations did not help the new immigrants, that the ethnic fraternals did not really do anything and therefore "looked like the communist system in Poland." At that statement, roughly half of the audience of one hundred clapped. In one article published in a Polonian magazine, a new immigrant wrote, "The pressure of social conformity here is no less effective than censorship in the PRL" (Wierzynski 1989, 11).

Many immigrants criticized the way that leaders were chosen for the PAC. The national PAC had a nominating committee that suggested a slate of candidates. The standard procedure was that the slate was either accepted or rejected at the National Council of Directors meetings. In reference to the PAC elections, one new immigrant said that because the voting was done by raising hands and not by secret ballot it was "like the communists do in Poland." The appointment of people to positions in the PAC was called "negative selection," which one immigrant described as "an expression from Poland, the Party selects for the president of a company or dean of a university the people who will follow the rules which are stated for them." One new immigrant, referring to the elections said, "I don't think there is much difference in the actions in Poland and the actions here." Another said, "I don't see in PAC enough democracy. I think there is no democracy, their, uh, elections is not democratic because there are some people nominated by previous president, they are not chosen from the people."[8] These quotes are not meant to imply that the new immigrants thought that the PAC was a communist organization but only to show how their experiences in the communist system influenced the way that the new immigrants thought (or at least talked) about Polish American organizations. The new immigrants superimposed the image of the rigid authoritarian structure of the communist regime onto the centralized bureaucracy of organizations like the PNA and the PAC. New immigrants did not appreciate these structural characteristics, and preferred not to join these formalized, centralized, and bureaucratic organizations.

Another reason new immigrants did not join was because they saw no benefit to joining. The immigrants wanted and needed organizations that would help them satisfy newcomer needs. The established organizations, however, were ethnic organizations set up to service ethnic needs. Ethnic needs included maintaining a cultural attachment to an ancestral homeland, fighting for state resources distributed on the basis of ethnic identification, working to maintain and increase their share of decision-making positions (that is, as elected and appointed public officials and top managerial and executive positions in the private sector), and fighting to minimize ethnic prejudice and discrimination.

The sorts of ethnic goods the organizations provided is reflected in their activities and goals: They sponsored Polish American Heritage Month activities; they published pamphlets on Pulaski and Kosciuszko, both heroes of the American Revolution; they organized parades and festivals, cultural tours to Poland, and fund-raisers for the renovation of the Statue of Liberty. Ethnic projects the PAC was involved in during the 1980s included: an

---

8. At the national meetings in November 1988, the PAC had to choose a new president to replace the twenty-year president Aloysius Mazewski, who had died. A motion to vote by secret ballot for the president and to elect the president from a number of candidates running for the position, rather than accept or reject the entire slate of candidates, reflects the fact that this was a new procedure.

> Council member: Mr. Lukomski and delegates, with the death of our late president, it brings us to a very important turning point in the Polish American Congress. Right now, I think the Polish press and radio, the Polonia, are looking at us, to see how we will elect our next president. Will it be in the democratic form? Will it be in the suggestive form as it was in the past? . . . We're talking all the time about democratic opposition in Poland, we want free elections—at least the highest ranking person should be elected by this body.

Even within the PAC, the framework of democracy and communism was used to promote or sanction behavior.

examination of the unfair and prejudicial portrayal of ethnic groups in the media; a nationwide library project entitled "Not For Polish-Americans Only" (1983–84); support for parochial schools in America and the Polish seminary at Orchard Lake; and funding for ethnic studies programs. The purpose of the Copernicus Center, as stated in their public relations pamphlet, was: "Our generation will construct the Center as an expression of the pride we have in them and our heritage." Activities at the Copernicus Center included Polish language classes, polka classes, an art fair, and the Taste of Polonia summer festival. President Mazewski describing the PNA stated, "We are more fraternal than anything. We just got two new dance groups, from two lodges. We spend a lot of money, over a million dollars on fraternalism, on dance groups and choral groups, and youth and sports clubs. This is all fraternalism." A pamphlet, describing the Polish Women's Alliance (April 1986), stated that "this fraternal has worked to preserve Polish customs and traditions and Polish culture." Toward this end the "Alliance sponsors Polish Language, literature, folklore, history and craft classes as well as Polish song and folk-dance lessons, festivals, commemorative programs and quadrennial youth conferences." The pamphlet of the Polish Roman Catholic Union fraternal states that it "promotes Catholic action, fosters Polish language, and maintains Polish traditions, promotes various sports activities, provides various activities such as folk dancing, singing, hobby classes, youth festivals, and language classes, [and] works to enhance the image and prestige of Americans of Polish descent." Organizations serving ethnic needs concentrate on the needs of an ethnic group in a pluralist nation: cultural maintenance, ethnic discrimination, political representation, and securing state resources for such things as museums and public festivals.

The new immigrants, however, were not yet ethnics. While their children may have needed Polish language classes or to learn about their Polish heritage, the new immigrants did not. Immigrant needs were attached to their newcomer status. They needed help resettling in a new culture and society; in this case, Poles had to learn what it meant to be American and how to live in the United States. Organizations serving immigrant needs would do things such as teach English, help newcomers fill out immigration and residency documents, and disseminate information regarding practical concerns (city transit schedules or instructions about utility company policies, for example). Teresa Golebiewska, at the time a graduate student in geography and a new immigrant herself, studied the residential choices of new immigrants. She noted the problems immigrants had deciding where to live.

> In Poland they assign you a place to live, you don't choose it. Therefore there are not things like good and bad neighborhoods, at least not in the extreme sense that we know of it. Someone is just lucky to get an apartment, they don't care where it is. Because people don't have a choice, they are not judged by what their building looks like, or what neighborhood it is in, instead they are judged by what it looks like inside, something they have control over. When they come to America they have to learn what "good neighborhood" means, they have to learn how to choose a good neighborhood, but first they have to learn that there is a thing such as good and bad neighborhoods, and then how to know what is the good one.

While all Americans have to find a place to live, Americans do not have to learn that there are differences between good and bad neighborhoods, and established residents in a city already know where these good and bad neighborhoods are. Another institution immigrants needed to negotiate was the education system. Hubert Romanowski, the director of the Polish University Abroad, said that he set up information seminars for new immigrants because, "the biggest problem for the new Poles is a lack of information about how to use the educational system." Immigrants did not know how to recertify foreign degrees or prepare for college entrance exams. Moreover, similar to the problems with residential choice, immigrants did not realize the importance of the different prestige levels of universities, that not all college degrees were equivalent. Finding a good neighborhood and knowing that a degree from Northwestern University was worth more than one from a community college were not things Polish Americans had to learn. Newcomers to a society have to learn new routines and new values (even if they decide not to adopt them), and they have to establish new networks.

Immigrant needs were concrete and immediate, involving the routines of day to day life. Ethnic needs were cultural and less exigent. The two identities—ethnic and immigrant—are not mutually exclusive. The newcomer status that structures immigrant choices fades over time and the ethnic identity matures. In between new immigrants and the established Polish American ethnics were the World War II émigrés, who, by the 1980s, represented a group of immigrants who were no longer newcomers. They expended more effort than did the immigrants at maintaining a cultural identity, but were also more directly tied to the homeland than were the ethnics.

The PAC addressed immigrant issues on a national level but not on a local level. The PAC lobbied to increase the number of slots for Polish refugees and change immigration laws to make them more favorable to Polish immigrants. The PAC Washington D.C. Office Report, covering the period November 1988 through May 1989, outlined the main activities of the lobbying arm of the PAC, which included efforts on behalf of Polish refugees to bring them to the United States and support of other immigration legislation (Immigration Reform and Control Act [IRCA], Bills S.358 and S.448) directed at altering the immigration quota preference system. In 1988, the PAC helped pass legislation that allowed Polish immigrants with Extended Voluntary Departure status to be granted temporary, and then permanent, residency in the United States. This national level action, however, did not directly address the immediate needs that immigrants faced upon arrival in this country. The only immigrant-oriented activity that the PAC Illinois Division undertook in the late 1980s was to provide ESL classes to the immigrants who received residency status through the IRCA. The PAC received government funds for these classes, so it was a profit-generating service. The PNA provided a few other immigrant services; for example, it organized a Polish Information Center in the late 1970s to assist members of Polonia. At one conference in 1988, held for delegates from various foreign countries interested in immigration affairs, the director of this PNA program described the goal of the center: "The principle of our program is not to give out food but to give information." The information provided, however, was directed toward the elderly members of the community (information on pensions, health insurance, Medicare, federal supplements, social security income). They did provide some services for new immigrants—mostly information about how to contact local, state, and federal agencies and programs, and help filling out forms. Still, the PNA was not an employment agency and it did not help immigrants find housing.[9] In general, organizations like the PAC and the fraternal organi-

9. The churches provided more immigrant services than did the ethnic organizations. For example, in 1987–88, when illegal immigrants could apply for residency through the Immigration Reform and Control Act (IRCA), the largest Polish church in Chicago, St. Hyacinth (*Kościół św. Jacka*) in *Jackowo*, held community meetings after its masses and brought in city

zations were not set up to help new immigrants.[10] In President Mazewski's response to Lukomski's plea to help the new immigrants (quoted at the beginning of the chapter), he did not mention anything the PNA or PAC could do to help them, but simply stated there needed to be an assessment of organizations providing immigrant services and a plan drawn up to procure increased funds for these needs. But the ethnic organizations themselves could not help the newcomers. Even if they wanted to, they were not set up for that function. As one director of the PAC said, "None of us are in a position or have the power to hire these people."

Several Polish immigrant service organizations existed in Chicago, such as the Polish Welfare Association and the Polish American Immigration and Relief Committee, but these were not membership-based organizations.[11]

---

officials and representatives from agencies to provide information and help the immigrants through the legalization process. It also had nightly ESL classes and programs that assisted immigrants who wanted to become naturalized citizens. The focus of this study was not, however, on churches, and so I cannot argue that this institution was more effective than the ethnic organization in serving immigrant needs. Several immigrants complained as bitterly about the Polish American churches as they did about the ethnic organizations, but for different reasons. Mostwin (1991) discusses new immigrant relations within old Polonian parishes more completely . She argues that the churches did not successfully meet the needs of new immigrants because the role of the priest was based on traditional models and suggests that the Polish American parish needed a new type of priest that was more sensitive to the psychological and social needs of new immigrants.

10. It should be mentioned that none of the ethnic organizations were financially well-off. Yet, I do not think that a tight budget necessarily explains the conflict. The organizations chose to direct their funds (however meager they were) toward ethnic functions. They funded ethnic and choral groups rather than employment service programs. I am also not arguing that they *should* have provided for immigrant needs but only pointing out that new immigrants made demands on the organizations because they were "Polish," ignoring or not understanding the fact that they were ethnic organizations, not immigrant organizations. Perhaps, however, if they had been resource-rich organizations they could have provided for both ethnic and immigrant needs.

11. The Polish Welfare Association provided for specific immigrant needs including counseling services for newcomers, food and clothing banks, employment services, translation services, English language classes, and assistance negotiating American institutions, primarily government programs and the legal system. In the six-month period between July 1985 and January 1986, this agency served 631 Polish newcomers, 41 percent of whom were refugees (Cichon, Gozdziak, and Grover 1986, 31). Unlike the early fraternal organizations that were strictly in-house operations, this agency was funded mostly be state and federal programs. It occasionally received modest donations from the larger Polish American fraternals but this made up only a small percentage of its annual income. In 1989, almost two-thirds of its funds came from the state and federal governments, and only 4.7 percent came from the Polish American fraternals (*Annual Report of the Polish Welfare Association*, 1989, 15).

The Polish American Immigration and Relief Committee, Inc. (PAIRC) was founded after

The conflict in the community centered around the fact that new immigrants were not joining ethnic organizations and large ethnic organizations, such as the PAC and the fraternals, were not helping new immigrants.
This conflict is well summarized in the following quote from a woman who
emigrated as a child in the late 1940s and was a secretary to the president
of the PNA.

> We are all Poles but very different. There are the ones that came a
> long time ago, and the ones that came in the 1950s, and then now.
> People that I meet at work now are recent arrivals. These new
> arrivals think that Polonia owes them everything. When it doesn't
> give them everything then they are very disappointed and discour-
> aged. They expect a lot from these organizations. But these are
> private institutions, not like in Poland where they are owned by the
> state. I have had contact with these new arrivals at the PNA, they just
> want a job and they want the organization to do something for them,
> all the time making demands and saying they want, they want. It's
> not like the post–World War II Poles. When they came they had their
> tails between their legs and they were meek and humble and they
> were willing to take any work at all. With these recent arrivals, if the
> organizations don't do what they want then it's very difficult to get
> them to join the PNA. What do they need insurance for, they aren't
> used to buying insurance. In Poland the state pays for everything—
> life and medical insurance. It's hard to convince them that they
> should buy this insurance. For most people the main interest is to
> make money to live here or to go back to Poland. That's why they
> have two or three jobs. See the problem is that they were raised in a

---

World War II to help resettle Polish refugees. It helps only refugees, not all immigrants. In the
1980s, the PAIRC was one of the official resettlement agencies in the United States and it
received its funding primarily from federal funds appropriated through the Office of Refugee
Resettlement. During the 1980s it resettled an average of five hundred Polish refugees a year.
PAIRC's "paramount aim" was to help "newcomers become self-sufficient and productive
members of their new homeland and not a drain on its economy" (Refugee Resettlement
Program, Report to Congress, 1983, 63). The PAIRC was not dedicated to helping refugees
find employment in fields similar to the ones they had in Poland, but instead to getting them
jobs as quickly as possible. Polish refugees who were resettled by PAIRC complained that this
agency was more concerned about getting them any job than getting them a good job. To
restate what Lukomski said in his letter to Mazewski, quoted at the beginning of this chapter,
the PAIRC was not "handling the problem satisfactorily, appearing to regard the refugees as a
troublesome burden."

communist country so they have been brainwashed. They have a communist mentality, they don't understand how things work over here. And there is a lot of problems because they don't want to join these organizations but they only want the organizations to help them.

Requests for assistance were interpreted as artifacts of communist socialization rather than as immigrant needs. Immigrants, she believed, asked for help because they came from communist Poland not because they were newcomers in America.

Symbols of Polishness and Cultural Borders

Although immigrants did not join ethnic organizations, they did form their own. In Chicago, new immigrants helped rebuild the Polish University Abroad (PUNO), and they created a chapter of the Club of Catholic Intelligentsia (KIK, *Klub Inteligencji Katolickiej*), modeled after a similar organization in Poland. They also formed numerous political organizations, discussed in detail in Chapter 4. In addition, the immigrants organized several new PNA lodges (and in this way did in fact "join" the fraternals, but they did not do so in large numbers). President Mazewski identified seven new fraternal lodges formed by new immigrants by 1988. Other new immigrant organizations included the Polish American Economic Forum, Polish Art's Club, Joseph Conrad Yacht Club, and *Klub Samotnych* (Single's Club).

The creation of new organizations was not as troublesome as their failure to join established organizations. The World War II émigrés themselves had created their own organizations (Blejwas 1981), so it was difficult for them to criticize the newcomers for the same behavior. Jan Nowak, a prominent World War II émigré, argued that new immigrants had different attachments to Poland and thought in different "categories" than did Polish Americans; they needed to form their own associations so as to ward off threats of dispersion and inactivity.

People who share the same experiences and memories easily find common ground and become exclusive, often without realizing it. The younger generation which was raised in Poland, finding itself in a foreign land, instinctively is drawn toward groups of their countrymen, but soon see that they are only marginally tolerated. They often do not understand the old structures and symbols, to which the past soldiers emigration [World War II cohort] is so attached. . . . Criticizing the old emigration and Polonia is also useless. Let's take people as they are. Let's not expect an American (second- or third- generation of Polish decent) who still feels some attachment with Poland to think in the same categories as a young, newly arrived Pole. Let's not expect from him, for example, the same degree of loyalty towards democratic movements in Poland, as we expect from ourselves. (1980, 3–4)

Polish American leaders also agreed that new immigrants needed their own organizations. Explaining the formation of new fraternal lodges, PNA President Aloysius Mazewski said:

See, it's better for them to have their own lodges because they understand each other. You see if it's an old lodge, you see, then there's some animosity, you know. And they have set ways of doing it. And even these newcomers have a different language. See the Polish language of the old is different, they have their particular style that has to be catered to.

The new immigrants strongly advocated their right and desire to form their own autonomous organizations. The new immigrants wanted to distinguish themselves from the already existent ethnic group. One founding member of Pomost, a new organization, wrote that this organization's goal was "to unite the politically active members of our generation and enable them to express their own judgments and to act outside the constraints of the current émigré routine. . . . Each new generation of emigrants must emphasize its own distinctive features" (Wlodarczyk 1980, 40). The two groups—Polish American ethnics and Polish immigrants—needed different organizations because they saw themselves as different. These differences originated in their different group biographies, which produced different symbolic meaning systems.

   Within the community, this difference between the new immigrants and Polish Americans ethnics was at times described as a class difference. There was some consensus between the groups that class differences were important, but there was no consensus as to which group had the higher status.

Both the immigrants and the Polish Americans believed they were of higher class. The educated immigrants compared themselves to, as one man said, "the sausage-selling grandchildren of the early peasants"; the suburban-dwelling Polish Americans compared themselves to "ghetto-dwelling hordes" of *wakacjusze* living and drinking in *Jackowo* "wearing funky nail polish" and living "like animals in a barn."[12] The fact is, there was more variation within cohorts than between cohorts. Both groups were economically, educationally, and occupationally diverse. As a migrant cohort, the new cohort was better educated and more cosmopolitan than the earlier "peasant" cohort. On average, however, the new immigrants did not have higher paying jobs or more wealth than Polish Americans. They were newcomers. Yet class is also related to education. Data in Chapter 2 show that new immigrants were often highly educated—more than half of them had some postsecondary education. Polish Americans had rates of educational attainment similar to those of other ethnics of European descent in America—roughly a third of the population attended some postsecondary school (Lieberson and Waters 1988, 107–8). In America, however, education is generally linked to class through occupation. More schooling leads to better jobs with either higher wages or more prestige and most often both. This relation between education and occupation was more direct for native-born Americans than immigrants. New immigrants seldom worked in the occupations they were trained for or at the level they had before they emigrated. As also noted in Chapter 2, emigration represented a decline in occupational status for most immigrants. Comparing the two groups in terms of income and occupation, Polish Americans fared better than immigrants; comparing the two groups in terms of education, the immigrants surpassed the ethnics. In a strict analysis that defines class only in economic terms, immigrants fell behind ethnics. However, immigrants had fewer resources because of their newcomer status, not because they had less education or fewer occupational skills.

Class also has a cultural component. Polish immigrants often remarked that they had a greater appreciation for "high culture," meaning art, operas, symphonies, and literature, and defined Polish Americans as having ties to a "folk culture" Polishness. Yet, the new immigrants' appreciation for

12. Like most Americans, they used class as synonymous with social status or prestige. I would like to thank Peggy Malecki for providing me with the tapes of three interviews she conducted with Polish Americans in the fall of 1986. This last quote came from one of her interviews.

high culture was not primarily related to their class position, but to their experiences in communist Poland. Polish Americans had less exposure to high culture because they lived in an American capitalist economy with a market-driven mass media culture, and had a greater affinity for Polish folk culture because they were descendants of a mostly peasant cohort. High culture is the domain of the middle and upper classes in America, where tickets to symphonies and operas are expensive. In contrast, the communist government in Poland provided inexpensive and accessible admissions to concert halls and theaters (Goldfarb 1982). Moreover, Poland's state-controlled television had only two channels, which, while showing some sports, slapstick comedies, and Hollywood serials (*Dallas* did make it to Poland), for the most part offered educational shows, documentaries, and musical entertainment. The offerings on Polish television resembled America's Public Broadcasting System. Americans would also be exposed to more "high culture" if the only television channel was PBS. Polish Americans' lack of appreciation for high culture is related to their predominantly working-class position in capitalist America.

The ethnic culture that working-class Polish Americans celebrated was the folk culture of their ancestors who came from rural Poland. Obidinski writes that Polonian customs are "residues of Polish American immigrant community activity derived from native peasant folkways" (Obidinski and Zand 1987, 138). Helen Stankiewicz Zand describes some of the folk traditions that have survived in American Polonia. "We see that the dances, the 'polka' as a ballroom dance and the 'krakowiak' as an exhibition dance, have a great vitality and are likely to last for a long time. The 'krakowiak' costume, somewhat stylized but very close to the original, has almost become a conventional symbol of the Polish people" (118). The dances and costumes are descendant from a rural peasant culture and persist, especially the polka dance, primarily in the culture of working-class Polish American communities.

Not all Polish Americans are working class. Charles Keil argues that class divisions within ethnic Polonia are reflected in the types of culture they cele-brate. He argues that most Polonian scholars and Polonian leaders prefer to emphasize high-culture Polishness, which connects descendants not to peasant roots but to aristocratic roots. Middle-class Polish Americans imagi-natively romanticize themselves as "heirs of Polish kings and knights with ancient codes of chivalry and honor to uphold" (1979, 43). Keil writes that middle-class Polonia "hates the polka with a passion" and shuns the corner bars, bowling alleys, and Knights of Columbus halls of the Polish American working class (38–39). Within Polonia, these middle-class values and culture are reinforced by the smaller elite intellectual strata and the World War II émigré cohort (Obidinski 1975; Gross 1976). This culture prefers to listen to Chopin rather than 'Lil Wally's Polka Band, they spend their time at the Polish Cultural Garden Club rather than the fraternal sports clubs, and with the Halina Singing Society rather than at the *Dom Polski.*

Whether it is a working-class tie to the peasantry or a middle-class tie to the aristocracy, Polish American culture nonetheless originates in nineteenth-century Poland. The cultural identity of the new immigrants is also rooted in their ancestors (no culture is ahistorical; they read Adam Mickiewicz and dance the Polonaise), but their cultural identity was transformed in twentieth-century Poland, so it has a contemporary as well as historical base in Poland. In contrast, the meaning of Polishness for Polish Americans was not modernized in Poland. At the Polonaise festival in July 1986, sponsored by the PAC Illinois Division, the brochure describing the Miss Polonaise contest stated, "Polish women kept the Old World Traits alive. They kneaded the *pierogi* and rolled the *gołąbki.*" Over the century, however, the "Old World" changed. The women in the new immigration wcrc defined not by their kneading and rolling, but by their behavior in contemporary Poland. Polish women were accountants and doctors, they managed households when their activists husbands were sent to prison, and they themselves were union organizers. Moreover, Polonian culture rooted in peasant traditions was not familiar to new immigrants who came from urban areas in Poland; this folk history was not their history, so the symbols of this culture held little meaning for them.

The cultural and social landscape of Poland changed over the last fifty to one hundred years, and with it the symbols associated with Polishness. One new immigrant couple living in Michigan talked about thcsc cultural differences between new immigrants and Polish Americans that became evident when they joined a Polish American organization. They started by saying they "cannot communicate with" Polish Americans. The husband said:

> Many [Polish Americans] do not speak correct Polish. And not only that, even people who came here thirty years ago, we are different. We have different values, we come from a different Poland. Poland now is all industry. There are no more farmlands. We all live in the city. My whole life I am living in the city.

And the wife said:

> And we cannot even talk to them. They are different. For example,
> we come here and everyone is having polka parties. In Poland no
> one polkas, oh maybe some folk groups, or for special ethnic days,
> but we dance the same dances as the Western world do now. And
> when we are together, I remember this one time we went to some
> thing at the Polish Heritage Foundation, and there were like two
> different cultures. The old Poles all sat on one side of the room and
> we sat on the other side. . . . And at the Polish Heritage Founda-
> tion they do not even speak Polish!

Another immigrant complained because the PAC chose to finance the
publication of a nineteenth-century novel rather than something by a more
well-known contemporary Polish writer.

> It's really stupid, because it's something like the novel about in this
> country, if we can compare, the Wild West, with all the shooting and
> riding horses. It was great, OK, but when I was fourteen. And they
> consider this a great novel. Oh. I don't know. It's a little bit different
> situation, because in some point in Polish history it was the impor-
> tant book. But not right now. We have world-wide recognized writers.
> Why don't they print these things? Because they don't know.

Polish culture for new immigrants included contemporary symbols and
figures. Polish culture for ethnics was rooted in the past.

Culture is not a static identity; it changes and evolves within a sociohistoric context. For Polish Americans this was an American context, and for
new immigrants it was a Polish context. The best illustration of this is in
language. Speaking a common language is often one indicator of shared
identity. In Polonia, however, the Polish language was not a shared symbol
system but a source of internal group borders. Many Polish Americans did
not speak Polish, and when they did, it was often grammatically incorrect,
full of outmoded expressions, with a heavy American accent or representative of regional dialects. One immigrant said, "You know we are a different
group from these older Poles. . . . Many Poles do not even speak Polish,
and some that do speak Polish, speak it very bad." Another newcomer said,
"The old Poles are different; they are like chop suey. Not really Polish; not
really America. When I hear them speak, I say, 'What's that? I never heard

that before.'" One new immigrant referring to several directors of the PNA said: "It's really beautiful, their Polish, it has all these old phrases, but it's not the Polish spoken today. Some have these old accents that make it hard for you to understand them." And another immigrant said:

> Some of these old Poles, [laughs] they are really funny, their Polish. It is not American, it is not Polish. Some I can not even understand. Those that came from the turn of the century from these poorer regions, mostly Galicia, they are speaking a different Polish than we do. And then they are here and it changes. It is really funny to listen to them. Some of them are so colorful. There was this one man, he knew some Polish and this man from Poland, some famous guy, came and he wanted to impress him so he wanted to use his Polish and he told the man to sit down in Polish and said, "*siedź na dupie*" which means "sit on your ass." And this man doesn't even know what he is saying, but that he thinks he is politely saying to this man to sit down, because maybe this is how he hears his father say it.

Communication between new immigrants and Polish Americans was difficult even when they were both speaking Polish. As the man I quoted in the introductory chapter stated, "There is still a language problem, even when I am speaking Polish with them." Languages are grounded in social contexts. The Polish of Polish Americans was an "old" Polish (grounded in nineteenth-century rural Poland), but it was also, in a sense, a "new" Polish because it was a language transformed in American. Languages are not dead as long as they continue to be used. The Polish used by Polish Americans was a hybrid, a new language: not Polish, not American but like "chop suey."[13]

The Polish language had changed over the generations in twentieth-century Polonia, but the new immigrants' use of language was also altered within the context of communist Poland. One of the ways this manifest itself

13. Helen Stankiewicz Zand offers a wonderful discussion of how the Polish language changed in America (Obidinski and Zand 1987, 40–49). She emphasizes that the Polish American tongue is distinct from the Polish spoken in contemporary Poland. Derived from mostly peasant origins, Polish American Polish reflects regional dialects and includes numerous American words (spoken with Polish inflections) referring to objects and concepts that did not exist in Poland around the turn of the century. Moreover, when a Polish American speaks Polish the pronunciation is softened—"It sounds muffled as though it were spoken through flannel" as vowels and consonants "lose their sharp contours" (43).

was in the writing styles of the new immigrants. One World War II émigré, a former editor of the Polonia newspaper *Dziennik Związkowy*, had hired new immigrants as staff writers. He connected the writing styles of the new immigrants to the state-controlled media in Poland. "They were born and they were raised and they know the Soviet style of journalism. . . . For example, they love to have interview, because in Soviets you have interview in the paper splashed all over, interview with Natasia Aleksandrownia who was the top tractor operator in some factory so she is a good hero, so interview in all the paper." He also believed that censorship in communist Poland shaped their writing skills so that they learned to write extremely long articles, "to figure out the space to talk and not to say anything."

The different writing styles became an issue in the Polish American Economic Forum (Forum), an organization established in 1989 composed of Polish Americans and new Polish immigrants. Several Forum documents, promotional letters, and information bulletins originally written in Polish had to be both translated into English and, as one Polish American said, "Americanized," which meant "changing the mood" of the articles. To put it into an American language meant to put it into a language that sells. For example, the Polish version of Forum's main promotional letter was six long paragraphs (five to six sentences per paragraph) and described in excruciating detail the inaugural meeting, the upcoming convention, Forum's offices, and membership fees. It was a very dry and boring document. The American version was only half as long, had ten short paragraphs (one or two sentences per paragraph), only briefly mentioned the inaugural meeting, convention, and membership fees, and focused mainly on the "extraordinary transition" occurring in Poland and the "inevitable opportunity" for profits. The American version was marked with punchy propaganda and included spicy adjectives and phrases about the "great change" and "urgent need" in Poland because the "alien system was being dismantled."

Language was also a source of divisiveness in the community when groups were forced to choose between Polish and English. Forum members debated which language to use (Polish or English) and, though the debate had certain practical tones, it also had symbolic meaning. Forum members spent half of one business meeting arguing over "the official language of Forum." A Polish American member identified this debate over language as "a philosophical question: Is Forum a Polish organization or an American organization?" In Forum's formative stages, the Polish American chairman (who spoke Polish) stated that English would be the official organizational language, although 98 percent of the members were not native English speakers and most were not proficient in English. In addition, most of the people in Poland with whom Forum negotiated did not speak English. In the beginning, despite the chairman's pronouncements, most of the literature leaving the office was in Polish only. The discussion of the official language surfaced again at the first board of directors' meeting. Although the majority of board members (78 percent) were native Polish speakers, the Polish American chairman decided that Forum was "an American organization. We should have English as the official language." He decreed that all board meetings were to be conducted in English. The result was that conversation was in English when the chairman was in the room, but in Polish when he was not present. Though the Polish Americans wanted to "Americanize" Forum, the nature of the membership base demanded that business be conducted in Polish. In the end, most business was conducted in Polish; however, the office staff meetings, literature, and the conventions were bilingual.

Language did not bring the two groups together. For Polish Americans, their Polish was tied to their immigrant ancestors and had transformed in American society; the new immigrants' language had evolved in twentieth-century communist Poland. In some instances, language became a site of struggle between the immigrants and ethnics as they vied for the power to define the situation as either American (English) or Polish. In the community, the Polish, Polish American, and English languages represented three different symbol systems, and these differences became in-house borders, or ways of defining "us" and "them."

Other symbols of Polishness were also not easily shared. One arena that illustrated symbolic differences was the May 3d Polish Constitution Day parade. This is "The" Polish parade in the City of Chicago. During the parade in 1988, over one hundred floats and groups marched down LaSalle Street, including Americans, Polish Americans, World War II émigrés, and new Polish immigrants. The first set of symbols displayed expressed Poland's contemporary struggles. In the "Solidarity group" (there was only one) most of the marchers (all new immigrants) wore T-shirts with the slogan "Alive *Solidarność*," and some had a number below this slogan that was the wearer's former prison number. The banners in this group reflected the contemporary political situation in Poland (for example, "*Solidarność*," "Free Elections in Poland, Jaruzelski Out," "Free Political Prisoners," a swastika and the Soviet emblem with an equal sign between them,

"Support Polish Strikes"). The group chanted political slogans (among them, "Solidarity—Yes, Communism—No," "Free Elections in Poland," "Stop Red Peril," "Lech Walesa," "*Solidarność*," "Jaruzelski Out"). This was the only group whose symbolic representation was based solely on contemporary Poland. Other groups displayed banners with symbols of Poland's opposition, however, these symbols of Poland's contemporary struggles were intertwined with ethnic or American symbols. For example, groups representing Polish American fraternal lodges and Polish Saturday schools also carried *Solidarność* placards, and the Illinois Right to Life group carried Polish flags and *Solidarność* placards. They used the symbols of Solidarity to complement and legitimate their own Polonian and American symbols.

A second set of symbols represented traditional Polish culture, much of which has found its way into Polish American (Polonian) culture. For example, people in the Krakus Ham float wore folk costumes, as did people marching to represent ethnic fraternal lodges. Others drew on Poland's political history of democracy, such as politician (and non-Pole) Tom Hynes, whose group carried a picture of him with the words, "We Salute the Polish Constitution." The constitution was written in 1791, just before the second partition of Poland and is a national Polish symbol of democracy and independence. The folk costumes and constitution are representations of Polish national history; these are symbols that have been incorporated into Polonian culture yet also remain meaningful in contemporary Poland.

A third set of symbols represented Polonian culture. For example, one group sang Bobby Vinton's song, "*Moja droga, ja ci kocham.*" Bobby Vinton is a popular singer in American Polonia with very little name recognition in Poland. Another Polonian association carried a banner that read, "Pride in our Country's Heritage." Pride and heritage reflect ethnic concerns in America. Other Polonian symbols of pride included T-shirts and pins with such pro-Polish heritage logos as: "Proud to Be Polish," "Half Polish Is Better Than None," "Genuine Polish Parts, Happiness Is Being Polish," and "Polish Power." These are not slogans one finds on T-shirts in Poland (except, perhaps, in shops catering to Polish American tourists). The fraternals, who sponsored the parade and whose lodges represented numerous groups in the parade, are themselves Polonian symbols. Fraternalism is an ethnic American institution rooted in late nineteenth- and early twentieth-century immigrant culture. The bands playing polkas also symbolized Polonian, not Polish, culture. In America the polka is almost synonymous with Polish Americans (perhaps to Polonian scholars and leaders it is synonymous with working-class Polish American culture, but to the rest of America it represents Polish American culture in general). The polka is actually a Czech dance that has become incorporated into Polish American culture. It is not a meaningful symbol of Polish national culture in Poland.

During the parade, new immigrants identified with the historical (the constitution) and contemporary Polish symbols but not the Polonian symbols. They wore buttons supporting *Solidarność* rather than ones that said, "Kiss Me I'm Polish." The new immigrants watching the parade joked when the "polka floats" passed, telling each other to go and join the music; "That's your group," they ribbed to each other and then laughed. Another said sarcastically, "Yes, yes, I loooove that music." These symbols of ethnic Polonia did not resonate with the new immigrant.[14]

In one exchange, a Polish immigrant who was a radio talk show host had to defend, or at least justify, to a confused Polish American woman why his radio program did not play polkas. The Polish American woman suggested, "You should spice it up a bit with some polkas. . . . What do you talk about anyway?" This was in the spring of 1988 and the immigrant mentioned the strikes in Poland and the activities of Solidarity. The ethnic responded, "I still say go for the polkas, they would add some life." For the ethnic, the polka was a symbol of Polish radio. For the immigrant, contemporary issues in Poland—social, political, literary, and economic—defined the content of new Polish media.

While immigrants have concrete ties to a contemporary homeland, ethnic ties are mediated through their ancestors. As a result, the two groups do not always share the same culture or even the same language. Social benefits such as friendship or entertainment that are derived from partici-

14. I cannot make any well-supported claims about the extent to which customs maintained in Polish American families are maintained in new immigrant families. I have observed some key traditions of Polish American culture that are also practiced by new immigrants; for example, *Wigilia* (the Christmas Eve supper), *Święconka* (the blessing of the Easter baskets), and *Kolędy* (Christmas caroling). These are national traditions, not specifically peasant traditions. There are other traditions that I have not observed but I cannot state authoritatively that immigrants do or do not practice them (for example, Dyngus Day, the bridal dance, visiting relatives' graves on All Saints Day). Many of these traditions are family traditions or private matters, and my data collection focused on organizations. While I participated in family gatherings with new immigrants, the data are too weak to make any strong claims. I am not arguing that there was no common culture between new immigrants and Polish Americans, only that some symbols of Polonian culture (such as the polka) were not meaningful to new immigrants. For a wonderful discussion of Polish folkways in America, see Obidinski and Zand (1987).

pation in organizations operate in those arenas where there is a like-mindedness among members. New immigrants did not experience a like-mindedness with Polish American ethnics, and therefore were unlikely to join an organization for its social benefits. Moreover, one primary goal of ethnic organizations was to promote cultural maintenance. Even if the immigrants decided they wanted to work on maintaining their culture, they did not necessarily agree with the Polish Americans on the symbolic basis of Polishness. These symbolic differences interfered with the practical problems of working together in the same organizations, and partly explain why new immigrants formed their own organizations.

Was Forum a Polish or an American organization? Symbols identify and maintain borders between groups. Much the same way that Pierre Bourdieu (1989) discusses borders between class groups, borders between social groups—in this case ethnics and immigrants—are also symbolically produced. Symbols are used by members of a group to define who they are as well as who they are not. Each group in Polonia fought to preserve its definition of Self; and ownership of the community depended in part on each group's power to symbolically define the public arena. The new immigrants would find themselves outside the community if Polonia were defined as speaking English and celebrating folk culture; the Polish Americans would find themselves shoved aside in a polka-hating, Polish-speaking community.

Conclusion

Contentious conflicts in the community were over the new immigrants' unwillingness to join ethnic organizations and with the ethnic organizations' inability to satisfy new immigrant needs. The established Polonians used a discourse of communism to explain what they considered undesirable behavior. Socialized in a capitalistic-democratic society, they believed that pervasive, subtle, and cunning communism brainwashed its victims and made them unable to understand concepts like freedom and democracy, that the supply-market principles of the communist system destroyed the work ethic of its citizens, and finally, that communism fostered an attitude of dependency. While members of the new migrant cohort seldom became dependent on state resources, they did expect the ethnic community to help them. The ethnic community, however, was structured to satisfy ethnic needs, not newcomer, immigrant needs. As a result, the new immigrants saw no immediate reason to join the ethnic organizations. Moreover, the immigrants did not feel a solidarity of likeness with Polish Americans. The two groups had different experiences, they had different social identities (ethnic and immigrant) that occasioned different needs, and they had different understandings of Polishness. Immigrants had direct experience with communism, while Polish Americans experienced communism filtered through an American lens. Immigrants experienced being newcomers to a society; ethnics experienced being established members of a society. Polishness for ethnics (its language and symbols) reflected nineteenth-century Poland; immigrants had a more up-to-date version. The immigrants and ethnics shared an historical identity but not a contemporary one.

4

A Solidarity of Differences

I see we need them. They know how to write letters, how to call Senators and who to contact. For me even the simple letter is big job. I don't know if I'm saying right, not just vocabulary and grammar but appropriateness. But, for them [Polish Americans], Solidarity and Poland are very loose terms. They can't imagine what it's like there, so everyday I'm explaining to them who this is, what that is.

—*a Solidarity refugee*

Differences between new immigrants and established ethnics were not always problematic. In fact, under certain conditions, differences facilitated organizational cooperation. While the two groups shared an historical ancestry and common goals, the organizational linkage was actually based on a solidarity of differences. In many ways this linkage resembles what Emile Durkheim called "organic solidarity"—an interdependence among diverse parts. This interdependency came about when new immigrants and established ethnics needed each other. Needing each other was a necessary but not sufficient condition for cooperative action. As shown, the new immigrants needed help overcoming their newcomer status and the ethnic organizations needed new members—yet this did not result in them working together. One reason was because the established organizations did not have the resources to satisfy the new immigrants' needs (for example, organizations like the PNA that needed members did not offer employment or housing services). The second condition necessary for cooperative actions, then, was that each group had to have the resources that the other group wanted and was willing to exchange.

Researchers have argued that new organizations, disadvantaged by low levels of resources (funds, members, legitimacy), find it useful to link up with preexisting organizations to gain access to their resources.[1] In the asymmetric relation between new and established organizations, the established organization usually has more to offer in the exchange. But cooperation is more likely when both parties find it beneficial. Optimally, both parties exchange resources they have for resources they need (Boulding 1941; Blau 1963 [1955]). When examining interorganizational cooperation between new and established organizations, we also need to examine what new organizations bring to the table, an issue much less discussed in the collective behavior literature.

In Chicago Polonia, ethnics and immigrants had different resources to share because their biographies were located in different environments—the former in America, the latter in Poland. Their locations influenced their networks and, consequently, the resources available to them. For example, ethnics had stronger links to American institutions and knowledge about "how to write letters" and "who to contact" in the U.S. Senate. Immigrants had stronger links to opposition activists and thus had knowledge about "who this is" and "what that is" in Poland. Because the borders of communist Poland were not always easily traversable, especially after the imposition of martial law in 1981, the informal and personal ties that the Solidarity refugees had to the underground opposition were valuable. Having different resources gave the groups something to exchange; and having different networks minimized competition because they were operating in different environments.

New Political Organizations

Members of the newest immigration cohort created their own political organizations in the 1970s and 1980s. The three most active political

1. Linkages with established organizations are useful to a new organization or incipient social movement because preexisting structures can provide such things as a resource base, an infrastructure of solidarity, communications networks, experienced leaders, strategic know-how, ideological orientation, legitimacy, and selective incentives (Oberschall 1973; Freeman 1973; Curtis and Zurcher 1973; McCarthy and Zald 1973; Gamson 1975; Jenkins and Perrow 1977; Aveni 1978; Walsh 1981; Tierny 1982; Hardin 1982; Morris 1984; Nielson 1985; Wiewel and Hunter 1985; Hunter and Staggenborg 1986; Staggenborg 1987; Klandermans 1989; Buechler 1990). Researchers have most thoroughly documented the importance of preexisting organizations for participant mobilization (Snow et al. 1980 and 1986; Oberschall 1973; Walsh and Warland 1983; Jenkins 1983; Taylor 1989; Fernandez and McAdam 1989). In

organizations of new immigrants in Chicago were Pomost (which means "footbridge" in Polish), created in the late 1970s; and Freedom for Poland and Brotherhood of Dispersed Solidarity Members (*Wspólnota Rozproszonych Członków NSZZ Solidarność*), both created in the mid-1980s.[2] A fourth organization, the Polish-American Economic Forum (Forum), was founded in the fall of 1989. These organizations themselves were never as large as the established Polonian organizations such as the PAC, nor were they immensely influential, and eventually they all disbanded. Nonetheless, in Chicago in the 1980s, they were the key organizations of new immigrants acting for Poland's independence. These organizations are sociologically important because they provide a context within which to analyze the culture, resources, and status of the politically active new immigrants.

As the events in Poland escalated in the late 1970s, new immigrants mobilized to support the opposition. The future leaders of Pomost first became acquainted with one another at the University of Illinois, Circle Campus, where they had organized the Polish Student's Association. In 1979, this group, which included its founders and leaders Christopher Rac, Waldemar Wlodarczyk, and Marian Sromek, decided to publish a "social-political" quarterly called Pomost for a Polish reading audience (92 percent

---

addition, they note that preexisting structures that support new movements are often found within an indigenous organizational base (Oberschall 1973; McAdam 1983; Jenkins 1983; Morris 1984; Taylor 1989). The general message is that new movement organizations are developed and maintained within an existing network of organizations.

2. Across America, numerous small groups of mostly new immigrants were organized for the purpose of helping Poland. Another new organization in Chicago was the Alliance for Independence. Members from this group were interviewed for this study, as well as members of new political organizations in California. In America there were twelve groups as of 1989 known as Support of Solidarity (SOS) committees (in Boston, Philadelphia, New York, Cleveland, New Haven, Connecticut, Ohio, Southern California, Los Angeles, Berkeley, western Massachusetts, Detroit, and Arlington, Massachusetts); seven chapters of Solidarity California (in Orange County, Concord, Los Angeles, San Diego, Sacramento, Santa Barbara, and central California); and another twelve groups created to support Poland's opposition — Freedom California, Maryland Action for Poland, Central New Jersey Solidarity, Solidarity International (in New Britain, Connecticut, and New York City), North Carolina Committee for Solidarity with "Solidarity," Friends of Solidarity (Washington, D.C.), Solidarity Support Committee of Rhode Island, Committee of Solidarity—Former Political Prisoners (Maywood, New Jersey), Friends of Solidarity Families Project (Buffalo, New York), Friends of Solidarity, Inc. (Vienna, Virginia), Polonia Solidarity Association (Reading, Pennsylvania), Solidarity and Human Rights Association (Buffalo, New York), and *Solidarność* Association (Seattle, Washington). The most prominent international organization was the Conference of Solidarity Support Organizations (CSSO) with which Brotherhood was affiliated. In the late 1980s, there were seven CSSO coordinators in four countries. In addition, there were at least twenty-six Solidarity support organizations in Canada, twenty in Europe, and organizations in Japan, Australia, New Zealand, Venezuela, and Mexico.

of the articles from 1979–84 were in Polish). The impetus for publishing the *Pomost Quarterly* came from an activist in Poland. In the lead article of the first issue, the editors noted that during a visit to Chicago in 1979, Pawel Bakowski, "an authentic representative" of the opposition in Poland, stressed the need for publicity as well as financial support for the movement. Between 1979 and 1984, Pomost circulated fifteen hundred to two thousand copies of each quarterly, except during martial law times (1982) when they printed nearly seven thousand copies. The quarterly was devoted to Polish issues and often printed articles written by opposition leaders in Poland. Between 1979 and 1984, 52 percent of the articles were about events in Poland, 31 percent were about Poland-Polonia or Poland-U.S. relations, and less than 6 percent of the articles concentrated solely on Polonia.

In 1982, the group became incorporated in Illinois as a charitable educational organization. The main purpose of Pomost was to support the democratic movement in Poland.[3] One Pomost member told me that Pomost attracted supporters because it was "unequivocally intolerant of communism. It was purely political. Whereas some of the other Polish organizations had a lot to do with different things—dance, and banquets and all this—Pomost basically stuck to politics." The reason for the "straight Poland" agenda was that the founders were immigrants. Although Pomost did attract some young Polish Americans and World War II émigrés, the three founders had immigrated to the United States in the late 1960s, and the majority of its members had arrived in the 1970s and early 1980s. During its peak years in 1982–83, Pomost boasted having six thousand sympathizers nationwide and nine hundred dues-paying members. Their main activities were publishing the quarterly, organizing demonstrations in

3. Pomost was a political organization concerned with Poland, not Polonia, as reflected in its goals set down in its articles of incorporation:

1. To give complete support to the government of the United States in its efforts to win and maintain a just and durable peace and to promote democratic principles throughout the world.
2. To actively participate in the political life of the United States and to develop and forge close and direct contacts with democratic movements in other countries, especially in Poland and Eastern Europe.
3. To perpetuate and to enrich the democratic ideals as reflected in the moral renewal of the Polish Solidarity Movement.
4. To develop and coordinate work with other groups in the United States in order to promote principles of freedom, liberty and justice for all. .
5. To attract all men and women of good will who share a concern for human rights in Poland, with the belief that such concern assists the pursuit and development of human rights generally, and peace throughout the world.

Chicago, raising funds for the opposition, and eventually engaging in lobbying activities to influence U.S. foreign policy toward Poland.

During the mid-1980s, the opposition movement in Poland experienced its lowest period of activity. World attention had turned away from Poland. Martial law had been lifted in July 1983 and most political prisoners had been released by 1984. People in Poland were increasingly affected by deteriorating economic conditions, and they became more occupied with economic survival than oppositional activities. The regime outlawed Solidarity in October 1982, and the opposition was operating underground as the Temporary Coordinating Committee of Solidarity (known as TKK, *Tymczasowa Komisja Koordinacyjna*). Other opposition groups (some organized in the pre-martial law period and others after martial law) were also working underground. The actions of these underground organizations were greatly limited during the repressive mid-1980s. No serious strike activity occurred until the spring of 1988. The most significant opposition activity during this period was the proliferation of underground publications.

Solidarity refugees founded several new organizations in the United States in the mid-1980s during this period of limited opposition activity, international inattention, and repressive state sanctions. Freedom for Poland (Freedom) was founded in October 1984 after a communist officer murdered Father Jerzy Popieluszko, a Roman Catholic priest in Poland and vocal advocate of Solidarity and human rights. Freedom was incorporated in Illinois in March 1985 as a nonprofit charitable and educational organization. One Freedom leader said its main goal was "to help Polish people fight the communist regime," which its bylaws stated it would do by promoting anticommunism and working with other anticommunist groups. By the late 1980s, Freedom mainly supported a more radical wing of the opposition, Kornel Morowiecki's organization Fighting Solidarity (*Solidarność Walcząca*). Freedom's main activity was to collect money and send it to the underground opposition in Poland. Money was collected outside of churches, at festivals, political meetings, demonstrations, parades, and other public events in Polonia. Members also paid dues ($5 per month). In addition, Freedom members organized demonstrations, circulated petitions, and sponsored opposition leaders' visits to America. Many of Freedom's roughly one hundred members were Solidarity refugees.[4] Freedom

4. Its leaders said that in 1988 Freedom had about one hundred members in Illinois, with sympathizers in California, New Jersey, Arizona, and Connecticut, but that on the average only

had a working-class tone that came from the occupations (skilled laborers in both Poland and America) and educational level of its active members (most had technical vocations rather than university degrees), and its method of fundraising (collecting change in cans at public functions). Freedom was intimately connected with Solidarity in Poland. The founding president of Freedom, Andrzej Dudek, had been a member of the National Coordinating Commission of Solidarity. Other key players in Freedom were Waldemar Kaszubski, Witold Szawlowski, and Jozef Krynski.

The Brotherhood of Dispersed Solidarity Members (Brotherhood) was started in the fall of 1984 by Solidarity activists Jaroslaw Cholodecki, Hubert Romanowski, and Wojciech Sukiennik. The main goals of the organization were to help the opposition in Poland and unite Solidarity refugees. A moral tone of obligation to Poland underscored Brotherhood's (and Freedom's) stated purpose. A letter sent to Brotherhood members dated March 31, 1985, states:

> We are in emigration, outside of Poland, and each of us had his own reason for departure from the country, and to even try to morally evaluate these decisions is unnecessary and injurious, and it is not important; what is important is HOW and WHAT we can do to help those who stayed. Poland can be helped in two ways: first, by pressuring the state, international organizations and public opinion against the PRL government, and second, to send direct material-technical aid to the underground.

The organization was never officially incorporated. Brotherhood was a loosely-knit group of about twenty people, operating mostly in Chicago. In contrast to Freedom members, Brotherhood members had professional occupations in Poland and had received higher educations. Several of them also held prominent positions in Solidarity: two had been on the National Coordinating Commission of Solidarity, two were regional chairmen, and one was a regional vice-chairman. In the national Brotherhood organiza-

---

twenty-five to forty members were active. Freedom leaders said that 80 percent of its members arrived in the United States after 1980, the others came in the 1960s and 1970s, and two were members of the World War II cohort. A few of the more active members were 1970s immigrants who had originally been members of Pomost; some new immigrants even referred to Freedom as "a splinter organization of Pomost." Freedom leaders estimated that 25 percent of their members were former Pomost members.

tion, nine members had been chairmen or vice-chairmen of regional Solidarity committees.

Brotherhood's recruitment letter stated that the membership was to come "exclusively from among the members of NSZZ Solidarity who have, in our opinion, high moral virtue" (Brotherhood letter, January 1985). Brotherhood members used their premigration links to help them reorganize themselves in America; in fact, the basis for organization was in part to preserve these premigration links. The recruitment letter stated, "The goal of the Brotherhood is to unify the members of NSZZ Solidarity in America."[5] The ideological ties of Brotherhood to the Solidarity union were also evident in how it assessed membership dues. Brotherhood dues were considered union dues. The basis for the dues was set by the same standard used for union dues in Poland; that is, 1 percent of their income (roughly $15–$20 a month in America). In addition to dues, strategies for collecting money included radio-thons, banquets, and selling paraphernalia with Solidarity logos (such as bumper stickers, T-shirts, and pins) at Polonian festivals. The money raised was sent to Poland to support regional and local underground publications and centers of activity. Other Brotherhood activities included organizing lectures, demonstrating, and circulating petitions.[6]

In the late 1980s, the deteriorating economic conditions in Poland, the weakening power of the USSR, and the escalating strike activity contributed to the Polish Communist Party consenting to partially free elections in June 1989. The overwhelming victory of the Solidarity candidates and the

5. In the first financial statement sent to members, three months after Brotherhood's founding, a cofounder of the organization wrote that Brotherhood was important for keeping this special group together. "It is very important that the representatives of the Solidarity emigration take some form, we must not allow its existence to break apart as a physical concept." In addition to keeping Solidarity refugees in America together, Brotherhood maintained ties to other Solidarity refugees and organizations around the world. Brotherhood was connected to the Solidarity Information Office in Toronto and the larger Conference of Solidarity Support Organizations (CSSO).

6. Brotherhood members also operated through a second group, the Club of Catholic Intellectuals (known as KIK from its Polish name *Klub Inteligencji Katolickiej*). KIK in Chicago was modeled after KIK in Poland, an organization created in the late 1950s for discussing social, economic, and religious issues. In Chicago, Brotherhood leaders and other new immigrants who considered themselves members of the intelligentsia founded KIK in 1986 to serve as a discussion group, and hopefully to bring together members of the intelligentsia from all Polonian cohorts. KIK was composed of roughly thirty to forty new Polish immigrants. In addition, half a dozen World War II émigrés regularly attended meetings, and some younger Polish Americans were occasionally present. All Brotherhood members were KIK members, but not all KIK members were Brotherhood members.

election of Tadeusz Mazowiecki, a member of the opposition, to the position of president, paved the way for changes in the Polish economy. Poland began dismantling its state-owned system and allowing free market practices. To assist Poland in this direction, the Polish-American Economic Forum (Forum) was organized in Chicago in the fall of 1989 with the objective to promote foreign investments in Poland and Western economic assistance for Poland. The president of Forum was Jaroslaw Cholodecki (a Brotherhood leader), and the chairman was Mitchell Kobelinski (a Polish American). In contrast to the smaller organizations like Freedom and Brotherhood, Forum became relatively large and formalized in a very short time. Forum had 170 members, each of whom had paid a $100 annual membership fee by the time of its inaugural meeting in October 1989. Two months later, Forum had increased its membership by 200 percent, secured the appearance of Lech Walesa at its first annual convention, elected a twenty-seven-member board of directors, and set up offices in Chicago and Warsaw. Moreover, Forum attracted the attention of officials and politicians in the United States and Poland, as well as local, national, and international news agencies.[7]

The rapid pace at which the leaders of Forum were able to get Forum established is in part a result of timing. Forum operated in an organizationally open environment. At its inception, there were few member-based organizations oriented toward the new private market sector in Poland. Forum emerged at a time when the new government in Poland was transforming its economy to a free market system. Lech Walesa was urging the Western world to help "jump start" the Polish economy. Poland needed capital, market skills, and technology. At a time when Poland's leaders were looking for foreign business partners, Forum was unfolding as an organi-

7. Press coverage in the United States included articles in local newspapers (*Chicago Sun-Times, Chicago Tribune,* and *Northwestside Press*), national and international presses (*Time, London Daily Herald*), and in the Polish-language print media (*Kurier, Dziennik Związkowy,* and *Nowy Dziennik*). There were also articles about Forum in the Polish-language presses in Poland (*Tygodnik Solidarność, Gazeta Wyborcza,* and *Rzeczpospolita*). Forum and its leaders received television and radio attention. The president of Forum was invited to be on *The Today Show* in October 1989 (he was bumped because of the San Francisco earthquake). CNN broadcast a segment about Forum, and local TV stations in Chicago covered the visit of Walesa to the Forum convention, the opening of the Forum office in Chicago, and interviewed Forum leaders. Voice of America and Radio Free Europe as well as local Polish-language radio programs (*Studio D, Na serio,* and *Rozmawiać*) also interviewed Forum leaders. While they were in Poland in January 1990, Forum leaders gave several interviews to the Polish radio, television, and press.

zation promoting and facilitating investments in Poland's private sector. Organizations like Forum complemented the U.S. administration's strategy (an $800 million aid package for Eastern Europe to be used primarily to build up the private market sector) and capitalized on the demand for economic information about Poland.

The main established organization was the Polish American Congress (PAC), founded in 1944. The PAC began to support the opposition in 1976 after the formation of KOR, the first public opposition organization in Poland. Besides the Roman Catholic Church, it was the first concrete non-regime-sponsored organization that Polonia could officially recognize. The national PAC leaders publicly praised KOR leaders and the striking workers, pressured the United States to continue support for Radio Free Europe, and provided moral support for what they referred to as "the human rights movement" in Poland. In 1976, the Illinois division of the PAC created the Assistance Committee for the Support of Human Rights in Poland (*Komitet Pomocy Obrońcom Praw Ludzkich i Obywatelskich w Polsce*), which collected money for striking workers and their families. As the opposition movement in Poland gained momentum in 1980, the PAC became an active and vocal supporter of the union, a position very much in line with the rest of American society. The Solidarity movement enjoyed support from diverse sectors—labor supported it because it was a union, and both Republicans and Democrats supported it because it was an opposition movement in a communist state. The PAC organized demonstrations to support Solidarity and helped orchestrate a massive humanitarian aid program that sent millions of dollars worth of food, clothing, and medicine to Poland.

All the groups agreed that specific directions on how to help Poland should come from the opposition or Church in Poland (the two legitimate organizations). Most felt that Polonia should not be telling Poland what to do.[8] The organizations were in general agreement on this principle that direction should come from Poland and that Polonians, even immigrants, had no right to criticize the opposition from the comfort of their warm Chicago bungalows. One Polish American stated: "We can't make hard choices for them, it's as stupid as trying to run the Vietnam war from

8. One exception to this surrounded the issue of lifting the economic sanctions the United States had placed on Poland after martial law. Pomost leaders wanted the sanctions to remain in place even after Solidarity leaders in Poland gave their blessing to lift them. See Chapter 5 for a discuss of foreign policy regarding sanctions.

Washington, D.C. . . . to run the Polish freedom movement from Chicago. We can only support them, and that's all." New immigrants voiced
similar sentiments. One said: "Whatever happens, will happen in Poland.
We can help. We *can* make a difference. But they will do the fight, in
whatever way they will go, whichever route they will take, if evolution or
revolution. It would be them who would decide and bring the change." And
another said, "I think that only people in Poland have right to decide what
have to be done in Poland. It's impossible to say from this side of ocean
what people in Poland have to do. It's impossible. It's very very easy to say
they have to do this, they have to do this. Why they do this, why they do this,
why they don't try this? If you are so wise, go to Poland." The PAC agreed
that Polonia should follow the lead of Poland. For example, after the round
table agreements in 1989 the PAC published a declaration in the *Dziennik
Związkowy* regarding its position toward the upcoming elections: "Decisions
related to the details of the agreement can only be made by authentic
leaders of the Polish society who take responsibility for them. These
decisions should not be influenced by outside factors, such as American
Polonia or emigrants, who do not have to deal with the consequences of
their decisions" (PAC 1989a, 1).

This was also the opinion of the opposition in Poland. Opposition leader
Adam Michnik pointed out that the London Government-in-Exile was
ridiculed for trying to govern from the comfortable position abroad during
World War II. He said that the "dominant view was that in order to speak
about the most important Polish issues one had to be here" (1985, 17).
Polish immigrants and Polish Americans agreed. For this reason they
followed the lead of the opposition movement rather than trying to direct
it. One implication of this policy was that Polonia needed open and
ongoing communication with the opposition.

The Exchange of Resources

Pomost, Freedom, and Brotherhood engaged in some cooperative activities
with the PAC, especially with the leaders from the Illinois Division with
whom they co-organized demonstrations and fund-raising events. They
cooperated because they had different resources to exchange. The different resources of each group illustrates differences in their identities. The
immigrants had ties to the new immigrant community as well as the

opposition in Poland; the ethnics had ties to American public officials, the American media, and the Polish American community.

The new immigrant and established ethnic organizations shared legitimacy and activists. An organization's "good name" is built on its reputation (which implies that it must have been around for a while) and provides legitimacy. Using the name of an established organization is particularly useful for new organizations that have not yet established a reputation. For example, the PAC provided legitimacy and publicity to Pomost. One of the Pomost founders told me that, in the beginning, the PAC helped Pomost get "contacts" and "spread it around that we are the good guys." Jan Nowak, a prominent World War II émigré aligned at that time with the PAC, wrote a supporting article for Pomost that appeared in one of its early quarterlies.

> [Pomost] can help form an association of people who think similarly, who think in Polish and still feel a fresh bond with the homeland. . . . This kind of association, organization or community, must be independent of the structures of the old emigration, which does not necessarily constitute competition or war between the two. That would be a senseless waste of time and energy. (Nowak 1980, 3)

The PAC and established Polonian leaders had the authority to condone (or discredit) a new organization. Those organizations that received the blessing of the PAC gained a degree of legitimacy.

In exchange for legitimacy, the new immigrants gave the PAC, as one new immigrant said, "an audience for the leaders and activists at the demonstrations." What the established organization needed was a younger cadre of organizers and activists. The PAC needed members, especially active members (as opposed to members on paper) to participate in collective action. Immigrants were more concerned about the politics of the home country than ethnics. From 1985 to 1988, almost all of the thirty regular members of the PAC Illinois Division's Polish Affairs Committee were immigrants; however, most of them were World War II émigrés. Still, this committee did attract a few new immigrants. Despite the nonjoiner behavior of new immigrants in general, the refugees did work with the PAC when the activity was related to Poland. PAC leaders explicitly expressed their desire to bring in young immigrants from the new Polish cohort to replace the aging World War II émigrés. In a self-critical article, several national directors of the PAC mentioned the importance of involving the Solidarity immigrants in

Polonian activity because "the post-World War II veterans are dying and there comes a time in the relay race of generations to pass on the baton to the next generation" (Lerski et al. 1988, 3). PAC vice-president Lukomski also acknowledged that the PAC needed involvement from the new cohort, which he referred to as "new blood" and "younger energetic people." At each of the thirteen demonstrations I attended in Chicago Polonia from 1986 to 1989, 90 percent or more of the participants were immigrants. The new immigrants had the energy and dedication that the PAC needed to conduct activities on behalf of Poland. As a result, new organizations often traded vigor and activists for the established organization's "good name."

The best example of trading legitimacy for activists was in the organization of demonstrations. Pomost and the PAC co-organized three demonstrations in 1980. An article in the *Pomost Quarterly* described the division of labor and complementary resources for the first big demonstration in Chicago (approximately one hundred thousand people), held in August 1980, to show support for the striking workers in Poland (Kobylanski 1980, 13–14). At a PAC Illinois Division meeting, Pomost members presented a resolution calling for a demonstration, and PAC members supported the resolution. Because the PAC had the established reputation of being the main representative of Polonia, it attracted media attention during this sensational news period. A CBS television crew was at this first PAC meeting, and both ABC and NBC crews were at the second meeting two days later. The *Pomost* article stated that for the demonstration, the "role of organizer was filled by Pomost." Pomost members disseminated information about the demonstration to the Polish media, printed flyers and painted banners, sewed a replica of a Soviet flag (to be burned), and set up the sound system. The Polish American PAC leaders took on the following tasks: disseminating information about the demonstration to the English-language media; obtaining the parade permit; inviting the mayor, governor, and representatives from Washington; and preparing the official program. In general, the Pomost members internally organized the event by doing the technical work and the public relations work in Polonia. The PAC leaders externally publicized and legitimated the event by securing the presence of U.S. politicians and the English-language media. The cooperation was possible because both organizations had things—though different things—to contribute. The two organizations had different audiences, different networks, and different skills.

In the mid-1980s, other new immigrant organizations also helped the

PAC raise money. Freedom gave continuous financial support to the PAC Committee to Support Democratic Opposition, and both Brotherhood and Freedom helped raise funds for special PAC drives. One Brotherhood leader, Jaroslaw Cholodecki, used his radio program to help raise money for the Striking Worker's Fund (PAC activity), the Home Army Foundation (a World War II veteran organization), and the PAC Charitable Foundation by inviting guests on his show to promote the funding drives, by having radio-thons to collect money, and by simply urging his listeners (mostly new immigrants) to donate. When immigrants and ethnics agreed on strategy, the differences in audiences worked to their benefit by simply increasing the potential resource pool.

In return for activists, organizers, and material resources, the PAC provided the new organizations with legitimacy and connections. A new organization can gain legitimacy in the eyes of the community by working with an already legitimate organization, which the PAC was. Freedom members said that working with the PAC helped them get permission to solicit funds outside of churches and at festivals. Brotherhood and Freedom also took advantage of annual events organized by the established community (such as parades and festivals) as opportunities to solicit funds and to inform the community about the opposition movement in Poland. For example, new organizations often had booths at the annual Festival Polonaise sponsored by the PAC Illinois Division. One notable case was the Independent Culture in Poland exhibit at the 1989 Festival Polonaise. Freedom and Brotherhood also had smaller booths at festivals during 1986–89 where they collected money and passed out information. The new immigrants also marched in Chicago's annual May 3d Constitution Day parade, sponsored by the Polish National Alliance ethnic fraternal. They used these preestablished venues (festivals and parades) as forums to advance their cause (to raise money, recruit new activists, and disseminate information). Inserting themselves into established Polonian routines, the new immigrants' activities were more accepted. They were able to capitalize on the legitimacy that is conferred on tradition.

In addition, the PAC had connections to the media and local American politicians that the new organizations did not have. As with Pomost, the PAC provided the name recognition that brought television crews and local politicians to demonstrations. Talking about how Freedom organized a demonstration, one Freedom member said they worked with the PAC because the president of the Illinois division, Roman Pucinski, had access.

"Pucinski is a big plus. First he can rally for us. When Morawiecki [the leader of Fighting Solidarity] was here, he set up a meeting with Mayor Sawyer. He set up the meeting with some others. He's got a lot of access. . . . Freedom for Poland could never do much on their own except collect money."

The new organizations needed the PAC name to attract attention to their events. The established ethnic leaders were known to American journalists and these leaders knew how to contact important American leaders. In return, the new immigrants gave the PAC activists. The PAC would not have been able to organize the demonstrations or raise funds as successfully without the contributions of the new immigrants. Ethnics were simply less interested in the homeland than were immigrants.

One difference among Pomost, Freedom, and Brotherhood was that the latter two were composed of political refugees, who also supplied legitimacy to the PAC. Brotherhood and Freedom members had been members of Solidarity, while the founders of Pomost were immigrants who arrived in America in the 1960s and 1970s before Solidarity had been formed. Some of Pomost's members in the later years (that is, after 1982) had been involved in Solidarity, but for the most part Pomost members were not political refugees. The prestige connected to the status of refugee provided more resources than the status of immigrant. Politicians in the United States defined these refugees as freedom fighters, and were eager to use them to bolster their own image as being strongly against communism. For example, in 1984, the Democratic Party invited Leszek Waliszewski, a Solidarity refugee, to their platform committee hearings in New York. One Brotherhood leader said: "We are legitimate people from Poland who are anticommunistic. . . . Leaders from American agencies and the government are asking leaders of Polish American organizations, 'What is your position and how do you manage relations with the new immigrants?'" So while the general trade was legitimacy from the PAC for activists from the new immigration, the refugees could also supply some legitimacy to the PAC.

New immigrants and established ethnics also cooperated to support the first partially free election in Poland in June 1989. Cholodecki, from Brotherhood, then acting through a new organization called Solidarity Election Committee, used his radio program to raise funds for the campaign in Poland. He then linked up with the PAC Illinois Division. Pucinski said that Cholodecki "called me and said, 'Look, can we use the Polish

American Congress as a transmission valve to give help to Poland?'"
Cholodecki's radio-thon fed both the national PAC and the Illinois Division
fundraising campaigns. The fund-raising efforts of the new immigrants
gained a stamp of legitimacy by using the PAC as a "transmission valve." In
addition, other, younger Polish Americans worked together with these new
immigrants. The Polish Americans who founded Fair Elections in Poland,
Inc., gave Brotherhood $3,000 to buy three fax machines to ship to Poland
for the purpose of domestic and international communications. The new
immigrants carried the equipment to Poland themselves and distributed it.
The new immigrants knew their way around the political terrain in rapidly
changing Warsaw; they understood political alliances and could identify old
communist wolves in sheep's clothing. This help was illustrated in a letter
sent by Polish American Tom Gobby, president of Fair Elections to Nancy
Soderberg, the foreign policy advisor to Senator Edward Kennedy, which
stated, "We have also been working with the 'Brotherhood of Dispersed
Solidarity Members' headquartered in Chicago . . . [which] has been
most helpful in providing us with current and accurate information as to
conditions and developments in Poland." In return, the Polish Americans
contacted American politicians and wrote press releases and funding
letters. The Polish Americans and new immigrants worked together because they had different but complementary skills and networks.

Networks into Poland

The structure of the organizations and the networks of their members led
to different types of support for the opposition in Poland. The new
immigrants' organizations were smaller and more informal and the immigrants had personal ties to people in Poland. The PAC was more formal and
bureaucratic and it had impersonal ties to institutions in Poland. The
support each organization gave was influenced by their different experiences (which created networks) and organizational structures (which created constraints). The PAC provided mostly humanitarian aid, which was
sent through institutional channels (such as the Roman Catholic Church),
and they mostly (but not always) supported the national mainstream
Solidarity opposition. The new immigrants provided financial aid and
technical assistance to local and regional chapters of Solidarity, as well as
lesser known and more radical opposition groups in Poland. They had

more knowledge about the opposition movement in Poland than did the Polish Americans, and the immigrants who had been Solidarity activists had personal connections to the opposition groups in Poland. The established organization, composed mostly of native-born Polish Americans, did not have these connections.

The PAC had formal relations with Poland and worked only with what they considered legitimate institutions. They never recognized the communist regime in Warsaw, and so after World War II, the key legitimate institution in Poland was, for the PAC, the Roman Catholic Church. The national PAC did not financially support the opposition until it was formally organized in the Solidarity Trade Union.[9] This support for the opposition came after the Church conferred legitimacy on the opposition. The PAC was "committed to looking to the Polish church for leadership. The Church, whose support for the workers' movement had legitimized Solidarity in the first place, was seen to be of crucial significance. . . . The PAC and Polonia looked to its leaders for direction in fashioning an orientation toward Solidarity." From August 1980 onward the PAC, along with most of the Western world supported the Solidarity movement, primarily the mainstream wing of the opposition movement. "The stance of the PAC . . . involved supporting the moderate elements within the Solidarity movement who appeared to be interested in building a viable trade union movement in the country" (Pienkos 1984, 290).

Legal limitations made it difficult to get funds to Solidarity after it was outlawed in 1982. It was difficult to have institutional ties to an underground organization. To get money to underground Solidarity (the TKK) meant that the PAC had to engage in illegal activity (smuggling in money), or it had to find another legal organization that would itself smuggle the money into Poland. The PAC chose the second alternative. Between 1976 and 1989, the national PAC newsletters did not report any material support for the Polish opposition. This does not mean there was none, but it

9. In his discussion of the Polish American Congress, PAC historian Donald Pienko spends several pages covering the turbulent periods in Poland (1968, 1970, 1976) without mentioning any financial support that the PAC gave to the oppositionists during this time (1991, 167–76). In addition, the PAC newsletters did not report any support for the opposition until 1976, when it saluted the fifty-nine Poles who signed the letter condemning the constitutional changes proposed by the government. The PAC did take action on this, drafting a working paper for John Armitage, undersecretary for European affairs, claiming the proposed constitutional changes were in violation of the Helsinki Declarations on the Universal Rights of Man. In 1976, the PAC newsletters also applauded the formation of KOR, but there was no mention of financial support.

suggests that, if the PAC did send money to the underground, it was not publicized. In Donald Pienkos's book on Polish American efforts for Poland wherein he discusses in detail the activities of the PAC, the only mention of financial support for the opposition is placed in a footnote, and his source of information is an interview with one person (1991, 551–52). While this detailed history of PAC activity for Poland barely mentions any financial support for the opposition, other evidence suggests they did provide some funds. In 1976, the Illinois Division of the PAC formed the Assistance Committee for the Support of Human Rights in Poland as a response to the strikes at Radom and Ursus and the formation of KOR. This committee was dismantled in the early 1980s, but reappeared December 19, 1985, as a national PAC committee, with the title National Assistance Committee for Democratic Opposition in Poland. The chairman and committee members were all from the World War II cohort except one, and this exception was Andrzej Dudek, a Solidarity refugee and president of Freedom (*Dziennik Związkowy*, December 2–3, 1988, 9). This committee did send funds to Poland during the 1980s when Solidarity was an illegal organization; however, as I have stated above, this was never publicly mentioned in the PAC newsletters or in the newspapers.[10] To have done this openly would have been to admit to illegal activity. In response to the question "How does the money get into Poland, because Solidarity is no longer recognized as a legal union?" national PAC vice-president Kazimierz Lukomski said, "Well, that I truly don't know, and I don't want to know."

Pienkos (1991) and PAC officials noted that the PAC sent money to the underground via two other organizations. First the PAC channeled money

10. In a footnote, Pienkos reports from an interview with Bonewenture Migala (a World War II émigré) that the National Assistance Committee for Democratic Opposition in Poland gave more that $900,000 between 1976 and 1988 to support the families of striking workers and political prisoners and the underground press (1991, 551–52). This number seems high in comparison to other references to money sent to Poland. Documents distributed at the PAC National Directors' meeting in the fall of 1988 stated that the National Assistance Committee for Democratic Opposition in Poland opened an account in 1985 with over $20,000 (the national PAC gave the committee $10,107, the PAC Illinois Division donated $1000, and $9,539 more came from the elimination of the Moczulski Fund, which was collected for the medical treatment of Leszek Moczulski); and this committee collected another $51,000 between 1985 and 1988, and almost half of that came from the Illinois Division of the PAC. I want to repeat that the PAC did most likely send more than the roughly $70,000 noted in public records, but it is not public information. Even Pienkos (who wrote the book "on the invitation" of the PAC with its blessings and help [1991, 13]) received his information about money sent to the underground opposition from a personal interview.

into Poland through the National Endowment for Democracy, a nonprofit private organization that supported opposition movements in communist countries and that was funded mostly with U.S. federal funds.[11] The United States relied on Polish immigrant organizations in America and Europe to help smuggle the funds into Poland (Pear 1988, 1 and 6). Second, the PAC gave money to *Kultura*, a Paris-based literary-political magazine founded by Polish émigrés after World War II. The PAC could send money to *Kultura* through legal channels; *Kultura* then had its own covert channels for getting the money to the opposition in Poland. The PAC used these two legal organizations to get funds to the outlawed underground opposition.

The PAC's main partner in Poland was the Roman Catholic Church. As a result of this institutional linkage, the overwhelming volume of PAC support to Poland during the 1980s was in a form appropriate for distribution by the Church, namely, humanitarian aid. A PAC pamphlet titled "Relief for Poland, General Information on Background and Current Crisis" stated that, between 1981 and 1988, the PAC collected over $5 million in money donations that enabled them to send over $122 million worth of relief goods to Poland. PAC's humanitarian aid was distributed by the Polish Roman Catholic episcopate in Poland. The PAC sent clothing, food, and medical supplies to the Polish episcopate, who then distributed the goods. The aid was sent through legal shipping agencies and international aid organizations such as Project Hope and CARE. Because the goods were sent through legal shipping channels, the containers could have been checked by state officials before they reached the episcopate. This formal channel, then, did not lend itself to smuggling in illegal goods. For example, the PAC could not have sent such things as typewriters or Xerox machines (the types of equipment the underground publishing houses needed) because in communist Poland it was illegal to have unregistered printing equipment like this, and it was illegal to unofficially send it. The PAC did not send money to the Roman Catholic Church, and the Church did not give direct financial aid to the opposition. Supporting Poland through humanitarian aid distributed by the Church, then, was not necessarily support for the opposition, although it certainly was support for the people of Poland. The strategy of sending humanitarian aid through the

11. Between 1985 and 1988, the United States gave over $5 million in cash assistance to opposition groups in Poland to support underground publications (Pear 1988, 1). The National Endowment for Democracy gave almost $100,000 to the Conference of Solidarity Support Organizations in 1988–89.

Church was reasonable for the PAC because Polish Americans were familiar with donating money to church-sponsored charitable organizations, and it ideologically resonated with Americans because it implied that Poles suffered materially under the communist regime.

The actions of the PAC were constrained by its structure. Rules governing the behavior of the organization in part determine an organization's potential alliances and activities. A less formal organization has more freedom of movement than does a formal organization. The PAC had a formal structure—the bylaws specified who could be members, how members were represented, how policy was decided, how officers were elected, and how the meetings were conducted. Issues and policies were discussed in committees, and their proposals were voted on by delegates at a national convention. The PAC Charitable Foundation (PACCF) could not use any of the funds it collected for humanitarian aid to support the opposition movement directly. According to the articles of incorporation, the PACCF was "to operate exclusively for religious, charitable, scientific, cultural, and educational purposes" (Article 5.A) with no mention made of support for political groups or unions. When people donated money to help needy children, the PACCF could not send the money to underground publishing houses. In another example, Kazimierz Lukomski, the vice-president of the national PAC said that it was also impossible to send money to nonmainstream branches of the opposition from the proceeds of a fund-raising drive that collected money for Walesa and the striking workers. He said, "It is illegal to advertise that the money is going to one place and then we send it to another."

In contrast to the PAC, the new immigrant organizations had informal structures. Pomost's policy was decided by five people who appointed themselves executive directors when the organization was incorporated as Pomost Socio-Political Movement in 1982. Its articles of incorporation broadly and vaguely defined its goals as fighting communism and supporting Poland's right to self-determination. Many of Pomost's donors gave only general instructions about how their donations should be spent ("to support the opposition in Poland"), so Pomost leaders could decide themselves where to channel the resources. Moreover, at the height of its activism in 1982–84, Pomost had no voting membership or bylaws, and its leaders were somewhat lax in their accounting (a practice that eventually got them into legal trouble). Brotherhood's activities were organized informally by three members in Chicago. Brotherhood collected dues only from its members, so they did not have to answer to a public when deciding how to spend their dues. Brotherhood was not incorporated and operated as if there were no legal restrictions on its activity. They had an annual or semi-annual letter sent to other members that simply informed them of how much money was collected and to whom they sent the money in Poland. Freedom had the most formal structure of the three new organizations. By the late 1980s, Freedom members were meeting in a public setting (a hall owned by a World War II veteran's group), they held elections for officers, and they were incorporated in 1985 as a nonprofit charitable and educational organization in Illinois. Still, when Freedom collected money, it did so for the opposition in general, which gave its leaders the freedom to decide who in Poland it wanted to support. These new informal organizations did not have the same constraints placed on their activities as did the formal PAC.

While the humanitarian aid of the PAC supported the generic, and often faceless, "people" of Poland, the new immigrant organizations gave funds directly to the opposition, and even more specifically to particular people and opposition circles. The immigrants' networks into Poland gave them access to information about what the opposition needed, and operated as conduits through which funds and supplies could get into Poland. Pomost gave material support to the whole spectrum of oppositional activities in Poland. In the late 1970s Pomost supported KOR, underground publishing houses, and the striking workers; in the early 1980s it supported Solidarity and other lesser-known oppositional groups. Pomost sent funds and technical aid to twenty different opposition presses (*Robotnik, Bratniak, Głos, Opinie, Nowa,* and *Spotkania* being the largest recipients), as well as twelve different organizations (including Solidarity, KOR, Confederation for an Independent Poland [*Konferacja Polski Niepodległej*], Fighting Solidarity, and the Movement for the Defense of Human and Civil Rights [*Ruch Obrony Praw Człowieka i Obywatela*]). Though the amount of money sent was not large (roughly $22,000 divided, though not equally, among thirty-two groups, the exchange rate was favorable at that time (the average monthly salary was about U.S.$20). Pomost did not send humanitarian aid to Poland, but funded the underground directly. Pomost also used *Kultura* to get their funds into Poland but, unlike the PAC, they openly reported this in their quarterly.

During 1984–88, much of the opposition activity involved publishing uncensored books, journals, newspapers, and bulletins. One activist I interviewed in Poland in the summer of 1987 said, "These publishing houses are the core of the underground movement in Poland. This is all that is left of the active opposition. The trade union doesn't exist." The imposition of martial law in December 1981 initially created a boom in the underground publishing houses, though many of the largest houses were established in the late 1970s (such as *Spotkania,* in 1977; *Nowa,* 1977; *Głos,* 1979). The main publishing houses reached their peaks in terms of publications and sales in 1984–85 and began to decline in sales by 1987.[12]

Assistance for the underground presses required links to the people involved in the opposition movement. The new immigrants, especially the Solidarity refugees, had these links, while Polish Americans did not. During emigration, Brotherhood and Freedom maintained links to the opposition through mail and electronic hook-ups. Brotherhood and Freedom received underground publications that had been either personally carried to the United States or taken out of Poland and mailed from some other European country. One Freedom leader showed me a piece of literature that had a publication date only ten days prior to our interview. In every interview with new immigrants who were post-1980 refugees, I was given pieces of this underground literature. No Polish Americans, World War II émigrés, or new immigrants who came before 1980 showed me any underground literature or talked about receiving any. In addition, Brotherhood leader Jaroslaw Cholodecki had his own informants in several cities in Poland with whom he talked on an almost daily basis to get information for his radio program. Moreover, when the opposition leaders traveled to America they often stayed with Brotherhood and Freedom members because they had known each other in Poland.

Resources from abroad, sent by organizations like Brotherhood and Freedom, helped the underground publishing centers to survive. Because printing supplies could not be obtained easily or cheaply in Poland, the presses had to rely on the expensive black market (which required Western

12. In 1985 there were roughly seven hundred publishing "houses" (and they literally were houses or apartments), but the number had dropped to four hundred by 1987 (Newman 1987). In 1986, in the Krakow and Malopolska regions, the underground presses published an average of forty-seven newspapers, which dropped to thirty-seven newspapers by 1987 (Informational Service of Regional Committee of Solidarity in Malopolska, special issue, Krakow, February 5, 1987). While the *Tygodnik Mazowsze* sold one hundred thousand copies of its newspaper in 1983, it sold only forty thousand copies in 1987 (Newman 1987). One activist in a publishing house in Wroclaw said that in 1982 they could sell five thousand copies of a journal, while in 1987 they could sell one thousand at most. Sales of opposition literature declined because, in the weakened economy people had less money to spend, the journals became more expensive, activism became more risky, and covert networks were broken (Erdmans 1992b, 364 n. 13).

currency) or on materials smuggled into Poland. Immigrants received specific and current information about what the opposition needed. One unsigned letter from an activist in Poland in Brotherhood's files reported: "The only duplicating machine one can buy in Polish stores is a typewriter and carbon paper. Correction fluid, sieves, dyes, offsetting and photography materials, IBM typewriters (in Polish and English) are all imported from the West."[13] In 1986, the Polish government changed its policy toward violators of the censorship code. Instead of imprisonment, violators were fined or had their cars or apartments confiscated.[14] Brotherhood responded to this new policy by setting up an "insurance fund" to provide the activists in Poland with some financial support to continue their activity. There were other letters in the Brotherhood file and some personal letters from activists in Poland to Brotherhood members that requested specific funds (for a named publishing house, a family whose husband has been in jail for several years, and someone who needed medical attention) or told Brotherhood (and the rest of Polonia) that they were not doing the right things (for example, that they should be lobbying Washington and organizing more demonstrations). When leaders visited from Poland, they often spoke at private meetings and public forums about what Poland needed and who needed it. Information came from the underground opposition to Chicago Polonia via these immigrant networks. As things changed in Poland, the needs changed, for example, from correction fluid to an insurance fund.

The new organizations supported the opposition at local and regional levels rather than at the national level. A January 1985 newsletter to Brotherhood members stated that because most foreign aid going to Poland was going to help the national and executive committees of Solidarity, Brotherhood would support the regional and local committees. In one published interview Cholodecki stated, "We sent $7,000 to $8,000, mainly to Krakow, Wroclaw and Lublin, because we were under the impression that a lot is happening there, and less help is getting there from official

13. Solidarity Endowment, an organization in the United States, also sent twenty offset printing presses to the underground publishing houses as well as transmitters and other broadcasting equipment to the illegal Radio Solidarity (Pear 1988, 6).

14. In 1986 the Polish government introduced Article 52a, a misdemeanor code that carried possible penalties of two to three months imprisonment and confiscation of the "instruments of crime" such as cars carrying independent literature or apartments that had printing presses or housed uncensored literature, as well as fines from U.S.$300–$5,000 (Erdmans 1992b, 365 n. 14).

European Solidarity channels. Obviously personal acquaintances play a role in this as well" (Krajewski 1989, 41). Brotherhood supported local and regional activists in the hometowns of its members—Krakow, Wroclaw, Opole, Lublin, and Gdansk—choosing recipients based on personal ties. The Brotherhood January 1985 newsletter stated money would be sent to Poland if someone "who is a friend of a member of Brotherhood, informs us that people in his area need money or equipment." For example, *Wroclaw Journal* was supported for two years because one of the Brotherhood leaders knew the activists publishing it. And once when they learned that someone just released from jail needed help, an informal vote among three of the leaders was taken and they decided to send him money. When Brotherhood sent money to Poland they did not use formal institutions, but instead used personal couriers.

In 1985–86, Freedom gave 80 percent of its money to Walesa and Solidarity; in 1987 it began supporting the Confederation for an Independent Poland and Fighting Solidarity. By 1988, more than 60 percent of Freedom's money went to these two organizations. Leaders of Freedom gave two reasons for the shift. First, the splintering of Solidarity in Poland in the late 1980s had a ripple effect in Polonia. By 1988, Confederation for an Independent Poland and Fighting Solidarity were accusing Walesa of bargaining with the communists. These groups wanted a more hard-line, no-compromise approach with the communists—they wanted them out of power. A Freedom leader told me that because Freedom's statutes specified that the organization's primary purpose was to fight against communists, they decided to support those organizations that they believed most upheld that goal—Confederation for an Independent Poland and Fighting Solidarity. The second reason that funds were shifted was that Walesa and Solidarity received money from other sources around the world. Freedom chose to support those organizations that did not have as many outside benefactors. As one leader said, "Fighting Solidarity is one of those groups that doesn't get any money from the State Department. That's why our group decided to support them. . . . We like Morawiecki [the leader of Fighting Solidarity] but apparently the State Department doesn't like him. They consider him too extreme." Though Freedom leaders acknowledged Walesa as the "true leader" of the opposition and Solidarity as its main union, they said that what Poland needed most in 1988 was freedom. According to them, Kornel Morawiecki's Fighting Solidarity had the best program for this. In fact, in 1988–89, Freedom saw their main goal as supporting Fighting Solidarity. Freedom had a special contract with Morawiecki to send him money; in return Fighting Solidarity would send them information about Poland.

To summarize, PAC's formal structure forced its leaders to be more accountable for how its resources were distributed, and they chose to support Poland by using other legitimate formal institutions like the Polish episcopate; in contrast, the informal structure of the new immigrant organizations provided their leaders with more latitude to support the informal, and at times illegal, opposition movement. The PAC supported mostly mainstream opposition groups on a national level and sent aid through institutional channels. The new immigrants had links to local and regional opposition activists as well as to nonmainstream groups, and channeled aid through personal networks. Brotherhood and Freedom's main strategic goal was to get funds to the underground opposition in Poland. They had their own connections to these opposition groups, and therefore did not need the established organization to implement their strategies. In fact, it was the established organization that needed the immigrants.

World War II émigrés and new immigrants working on the PAC National Assistance Committee for Democratic Opposition were responsible for establishing contacts with the opposition in Poland and finding out who needed financial support. Polish Americans usually did not have this knowledge or the necessary contacts; it was the immigrants within the PAC and working with the PAC who helped the PAC get these funds to the opposition. One organization that helped the PAC establish contacts with the opposition was the Studium North American Center for the Study of Polish Affairs (Studium) in Ann Arbor. Created in 1976 to educate and inform the American and Canadian populations about Polish affairs and to assist Polonian organizations in their efforts to help Poland, it was com posed mainly of World War II émigrés and young educated Polish Americans. Studium was a member of the PAC, and its members worked with the national Polish Affairs Committee directing policy toward Poland (Best 1982). Contacts that other World War II émigrés had with some members of the opposition were also useful to the PAC. In addition, the new immigrants' networks gave the PAC connections to and information about nonmainstream opposition organizations in Poland. In the late 1980s, the PAC began supporting several nonmainstream groups such as Fighting Solidarity, Confederation for an Independent Poland, and Rural Solidarity. At the time, Freedom members were working within and with members of the Polish Affairs Committee, and they strongly encouraged the PAC to support these groups. The new immigrants also influenced PAC support for these lesser known opposition groups by disseminating information about them (in their magazines and on their radio programs), and organizing American fundraising tours for their leaders and representatives (such as Kornel Morawiecki, Leszek Moczulski, Andzej Gwiazda).

While the PAC eventually gave some assistance to these other groups, for the most part it supported the mainstream opposition and supported it at the national level. And the new immigrants, while acknowledging the legitimacy of Walesa's Solidarity, gave more financial and technical support to the lesser-known opposition organizations, and at the regional and local levels. Having different operational goals (in this case, supporting different groups in Poland and supplying different types of aid) did not in itself lead to interorganizational conflict. If the goals are complementary, organizational differences can, in fact, strengthen a movement (Freeman 1973; McCarthy and Zald 1977; Morris 1984). Freedom's goal was to support a wide spectrum of activities in Poland. It did not intend to split the movement, but rather to make it richer and give it depth so that eventually there would be a multiplicity of bases from which to fight the ruling regime. The PAC at this time did not disagree with this view. Brotherhood members also thought it beneficial to have a lot of organizations pulling in the same direction but having slightly varied goals. Justifying why there was a need for Brotherhood to send money and materials to Poland when there were other organizations already doing this, its founders wrote: "It appears to us that the more channels the better, because it makes possible greater versatility of help" (Brotherhood newsletter, January 1995). One Brotherhood member said, "I think that there could be many organizations . . . that make some action for Poland—one can support the Polish people in Poland with money, another organization like the Charity Foundation can support people with medicine."

Brotherhood and Freedom supported nonmainstream or local and regional groups, not because they had a different ideology for liberating Poland than did the PAC, but because they had ties to these groups. The Brotherhood leaders supported those opposition circles in their home-towns in Poland. Freedom supported Kornel Morawiecki's Fighting Solidarity after he came to the United States and made a personal pact with its leaders. The new immigrant and established ethnic organizations had different connections to Poland because they had different group biographies. The history of the cohort in part determined what links to Poland were possible, and it was the linkages that influenced who received support in Poland. The Polish Americans, many of whom had never been in Poland, had only formal ties to organizations. The new immigrants, having recently come from Poland and having been intimately involved in the opposition, had personal ties to the activists.

Networks and Recruitment Strategies in Polonia

Competition is often a result of niche overlap and a limited supply of resources. The resource environments of the new and established organizations in Chicago Polonia did not overlap completely. New immigrants attracted members from the population of new immigrants, and the PAC and the ethnic fraternals drew in resources from the Polish American ethnic environment. Moreover, the resource environment was not tapped out. Activists estimated that at most 10 percent of Chicago Polonians were active contributors to the Polish cause. New immigrant organizations brought in some of the "latent activists," that is, previously inactive members of Polonia. Polonians were not switching allegiances. Instead, those who had previously never joined any organization were now joining organizations such as Pomost, Brotherhood, Freedom, and Forum. As a result, the organizations were not competing with each other for members. Formal and informal networks are useful in recruiting new movement participants (Snow et al. 1980; Klandermans and Oegema 1987a; Fernandez and McAdam 1989); and a multiplicity of networks increases the overall size of the potential mobilization or "reservoir the movement can draw from" (Klandermans and Oegema 1987b, 519). New immigrants could draw in activists through one set of networks and ethnics through another. This simply increased total activism for Poland.

The established ethnics and the new immigrants had different strategies for recruiting members. Recruitment does not always move someone from apathy to activism in one step. People are at different levels of activism and potential activism. The levels of activism range from (1) the inner core of leaders and activists, (2) members of organizations, (3) the informed media audience, and (4) the outer range of nonmembers and nonaudience. Activists are people who donate a significant amount of time and energy to the cause. Being a member of an organization does not automatically make one an activist. Organizational members may donate money or sign petitions but some are not much active beyond paying their dues. The media audience can contain nonactivists as well as activists who do not belong to any organization. Yet, to participate in some action—for example, a demonstration—requires at minimum that the person knows about the event. Those who are not connected to the community via organizations or media then must have at least informal social networks to other activists. Activation can be defined as movement across any of these levels: getting people to read ethnic newspapers, getting readers to become members of organizations, or getting members to become active in the movement. The established ethnics and the new immigrants used recruitment strategies that targeted people at different levels. Ethnics tended to recycle activists (targeting the upper levels); new immigrants tried to recruit latent activists (targeting people at the third and fourth levels). The recruitment strategies used by Polish Americans and new immigrants in the Polish-American Economic Forum effectively illustrates these differences.

Recycling Activists and Recruiting Latent Activists

The Polish Americans in Forum used the membership lists of other Polish American ethnic organizations to recruit people from the second level, while the new immigrants relied mostly on media links to bring in new members. Forum sent out over four thousand letters for the initial membership drive. The names and addresses were culled from the membership lists of numerous Polonian organizations. Because of past or present affiliations, Polish Americans in Forum had access to three thousand names (some duplicates) from the membership lists of eight established organizations: the Chicago Society, the Polish American Commercial Club, the Advocates Society, the Polish Arts Club, the Polish Welfare Association, the Polish Teachers Association, Inc., the Polish Institute of Arts and Sciences, and the state divisions of the PAC.

    The new immigrants also used membership lists, but because they were less established members of the community they had fewer contacts and less access to established ethnic organizations. Still, the new immigrants did get the membership lists from the Polish American Engineering Association and the Polish Medical Alliance. These organizations, although they had been established approximately forty years before, had significant numbers of new immigrants among their members. (New immigrants joined them because these organizations were composed largely of World War II émigrés not Polish Americans ethnics, and because these organizations could potentially help them with their careers.) Forum leaders had also spoken to these groups on several occasions. In addition, the new immigrants used a list of mostly World War II émigrés and new immigrants that had been prepared in 1989 for the visit of Cardinal Glemp from Poland (a visit later canceled). New immigrants also recruited members from the core of other new organizations, such as Brotherhood and the Solidarity Election Committee, an organization active during the June 1989 elections. New immigrants also used their links to Solidarity organizations throughout the United States to bring in new members. Altogether, the new immigrants contributed a quarter of the names to the membership mail drive, mostly names of other immigrants.

The established ethnics had access to many more names than the new immigrants, and they were also the ones who suggested using these preexisting address lists. Relying on these preexisting networks, Forum recruited established organizational members; that is, organizational membership was an implicit criterion for being invited to be a member of Forum. This strategy of recycling organizational members did not tap the estimated 90 percent of the population who were not members of organizations. Moreover, new immigrants had not generally joined these established organizations. In a survey of roughly a quarter of the Forum members, less than 20 percent of them were also members of other organizations in the United States. This strategy of recruiting from other organizations recycled members but did not bring in new members from the universe of potential Polonia activists (although it had the potential to activate inactive members by enticing them with new activities and a new orientation).

In contrast to the recycling strategy, the new immigrants' main strategy for recruiting members relied on the media. This strategy recruited Polonians from outside the levels of organizational affiliation. Jaroslaw Cholodecki, a founding leader of Forum, had been a radio personality in Polonia since 1987. At the time that Forum was being created, Cholodecki's Polish-language radio program in Chicago was broadcast three hours every day. Cholodecki's program was considered by many new immigrants to be one of the best programs during that time period; he had an estimated listening audience of almost thirty thousand, and he was a gregarious, charismatic radio personality. In addition to Cholodecki's own program, he helped to start and direct two other programs. The format of all three programs was news oriented, with discussion and listener call-in periods. Another leader of Forum, Krzystof Kaszprzyk, was the editor of one of the most popular Polish-language magazines in Chicago, *Kurier,* in which appeared numerous articles about Forum. Through advertisements, discussions, and articles, these new immigrant leaders used media avenues to recruit members.

In addition to these media sources, the new immigrants also recruited from the nonmember, nonaudience level by setting up Forum information booths at festivals and picnics in Chicago Polonia. Granted, many of the people attending these festivals had heard about the events through the Polish-language newspapers, radios, and organizational newsletters, which means they were from the levels of members and audience. However, these picnics were also advertised in the local English-language media and therefore attracted non-Poles and Polish Americans who had no other association with Polonia. Some Polish Americans hitherto unaffiliated with Polonian organizations were recruited at these functions. For example, one third-generation Polish American woman joined Forum after hearing about this organization from a group of new immigrants staffing a booth at Taste of Polonia, an ethnic festival. She had never been involved in a Polish organization, but she had read about the festival in the *Chicago Tribune* and decided to attend after watching a documentary about Poland on television (both sources of information show that she was really at the fourth outsider level in the community).

The ethnics' strategy of using organizational lists to recruit members recycled ethnic joiners, while the immigrants' strategy created new members. The strategies that ethnics and immigrants chose, however, depended on resources available. Established Polonians had more access to ethnic organization membership lists and less access to the new immigrant media. The converse was true for new immigrants.

Multiplicity of Networks and Resources

Ethnics had ties to other ethnics, American officials, and American institutions. Immigrants had ties to other immigrants, especially Solidarity activists, and the new Polish government. These immigrant ties represented premigration and postmigration networks. The Polish opposition represented an established network. For those in emigration who had been a part of this network, this was a premigration tie. If these ties could be reactivated in emigration, then immigrants could draw upon premigration ties to build new organizations in America. This is what the World War II émigrés did when forming their veterans' organizations, and what Brotherhood did when creating its organization of Solidarity members in emigration. Many important Solidarity refugees (that is, those who had held union positions in Poland) knew each other in the United States. The Polonia media made note of important Solidarity members who emigrated here, and refugees in America would often receive word from Poland that another refugee was arriving. Those who emigrated later (1984–87) had also sometimes heard about their predecessors while still in Poland. Underground presses that received some finances from abroad mentioned the activities of their sponsors who were often Solidarity refugees. Several refugees said that they had the names and addresses of Solidarity refugees with them when they arrived in the United States. And, finally, numerous Solidarity organizations in America were in contact with each other. This premigration network gave Solidarity activists links to potential activists.

Jaroslaw Cholodecki used these ties to other Solidarity activists when creating Forum. Several Solidarity activists became directors of Forum and played key organizational roles in their respective Polonian communities across America. For example, Walter Jermakowicz, a professor, was able to procure money and labor from a research center at his university. He conducted a questionnaire about the investment interests of Forum members and potential members at the expense of the research center. He also initiated a program of investment seminars, funded by his university but endorsed by Forum, with profits and recognition going to Forum. Once reestablished, premigration networks provided useful resources.[15]

The second population to which the new immigrant Cholodecki had

15. Some activists in Poland never became active in emigration because they settled in small towns in America and never connected with other immigrants or ethnics. In order to use premigration links, the ties must be reactivated, even if the linkage is serendipitous, as in the following example.

At the 1989 conference of the American Association for the Advancement of Slavic Studies, there was a panel discussion about the Polish economic situation. As a sociologist interested in Eastern Europe, I had connections to this academic community. I told Cholodecki about this convention and read him the names of the panelists. At the mention of one name, Walter Jermakowicz, he immediately decided to attend the panel discussion. Cholodecki said he had last talked to Jermakowicz on December 12, 1981, in Poland when Jermakowicz, an economics professor, addressed a group of Polish workers at a meeting organized by Cholodecki, then the regional vice-chairman of the Opole Solidarity Union. Jermakowicz had forgotten his hat at Cholodecki's house; but Cholodecki could not return it because, when martial law was imposed that next day, Cholodecki was imprisoned. Cholodecki spent the next year in prison and emigrated to the United States two years after that, without ever having spoken to Jermakowicz again. Jermakowicz also emigrated and began teaching at the University of Southern Indiana. Eight years later when they met for the first time at this academic conference, Jermakowicz's first words to Cholodecki were "Do you still have my hat?"

more access than did the Polish Americans was the group of new Solidarity-backed politicians and officials in Poland. These connections came from his activism prior to emigration and his occupation in the United States (as a radio program host, he kept himself in touch with the new leaders in Poland). Forum's Polish American chairman deferred to Cholodecki on matters related to Poland, often saying that the Polish side was in "Jarek's hands" (Jarek is the diminutive for Jaroslaw) because Cholodecki knew his way around the political labyrinth of the new government in Warsaw. Cholodecki arranged to have Lech Walesa and other opposition leaders and Solidarity-backed politicians attend the inaugural meeting and the First Annual Convention.[16] Cholodecki used these connections to gain exposure for the Forum and legitimate the organization in the eyes of the new Polish immigrants who composed the majority of Forum's membership. Moreover, the presence of the leaders from Poland helped increase attendance at Forum's key events. Finally, having leaders from Poland supporting the organization publicized Forum in Poland, which was important because the nature of Forum's goals—promoting investment in Poland—required that it attract investment partners from Poland.

These ties to Solidarity refugees, officials from Poland, and the new immigrant community in general provided Forum with members, leaders, and authority. As members, these people provided the resource of money; as leaders, they provided organizational skills; and as authorities, they provided legitimacy and exposure.

In contrast, the Polish Americans had links to the ethnic community and American institutions. Mitch Kobelinski, the Polish American president of Forum, had networks to U.S. officials, international agencies, and the ethnic community. Kobelinski had contacts with representatives from the U.S. Information Agency (USIA), U.S. Agency for International Development (USAID), the Overseas Private Investment Corporation (OPIC), the

---

Jermakowicz immediately became interested in Forum and his enthusiasm translated into resources.

16. Senator Celinski from Warsaw, Maciech Kozlowski (a Catholic journalist recently appointed consul for the Los Angeles Polish consulate), and Jan Gornik (a famous dissident) spoke at the inaugural meeting. The first annual convention had an even more impressive roster that included Lech Walesa, Janusz Onyszkiewicz (national Solidarity spokesman), Lech Jeziorny (vice-president of Krakow Industrial Society), Jan Bielecki and Andrzej Arendarski (parliament members), Michael Wojtczak (deputy minister of agriculture), and Dariusz Ledworowski (deputy minister of foreign trade). In addition, Cholodecki invited the minister of radio and television from Poland, Andrzej Drawicz, to the opening of the Forum office.

Import-Export Bank, the Small Business Administration, and the U.S.-Polish Economic Council (part of the U.S. Chamber of Commerce). Kobelinski's links to these agencies came from his profession (a banker and foreign investor in Poland since 1973) and his past positions as a director of the U.S. Import-Export Bank (1974–77) and administrator of the U.S. Small Business Administration (1976–78). His knowledge about the American market system, American federal agencies, and the Polish market system made him a good candidate for federal agencies looking for someone to direct American resources being invested in Poland. Kobelinski also had ties to financiers and businessmen. Because of his experience in foreign investments in Poland he was often a speaker at conferences on economic conditions in Poland. As a speaker at an investment seminar on Poland conducted by the U.S. Chamber of Commerce, he was able to talk about Forum to two hundred businessmen attending the conference. Through these links, Kobelinski presented Forum's agenda, invited representatives from these agencies to become involved in Forum's activities, and secured the presence of officials from these institutions to speak at the Forum Convention.

Kobelinski also had connections to local and state officials. As a leader of Polonia (he was the founder and president of the Copernicus Foundation, which established the Copernicus Cultural and Civic Center), he was in a position to influence voters and thus he attracted the attention of Illinois politicians such as Lieutenant Governor George Ryan, who was a candidate in an upcoming gubernatorial race. Through this connection to Ryan, Kobelinski secured bureaucratic resources (for example, Forum's Articles of Incorporation were approved in only forty-eight hours so that they would be ready for the Inaugural Meeting) as well as legitimating resources (Ryan spoke at the Forum Convention).[17]

Third, Kobelinski had ties to the Polish American community. Because he was respected by the Polish American ethnic organizations, and because

17. Although it was Polish American chairman Mitch Kobelinski who had most of the contacts with American politicians, it was Cholodecki who, because of the prominence of his radio program, attracted Illinois Senator Paul Simon (who was up for reelection in a district with a lot of Polish American voters) to the Forum. In September 1989, Senator Simon had just returned from Poland and was a guest on Cholodecki's program. Simon used the program to speak to voters, and in return Cholodecki asked Simon to speak at Forum's inaugural meeting. This link to American politicians was uncommon for new immigrants. It shows, however, that over time, as immigrants developed stronger networks in America, they began to moderate the limitations of the newcomer status.

he was a member of the established community, other prominent Polish American leaders worked with him even when they refused to support Forum. For example, when someone called the PAC asking for information on Poland's markets, the caller was often referred to Kobelinski. However, the caller was given Kobelinski's Copernicus Center phone number rather than his office phone number or Forum's office number. The Copernicus Center then referred the caller to Forum. In this way, the PAC referred people to the Forum through an established ethnic intermediary.[18]

The ethnics had ties to American institutions and the Polish American community; the new immigrants had ties to Polish institutions and new Polonia. Thus the networks of the new immigrants and the Polish Americans complemented each other. The new immigrants managed the Polish end of Forum and the Polish Americans managed the American and ethnic end. The Polish American ethnics knew how to get Forum established legally, publicly and financially. The Polish immigrants knew how to recruit members, leaders, and legitimating authorities from Poland, and how to organize market and publicity opportunities in Poland. These differences in networks strengthened the overall activism in the community because the networks gave them access to different resource arenas.

Conclusion

New immigrant organizations worked together with established organizations when they had resources to exchange, when they did not compete for members, and when differences in strategies complemented each other. Differences between ethnics and immigrants influenced the types of net-

---

18. In addition to Kobelinski, several Polish American men and women were very active in the Forum. The skills they brought to the Forum included public relations, grant-writing, legal, and editing. A Polish American with public relation skills undertook the English-language press relations tasks. She prepared articles for the local and city presses, arranged to have interviews of Polish officials in the Chicago business magazine *Cranes*, and suggested that the Polish politicians invited to the convention arrive a few days early so that Forum "can get some publicity mileage out of them." Another woman, trying to secure institutional financial support for Forum, wrote ten grant proposals to private foundations and federal agencies, such as the Rockefeller Foundation, the MacArthur Foundation, OPIC, USAID, and USIA. The secretary-counsel of Forum used his experience as a lawyer to draft Forum's bylaws. Other Polish Americans wrote the English-language documents for Forum: letters of invitation, speeches, membership forms and flyers.

works they had, which predicated the types of resources they had to exchange. New immigrants could turn to Poland more successfully for resources of legitimacy and information than could ethnics. This was especially true for former Solidarity activists who had premigration ties to the opposition. In addition, their ties to the immigrant community made it possible to mobilize the large numbers of people necessary for successful demonstrations, petitions, and fund-raising activities. The ethnics' resources included legitimacy as ethnic leaders in Polonia but also information about American procedures. They were more successful at raising large sums of money as a result of their ties to the established ethnic community. The ethnics also had more developed American networks that connected them to political, media, and organizational institutions. The PAC was able to use elected and media officials to promote their cause more ably than were the new immigrants. The organizations cooperated because they had resources to exchange that each other needed. Polish Americans got the parade permits, contacted the American media, and sent large sums of humanitarian aid to Poland through legal channels. The Polish Americans had an understanding of English grammar and political etiquette, and knowledge of whom to call and connect with in the American political system. New immigrants knew who the legitimate political actors in Poland were and how to read signals coming out of Poland. The new immigrants were also the grassroots organizers, disseminating information in the immigrant community, rallying enthusiasm, and mobilizing collective action. They sent much smaller amounts of aid to Poland, but it was more specifically targeted to local and regional opposition sectors as well as to individuals. The key reason why their resources differed was because they had different histories, which gave them networks into different arenas and as a result different resources. Cooperation was possible because of these differences, not in spite of these differences.

5

Power, Competition, and Ownership

The political life of Polonia in Chicago resembles a giant theater of the absurd. Before the gossip and emotion of one scandal fades another begins.

—Jerzy Bereszko (1989)

The United States was interested in Eastern Europe for national security, humanitarian, and business reasons. Both the left and the right political spheres applauded and encouraged the formation of the Solidarity union. The Carter administration took an interest in Poland, especially during Zbigniew Brzezinski's tenure as national security advisor. In September 1980, the Carter administration approved $670 million in agricultural and technical aid to Poland in the form of credits. Although President Carter sent a clear warning to the USSR that any military invasion of Poland would have serious consequences, the United States was never willing to intervene militarily on behalf of the Polish workers. The Reagan administration also ideologically supported the workers, and in 1981 approved a $1.2 billion aid package to Poland, authorized the sale of $71 million worth of surplus dairy products, and agreed to reschedule Poland's debt (U.S. Department of State Bulletin, August 1981, 76). When martial law was imposed December 13, 1981, the United States was sympathetic but not aggressive. President Reagan condemned martial law as a violation of human rights in his Christmas address on December 23, 1981, and his administration took punitive measures against the Polish and Soviet regimes in the form of economic sanctions. Sanctions applied to Poland included the suspension of agricultural and dairy surplus shipped to Poland, nonrenewal of the Import-Export Bank's line of credit to Poland, suspension of Polish civil aviation privileges, suspension of Polish fishing rights in U.S. waters, and further restrictions on high technology exports to Poland. In October 1982, when Solidarity was declared illegal, the Reagan administration suspended Poland's most-favored-nation (MFN) tariff status. The United States also placed sanctions on the USSR: they suspended Aeroflot services to the United States, closed the Soviet Purchasing Commission, suspended issuance or renewal of export licenses for electronics and high technology products, and postponed negotiations on grain and maritime agreements (U.S. Department of State Bulletin, February 1982, 3–8).

In his autobiography, Lech Walesa, the leader of Solidarity, wrote that most people in Poland initially saw the sanctions as "a clear gesture of support for us, and as one of censure against the government" (1987, 264). Walesa, whose autobiography was published for an American audience, wrote that the Polish people knew they would have to make sacrifices, that the sanctions would lower their standard of living, but that they supported them if they forced the government into a "compromise with Solidarity." He stated they did not want foreign credits extended to Poland because they were unsure whether the government would use them effectively, and that the Polish people would be the ones who had to repay them in the future (264–65).

In the beginning, both the PAC and Pomost supported the sanctions. By 1984 the attitude toward sanctions had changed. In July 1984 a general amnesty released most of the remaining political prisoners (martial law had been lifted in July 1983), and the United States responded by removing some of the sanctions (such as airline restrictions and the ban on scientific exchange). PAC leaders agreed with this decision and urged the United States to open discussions on Poland's admission to the International Monetary Fund (IMF) so that Western credits could be extended to Poland and thereby aid in the relief of its economic and ecological problems. PAC leaders argued that the remaining sanctions only hurt the people of Poland. Removing the sanctions would also help those Polish Americans with business interests in Poland. In Poland, Solidarity leaders (and the communist regime) also agreed with the lifting of the sanctions. Jan Nowak wrote that, by 1985, the PAC was on the side of "the Pope, the Polish Episcopate and Lech Walesa" in urging that the remaining sanctions be lifted (1986, 53). Pomost leaders, however, disagreed with the PAC, the U.S. State Department, the Pope, and Solidarity. Pomost wanted the sanctions to remain in place in order to pressure the Polish government to relegalize

Solidarity and to introduce real social reforms. Pomost leaders forcefully lobbied U.S. politicians to keep sanctions in place.

Washington was hearing two Polonian voices during this period and established Polonia thought this was problematic. The PAC firmly believed that Polonia should have only "one strong voice" in Washington. Its pamphlet distributed in the mid-1980s stated, "The Polish American Congress is the sole representative spokesman of all Polish organizations in the United States." At its 1989 National Council of Directors meeting, the PAC president stated:

> Today news of difficulty with establishing help for Poland came from Washington. One of the reasons is the lack of unity among Polonia. . . . There are people among us who take it upon themselves to talk to Washington. . . . This must end at all cost. One strong voice of Polonia is needed and that is the only way to realize contact with Washington and the opposition in Poland. (Bialasiewicz 1989, 16)

Zbigniew Brzezinski also supported PAC's drive for one strong voice stating that the best thing Polonia can do for Poland is to be united behind the PAC because "any fragmentation of its influence hurts the influence of Polish Americans" (*PAC Newsletter*, September 1986, 6–7).

New immigrants understood established Polonia's desire to present itself as a unified community but were also aware of the cacophony of voices. Jaroslaw Cholodecki said, "You see, here the myth of one Polonia is very much alive. There is the belief that our voice can be heard in Washington only if it's one cohesive and unified voice. If that's not there, Washington pushes aside the problem because it doesn't know who to listen to" (Krajewski 1989, 38). While new immigrants were mindful of dissenting voices (which were often their own), most of them accepted the dominant opinion that "one" voice or organization should represent Polonia. Accepting this opinion muffled discord and silenced dissent; not accepting it, however, led to acrimonious power struggles.

If immigrants agreed that Polonia had to speak as one, and that the spokesperson should be the PAC, then they needed to get inside the PAC if they were going to influence the voice of Polonia. If groups instead acted outside the framework of the PAC, and they advocated policies different from the PAC, then cooperative relations became problematic. Cooperation was possible when they shared material resources such as information and activists, but it was impossible when they tried to share power. When new organizations like Pomost began lobbying they placed themselves in direct competition with the established organization. Their lobbying activity challenged, and at times threatened, the Polish American leaders' positions. When new immigrants questioned the PAC's right to be Polonia's representative or disputed the effectiveness of its strategies and policies, they undermined its traditional authority. Whenever new immigrants presented an alternative definition of the situation or publicly disagreed with PAC policy, they brought upon themselves the defensive wrath of old Polonia. At one point, the PAC president labeled new immigrants "born-again super patriots who have targeted the Polish American Congress and Polish American organizations for take-over" (Moskal 1991, 5). At the center of the controversy was the struggle for community ownership. Who had the right to lead Polonia? And, who was Polonia?

Keeping Low the Voice of Newcomers

The PAC was the largest and most recognized political representative of Polonia. When the president of the United States wanted to strengthen links to Polonia, he turned to the PAC; when U.S. officials wanted advice or support on foreign policy toward Poland, they turned to the PAC; when Washington needed a representative of Polonia for public relations purposes, it turned to the PAC. To play a political role in Polonia, the new immigrants would have to secure decision-making positions in the PAC or set up a parallel organization that would inevitable compete with the PAC. The new immigrants never joined ethnic organizations *en masse*, however. Some new immigrants worked closely with PAC officials and others were involved with the PAC through their PNA lodges: Pomost had *Pierwsze Pokolenie* (First generation), Brotherhood had *Sierpień 80* (August 1980), and some Freedom members belong to the PNA lodge Giewont. The new immigrants participated mostly at the state division level and mostly in the Polish Affairs committees. Pomost members were active in the PAC Illinois Division Polish Affairs Committee between 1976 and 1981, and Freedom members were active in this committee after 1984. Brotherhood leaders had ties to members of the national Polish Affairs Committee but never held formal positions on this committee. A few new immigrants had strong working relations with top PAC officials, but they were informal and personal relationships. In the 1980s, no new immigrant secured a formal leadership position in the national PAC where important policy issues regarding Poland were decided.

The new immigrants were never able to gain a secure foothold in the PAC because its formal, hierarchical structure of representation restricted the role of newcomers. Explicit rules governing how newcomers entered the organization and the procedures for gaining access to decision-making positions ensured that the organization would not be taken over by new-comers. It was nearly impossible for newcomers to reach national positions in the PAC because its structure was based on organizational representation rather than individual representation. The PAC was a coalition of organizations, and large organizations had a stronger presence (and voice) than smaller organizations. In the 1980s, the PAC, as an umbrella organization, was composed of over three thousand member organizations.[1] Organizations could send from two to ten delegates (depending on the number of members it had) to state-level divisional meetings; and each division had one to six seats on the National Council of Directors, the main policy-making body of the PAC.[2] For example, an organization of fifty people had only two delegates to the divisional meeting and often no delegates to the

1. Traditionally, the PAC has consisted mostly of organizations, but in the 1980s they began admitting more individuals. Individual members were allowed to participate in the division meetings, and were entitled to one vote but no proxy. In divisions where there were fewer organizations, such as Washington, D.C., there were more individual members. PAC leaders, however, discouraged individual memberships. The Illinois Division president told me he recommended that people applying for individual membership "find an organization," because an organization brings in more members, more money, and more legitimacy to back up PAC's claim that it represents all of Polonia.

2. PAC bylaws operative in the 1980s outlined the following conditions for representation. There were 125 national directors who formulated national PAC policy, and the allocation of directorships depended on organizational size. First, each state division was allotted a certain number of seats on the national council based on how many organizations they had in their division. Divisions with less that eleven organizations had one director, and those with one hundred or more organizations had six directors. Additional seats were allotted to large national organizations (defined as organizations with chapters, clubs, or groups in at least two states and whose membership was more than 1000). National organizations that had between 1,000 and 10,000 members were given one directorship, and those with over 250,000 were given eight seats. In addition, ten directors were appointed at large if needed. Second, there was a national convention at which policies formulated by the national committees were voted on. The number of delegates an organization could send to the convention again depended on membership size and type of organization. For example, organizations national in scope with more than 5000 members could send ten representatives, those with 1000–5000 members could send five delegates. Branches or lodges of organizations could send from three to five

national meeting. This structure of hierarchical organizational representation limited the new immigrants' chances of having a strong voice or
influencing PAC policy.

Moreover, according to PAC bylaws, all delegates to the national meeting
must be American citizens. Since it takes a minimum of five years for an
immigrant to become a citizen, and many apply late or not all, this bylaw
limited the involvement of newcomers. Furthermore, even if a few new
immigrants did reach national positions, their voices would be weak compared to those of Polish Americans because of the numerical differences.
Polish American organizations, especially the fraternals, had the largest
representation in the PAC. At least 90 percent of the member organizations
were Polish American fraternal lodges and church groups. The large
national fraternals had a dominant voting bloc at the divisional and
national meetings. The fraternal-PAC connection was also evident in the
executive committee, where four of the five officers were required to be,
according to the bylaws, from the four largest Polish fraternals in America.
In addition, the president of the PAC had always been simultaneously the
president of the PNA fraternal because the PAC's low resource base
was inadequate to support a paid executive staff, and the PNA contributed
the most money and members. Since fraternals were the domain of
the established Polish American community, new immigrants had fewer
chances of gaining executive positions within the fraternal structures and
hence the PAC national structure. This PAC-fraternal connection effectively excluded most new immigrants from national PAC decision-making
positions.

The process of becoming a PAC national director usually took decades.
Kazimierz Lukomski, a World War II émigré, took fifteen years to be elected
to the national executive committee. (He was the only immigrant and
nonfraternal leader on the executive committee during my study.) Another
World War II émigré told me that in the 1950s his aunt signed him into a
PNA fraternal lodge; after six years he became a delegate from his local
lodge to the PAC Illinois Division; and only after thirty years did he become
a national director.

The new immigrants tried to get inside the PAC by the old-fashioned
route: through their PNA lodges (and maybe after fifteen or thirty years

---

delegates, and independent societies, clubs, or organizations could send two delegates, and
one additional delegate for each 100 members with the limit being five representatives.

some will hold prominent positions in the PAC). But new immigrants were annoyed that it took years to reach a powerful position, that is, an executive position at the national level where major policies regarding Poland were decided. They believed that action for Poland demanded immediate attention. Being the most recent arrivals from Poland, and being the members of Polonia who had lived in the communist system, the new immigrants argued that they had a better understanding of how to support the opposition movement. The freshness of their information would soon stale. As one new immigrant said, "In ten years everything in Poland may change." They felt that ownership of this information was sufficient for them to be included immediately in policy-making decisions regarding Poland. They did not want to spend ten years rising through the ranks of PAC's formal structure before someone would listen to them, because the longer an immigrant was in America the less he or she understood about what was happening in Poland. The new immigrants were frustrated by their inability to be heard. In one interview, Jaroslaw Cholodecki, a Brotherhood leader stated, "PAC plays a big role here. It's the institution into which we have tried to gain access. For now, this institution has disappointed us a little . . . We agreed that if any important matters arise concerning Poland, we will be informed, we will be able to express our opinion and to be able to organize some things. And it's not that way" (Krajewski 1989, 39). Most new immigrants were not interested in taking over the established organization, they simply wanted to have a voice inside the PAC.

PAC's connection to the Polish American fraternals, the hierarchical structure of representation, and the lengthy amount of time needed to rise within the ranks all limited new organizations' chances of influencing national PAC policy. Arthur Stinchcombe suggests that an institution ensures its continuation (and the continuation of its values) by controlling the succeeding generation. This it does by, among other things, choosing and socializing (training) its successors (1968, 101–30). People in power tend to choose people with the same values and interests to replace them (Selznick 1988 [1966]; Kanter 1977). The PAC required that the newcomers move up through the ranks so that it had time to resocialize them. The organizational structure safeguarded the values of the established members and in the process ensured the continuation of their values, but this structure also alienated the new immigrants and in doing so jeopardized the organization's continuation in the next generation.

The Definition of the Situation

The new immigrants were unable to shape PAC policy toward Poland and this became problematic when the new groups espoused opposing policies. In some cases new immigrants and established ethnics agreed upon the strategies for helping Poland, but there were also times when they disagreed. Simply having different strategies of action was not the problem. As seen, differences in strategy do not always have to be conflictual but may complement each other as was the case in the groups' different types of aid to Poland sent through different channels. New immigrants and established ethnics could organize in different arenas and support different groups in Poland without interfering with each others' activity. However, when they had opposing policies, they competed with each other to impose their definition of the situation.

Defining the Enemy in Poland

Polonia unequivocally rejected the communist government in Poland. Yet its leaders had no interest in severing all ties with the ancestral homeland. In order to maintain "legitimate" links, they meticulously extricated Poland from communist Poland. The PRL government (*Polska Rzeczpospolita Ludowa*, The People's Republic of Poland) was communist, the Polish people were not. Polonian leaders wanted to be sure that they did not hurt the people of Poland in their attempts to bring down the communist government; and conversely they did not want to inadvertently help the communist government in their efforts to help the people of Poland. When forced, however, established Polonia chose to help the people, or the nation as a whole, even if it did help the PRL. For example, in supporting Poland's bid for a seat in the United Nations, Roman Pucinski, the president of the Illinois division of the PAC said:

> We were very effective in getting Poland recognized as a nation when they denied Poland a seat at the United Nations in San Francisco, and ever since then we've been fighting for help for Poland, even though she was in the grip of a communist regime, because our position has been very simply, people don't change, governments change. People's needs remain the same. When we help Poland we help the Polish people. We never shut ourselves off. Others say,

"Well, it's a communist country," well we can't help that. The Polish
people are not communist, they never were and never will be. When
you help Poland you help the Polish people.

Although not always possible, Polonia nonetheless tried to keep a clear distinction between the communist regime in Poland and the Polish people.

PAC issued a memorandum at the 1988 National Council of Directors
meeting titled, "Recommendations on Language Usage," which outlined
the difference between the communist regime and the Polish nation. The
pamphlet stated that the words "Polish" and "Poland" should be used to
describe the Polish nation and people, while "PRL" should be used to
modify the actions of the communist government. The pamphlet gave some
specific examples:

1. Don't call PRL "Poland." Using Poland for PRL suggests that foreign
   rulers have a right to govern Poland. Not "government of Poland," but
   "government of PRL."
2. Poland refers to the Polish nation or society, its history, traditions,
   language and culture. e.g., "Poland lies in Central Europe." "Poland
   declared herself in favor of Solidarity."
3. Don't use "Polish" to describe the regime, its authorities or institutions.
   e.g.. Not "Polish ambassador," but "ambassador from PRL."
4. Use the adjective with care, e.g., not "the efficiency of Polish workers is
   low" but "the efficiency of the workers in the PRL is low."

The period of détenté beginning in the 1970s opened Poland's borders
to educational, scientific, and cultural exchanges as well as business relations. In order to participate in these exchanges, the PAC made explicit
statements about separating the Polish people from the communist regime,
affirming their desire to help the people of Poland while renouncing the
government in Poland. For example, in one newsletter PAC vice-president
Lukomski stated: "The PAC pursues a two-pronged policy relative to Poland; encouragement and support of the economic, technological and
cultural exchanges but at the same time strict opposition to the Communist
dictatorship" (December 1973, 8). In his keynote address at the tenth
national PAC convention, President Mazewski stated that while the PAC did
not "recognize the Communist regime in Poland," it supported "everything
that aids the Polish nation." He cautioned, however, that aiding the Polish
nation through cultural exchanges and economic aid "which in a long run

holds a promise for better life for the Polish people, require certain amount of official contacts. In the present set of realities they are unavoidable." Mazewski resolved the dilemma by stating that help for the people of Poland did not mean that one accepted the communist government. He said there were "many means to support the Polish people without strengthening the Communist stranglehold over the nation." He suggested as an example that in cultural academic exchanges the PAC should pressure the PRL to choose recipients based on merit, and that there should be reciprocity in exchanges of printed materials. Such efforts, he argued, would subvert the system while at the same time would help the Polish people (*PAC Newsletter*, April 1977, 3–4).

Relations with high-ranking communist officials were taboo for Polish American officials as they implied recognition of the communist regime. PAC leaders did not go to Poland, except when sent by U.S. leaders or invited by the Church or Solidarity. PAC president Mazewski stated, "I have never been in Poland, only once when President Reagan sent me there for a funeral of Cardinal Wyszynski, otherwise, I've never been in Poland. My mother's never been in Poland either." Jan Nowak, a prominent World War II émigré wrote: "I wouldn't accept an invitation to come to Poland from the government, but I'll happily go on the invitation of Walesa" (1989, 3). Even meeting with PRL leaders in American could be injurious to one's reputation. PAC leaders would not attend the ceremonies when First Party secretary Edward Gierek came to the United States in 1974 (Pienkos 1984, 283), nor when prime minister and First Party secretary, General Wojciech Jaruzelski appeared at the United Nations meeting in New York in February 1986. The PAC and Pomost boycotted and protested Jaruzelski's visit. Polish Americans who attended the reception for Jaruzelski in New York were strongly criticized because they "chose to turn a blind eye on the realities of Poland's communist dictatorship headed by Gen. Jaruzelski" (*PAC Newsletter*, March 1986, 3). The PAC publicly sanctioned the attendees by printing their names and occupations in its March 1986 newsletter.

Polonia treated the PRL consulate the same as they did the regime. One Polish American said: "The consulate is just a great place to demonstrate in front of. . . . Most Polish Americans stay away from the consulate because it represents a government that the people have not chosen. They go there only to get a visa." One new immigrant said, "See, you must understand the meaning of this, the symbolic meaning. If I go to the Polish Consulate's office here, if I have anything to do with the consulate then this means that I am accepting the government in Poland. This means, I will work with your people and your system if I use this consulate office. I do not want to give them that satisfaction." Kazimierz Lukomski, PAC vice-president, was invited to the Chicago consulate for the seventieth anniversary of the independence of democratic Poland. He declined the invitation stating:

> Any contacts or discussion whatsoever between leaders striving for an independent Poland and representatives of the PRL Communist regime depend in the first place on the conclusion by the PRL authorities of a public agreement with spokesmen of independent society, represented by NSZZ "Solidarność" and its head, Lech Walesa. . . . Our partner in Poland is Solidarity. (*Studium Newsletter*, December 1988, 5)

In addition to Solidarity, the other legitimate institution was the Roman Catholic Church. Jan Nowak, a prominent World War II émigré wrote, in regard to Polonian dialogue with Poland: "The mediators can only be the Church or the opposition because these two institutions are trusted by Polonia and the émigrés" (1989, 3).

It was fairly clear during most the 1980s who were legitimate partners (the Church and Solidarity) and who were not (representatives of the regime). This clarity was lost during the transition period in 1989—the period when reforms from the roundtable had been approved but the elections of June 1989 had not yet taken place. In the spring of 1989, LOT Polish airline, the PRL government-owned airline, invited Edward Moskal, president of the PAC and other PAC leaders on an all-expense paid trip to Poland on the inaugural flight from Chicago to Warsaw. Moskal initially accepted. Studium, an organization of Polonian professionals, many of them academics, from both the Polish American and World War II cohorts, sent Moskal a fax urging him "to reconsider your acceptance of the invitation . . . [and] to seek appropriate opportunities to visit Poland, including at the invitation of Solidarity or the Church, as an independent observer of the upcoming elections, or especially as a member of President Bush's delegation" (*Studium Newsletter*, May–June 1989, 1). Moskal did reconsider, but then Studium was criticized by Don Horkey, editor of the Detroit *Polish Daily News*. Mr. Horkey wrote that "he saw no difference between Mr. Moskal and Joe Private Citizen accepting such an invitation" and suggested that given the changes in the regime, Polonia should "bend a little" and start to "normalize" relations with the regime (*Studium Newsletter*, May–June 1989,

2). Studium responded with a letter to Horkey, which they also sent to the PAC Ann Arbor chapter, stating:

> Ed Moskal, as President of the Polish American Congress, is our leading politician and spokesman in the struggle for Polish freedom and independence. To say that his action's are no different from that of Joe Private Citizen's is to render the PAC meaningless. He needs to be able to deal with the Polish regime independently and on his own terms. (*Studium Newsletter*, May–June 1989, 1–2)

The PAC and most other Polonian leaders and activists made careful distinctions between the Polish people and the PRL Government. They were aware of the subtle nuances of language, the symbolic meaning of behavior, and the circumscribed links to educational and cultural institutions. For the most part, they all agreed that the PRL communist regime was not the Polish nation, they all recognized the Church and opposition as the only legitimate institutions in Poland, and they all defined the consulate in Chicago as an extension of the PRL regime. Where disagreements arose were in the economic arena. Polish Americans did not fully appreciate that in communist systems the economy and polity were much more intertwined than in capitalist-democratic systems.

Separating the Economy and Polity: American Style

Some Polish Americans and World War II émigrés who were avowed "anticommunists" were also entrepreneurs with business interests in Poland. They argued that "business was business" and that one could be politically against the communist regime in Poland and still carry on international trade relations.[3] The PAC encouraged contacts with the Polish *nation* through economic linkages (*PAC Newsletter*, December 1972, 6). A pamphlet published by PAC in 1988, "Relations of Polish Americans

---

3. Changes in legislation in Poland in 1976 made it possible for enterprises owned solely by foreigners or Poles living abroad to do business in Poland. The companies, called *polonijne* (Polonian) businesses, operated in "more favorable" conditions after 1979 when income tax was at 50 percent and they could employ as many people as they wanted. They were also able to transfer profits to other countries. In 1982, there were 230 new *polonijne* businesses and by 1984, "about 500 Polonian enterprises had started operating employing some 25,000 people" (*Studium Papers* 8 [October 1984]: 109–10).

with the Communist Regime in Poland," stated its stance on business
ventures.

> The Polish American Congress supports private business ventures
> and investments in Poland as a way to develop the independent,
> market-oriented segment of the economy. This obviously requires
> establishment of relations with Poland's governmental agencies.
> Polish Americans should put these relations, however, on a strictly
> business basis, shunning social, and other non–business-related
> activities, which create the appearance of their political support of
> the regime.

The PAC cautioned entrepreneurs, yet it nonetheless supported Polish
Americans business ventures in Poland because it believed they ultimately
helped the Polish nation.[4]

Some immigrants objected to these economic linkages. They considered
business relations with the Polish nation an acknowledgment of the legitimacy of the communist regime. One member of Pomost said the new
immigrants "couldn't understand why some [Polish Americans] were willing to cut deals, to set up businesses in Warsaw and had good relations with
the Polish communists." Another immigrant who arrived in the late 1970s
blamed the World War II émigrés:

> And these people, as I see, they start to open some travel offices,
> tourist offices, expeditions, like sending the packages. . . . And
> they, even though they were soldiers of the Polish army in the West,
> they were the first people who start to make contact with the Polish
> regime, because it was their business. They forget simply about the
> war, about that they are communists. They want to make money. So
> this is the problem, they are in PAC and many other organizations
> and they do not understand this kind of idea, they just want to make
> a business.

Another new immigrant said: "Even in the PAC there are divisions. On the
national level they are very anticommunistic. But on the local level this is

---

4. Though this policy statement was from 1988, Vice-President Lukomski told me that it
reflected the opinion the PAC held in the late 1970s and 1980s.

not true. Many cooperate with the government because they have some business with them."

The problem, these immigrants believed was not just that these Polonians had business relations with Poland, but that they were also leaders and members of Polonian organizations like the PAC. One new immigrant said, "You know these people, he do something here, he make business. . . . And after that he make the business with the communist country, you understand. He sent over there some stuff for the factories, something like that. They make business for the communist country. And these people been in the Congress too some of them, the Polish American Congress." His and others' criticisms of this practice centered on the fact that the people doing business in Poland did not have the luxury of being Joe (or Jane) Citizen if they were also active in the PAC. As PAC officials, they were public figures whose business interests in Poland were more than just private affairs. The new immigrants challenged the PAC on this matter. One immigrant, who had been a member of Pomost said that at a meeting in Kalamazoo in the late 1970s new immigrants reproached Polish Americans for this practice. He said that the topic of business relations was brought up and they decided that it "was obligatory for members of the PAC, if they are prominent, like the directors, they don't supposed to go to Poland and show off their presence there. . . . And they were agreeing on that. Let's say we can't have a business with a regime; or a prominent member of the Congress, not like soldier, but general, can't do business with regime. And they agreed." Nonetheless, he acknowledged regretfully that the practice did not stop.

The significant problem, they argued, was that by wearing both hats, they felt that at times business interests were influencing PAC policy. This accusation arose during the controversy about lifting economic sanctions imposed on Poland after martial law. Some immigrants insinuated that PAC's policy reversal toward the sanctions that, in 1984, led to its circumscribed support for their removal was motivated in part by some of its leaders private business interests. One immigrant said, "Because somebody have business in Poland, you understand, and it's why he like look for the communist country maybe better, he say, 'we support the communist country, come on Reagan, stop these, open the money everything send to the Poland.' This is been big conflict for the new immigration and for the old immigration." During this time, Mitchell Kobelinski, a Polish American businessman, president of Kore International Trade and Investment Company (which had business interests in Poland) and former president of the

PAC Illinois Division, wrote a letter to the Political Trade Committee that
argued that the Polish People's Republic should be returned to MFN trade
status. Magnus Krynski, a Pomost member, argued that Kobelinski's business interests in Poland, as president of Kore International Trade and
Investment Company, influenced his political stance (Krynski 1983). Krynski sent letters to both television journalist Sam Donaldson and the chief of
Voice of America, Polish Services, in September 1983 complaining that only
those "few Polish Americans who want to conduct business with the
Jaruzelski regime" were in favor of lifting sanctions. He named in particular
Mr. Piszak, owner of Mrs. Paul's Kitchen, who, Krynski argued, would
benefit from restoring fishing trade with Poland.

The difference in opinion about economic relations with Poland also
played itself out in attitudes toward the strategy of boycotts. Pomost took a
strong stance against economic relations with Poland. After the imposition
of martial law Pomost engaged in boycotts of Polish products and Polish
performers touring America. Pomost tried to get the PAC to support these
boycotts but the PAC leaders said the boycotts unfairly hurt the small
businesses in Chicago that sold Polish goods. Pomost also advocated boycotting American companies that continued to do business with Poland.
For example, they urged a boycott of PepsiCo to persuade its chairman to
"scale down his lobbying activities toward an economic détente" as well as a
"three-month round-the-clock picketing of the main branch of the Chase
Manhattan Bank in NYC" because it was the first bank to establish a Moscow
branch in the 1970s (Krynski 1984, 46–47).

Some even went so far as to accuse those with business interests in Poland
of being collaborators. As a representative of Pomost, Magnus Krynski
wrote on February 18, 1983, to Marek Maciolowski, director of Aid for
Poland in Chapel Hill, North Carolina, that there were some Polish
American "collaborationist elements, people who want to trade with Communist Poland, travel agencies which are working against the boycott of
LOT airline and other people of the same ilk." One new immigrant,
judging the credibility of organizations working for Poland, gave the
highest ranking to the organization refusing to do any business with
Poland, saying that "in Chicago there is only one program, Freedom
for Poland who program which not collaborate with no any commercial,
LOT, Polish ham, or travel bureau where you can apply for consulate
passport or something like that. It was good."

Another example of the different understandings new immigrants and
Polish Americans had regarding the relation between the polity and the

economy in Poland developed in the Polish-American Economic Forum (Forum). Established in the fall of 1989, new immigrants initially created Forum to show support for the new Solidarity government by promoting and facilitating foreign investments in Poland's private market. New immigrants still reasoned that support for the economy was support for the polity, but in the fall of 1989 the polity represented Solidarity. As Poland and other East European countries sought political autonomy from the Soviet Union through greater freedom in the electoral arena, they also sought economic autonomy and tried to disengage themselves from the state-owned communist economic system. National independence was interpreted first as democratic freedom and then as market freedom.

New immigrants were eager to show their support by helping the new government develop a new market economy. Forum leaders who were immigrants defined economic support of the private market in Poland as a political act. Investment dollars were cast as a form of political demonstration. One leader said, Forum "is nothing more than an idea to make another demonstration—only without the rotten eggs" (*Kurier* 1989, 6). The political theme of Forum was its emphasis that investment dollars would contribute to the collective good—an economically stable Poland. However strongly these economic objectives were emphasized, immigrants maintained that Forum was also a political organization and that supporting the new economy was a political act. In a questionnaire completed by 98 of the 170 people who attended Forum's inaugural meeting, 70 percent of the respondents said they became involved in Forum for political reasons (Kusak 1989, 4). For example, one respondent said, "It's our responsibility to bring help to our nation"; other respondents echoed this sentiment, describing their membership in Forum as a "duty" and "obligation" in order "to help" Poland "our fatherland" (4–5). In my survey of 109 Forum members, 73 percent of the respondents indicated that they had joined Forum "to help Poland."

As Forum developed it began to concentrate on the investment agenda, especially when a Polish American banker, Mitchell Kobelinski, who himself had business relations with Poland, became the chairman of Forum. Whereas Jaroslaw Cholodecki, the Forum president and a Solidarity refugee, stressed the political nature of Forum, Kobelinski emphasized the economic side. For example, some new immigrants proposed that Forum promote the purchase of Polish government bonds. Kobelinski asked, "How does this relate to the private sector in Poland? This is an organization for investment in the private sector." Cholodecki argued that the bonds would help the Mazowiecki (Solidarity) government become more stable. Kobelinski responded loudly, "I don't want to save Poland, I want to invest in Poland. A government bond is not a private investment." Polish immigrants, however, were also interested in "saving Poland."

New immigrants experienced the intertwined nature of polity and economy while living in a communist regime and they saw no difference between doing business in Poland and supporting the regime. Polish Americans perceived a line of demarcation between the PRL regime and the Polish market; they compartmentalized their ancestral sentiments from their American pocketbooks. Polish Americans, as Americans, thought of profit making as a rational activity divested of moral dilemma.

A Conflict in Strategies: Pomost and the PAC

Until 1981, the PAC and Pomost worked together organizing demonstrations, fund-raisers, and meetings. After the imposition of martial law, their relationship began to deteriorate—first they stopped working together then they started working against each other. After 1981, the PAC and Pomost no longer co-organized demonstrations (Table 5.1), later they began verbally attacking each other in public, and finally Pomost began independent lobbying activities.

The PAC and Pomost responded differently to the implementation of martial law. On December 13, 1981, when martial law was imposed, Pomost organized a demonstration; the national leaders of the PAC spent the afternoon in a meeting discussing what they should do. Two Pomost members attended the PAC meeting. They asked the PAC leaders to work with them to organize the demonstration along the same lines as they had cooperated earlier. The Pomost leaders were asked to leave the meeting because they were not national PAC directors. The Pomost leaders left and mobilized three thousand people to demonstrate in front of the consulate later that afternoon. Three days later, on December 16, the PAC sponsored a large demonstration in which Pomost members participated. Another PAC-organized demonstration on December 27 attracted over fifty thousand demonstrators.

Pomost criticized the PAC for not acting like a quick response strike force; however, formal bureaucratic organizations are often rigid and slow

Table 5.1 Organization of demonstrations in Chicago, 1980–1984

	Organized by Pomost	Organized by Pomost and PAC	Organized by PAC
1980	9	2	0
1981	7	1	2
1982	18	0	3
1983	13	0	2
1984	4	0	1
Totals	42	3	7

SOURCE: *Pomost Quarterly*, 1979–84; *PAC Bulletin*, 1980–81; *PAC Newsletter*, 1981–84; *PAC Illinois Division Bulletin*, 1980–84. Demonstrations include vigils and rallies. This table only refers to the sponsors. At most demonstrations, members from both Pomost and PAC were present. PAC here refers to the Illinois state division. Prior to 1981, Polonia demonstrated to show support for the striking workers and Solidarity; after 1981, they protested the mass arrests in Poland, the imposition of martial law, and the delegalization of Solidarity. After 1981, demonstrations in front of the Polish consulate took place mostly on Solidarity anniversaries: August 31, the date of the signing of the Gdansk agreements, which marks the birth of Solidarity; and December 13, the imposition of martial law.

to act (Morris 1984, 54 and 285). Pomost was able to organize more quickly because its small, informal structure made it easier for its leaders to reach a consensus. During this period, three to five leaders decided the policy, tone and actions of the organization. In contrast, the PAC Illinois Division, which organized the demonstrations in Chicago, needed to have its strategic decisions approved by roughly one hundred delegates. PAC policy issues were first discussed in a committee before they came to the delegates for a vote. Roman Pucinski, the Illinois Division president, explained the process: "The Polish Affairs Committee observes very carefully the development of events in Poland; discusses them at their committee meetings; and out of those discussions evolve resolutions, programs or recommendations for rallies and stuff. And then those recommendations are brought to the full membership and they vote on them." When a quicker response was required, as it was on December 13, decisions were made by the executive committee in conjunction with the Polish Affairs Committee; however it still required that decisions be made with some informal consultation of members.

The imposition of martial law radicalized Pomost. Pomost adopted a strategy of guerrilla-style demonstrating—small, frequent, and hostile protests. At one demonstration, a protester chained himself to the consulate fence and the Chicago police arrested him for disorderly conduct (*Chicago*

Tribune, December 19, 1981, p. 2). These disruptive actions began to irritate the wealthy American North Shore residents living in the vicinity of the Polish consulate (Shulgasser and Robinson 1981). At several demonstrations, the protestors threw rocks, eggs, and red paint at the consulate (Briggs and Cordt 1981). The PAC Illinois Division president said, "I regret the paint throwing. That's hooliganism, and I don't approve of it" (*Chicago Tribune,* December 28, 1981, p. 17). Eventually, police barricades were set up to keep the protesters away from the consulate. For several weeks after martial law was imposed in Poland, Pomost held daily protests, and throughout 1982–84 Pomost continued to hold small (fifty to one hundred people) demonstrations in front of the consulate on the thirteenth of every month, marking the imposition of martial law. It was also during this period that Pomost began boycotting products from Poland, and this boycott was not supported by the PAC who said the practice hurt Polish American businesses.

In contrast, the PAC implemented more moderate strategies of protest. They believed sufficient action was being taken in the form of U.S. economic sanctions imposed upon Poland after martial law. PAC leaders also thought these small, guerrilla-style demonstrations were unproductive. The PAC preferred large, well-planned demonstrations and engaged in only a few select demonstrations a year that attracted thousands of supporters. Roman Pucinski believed that Pomost's small and numerous demonstrations were ineffective because the protesters had lost their ability to attract the American media by demonstrating too often. He said the PAC preferred to have large, well-advertised demonstrations because the main purpose of the demonstrations was "not to annoy the Polish consulate," but instead to "bring attention to Poland's cause."

The antagonism between the PAC and Pomost went public. When Pomost planned a demonstration for December 31, 1981, the leader of the PAC Illinois Division actively discouraged people from attending (*Pomost Quarterly* 5 [1983]: 54). One Pomost leader said, "Mr. Pucinski was so active he got on three TV networks advising people not to go [to the demonstration] because there was going to be drunk people there, they may be beaten up." As an alternative to demonstrating, the PAC supported the more moderate strategy advocated by President Reagan of placing candles in windows as a show of support for Solidarity. A letter from David Wilke to Magnus Krynski (February 15, 1983), both of whom were Pomost members, details the growing dissonance between Pomost and the PAC. First, PAC president Mazewski refused to sign an open letter to President Reagan published in the *New York Times* (July 10, 1981) under the banner "Back the Courageous People of Poland Now." After it was published, "a group of PAC members discredited it to the State Dept. and other government officials." Second, "Pomost asked Mazewski to join in demonstrations at the Polish Consulate in Chicago on December 13, 1981. He refused saying that Pomost was conducting this activity for 'advertising' purposes." Third, the *Dziennik Związkowy*, the key Polish-language newspaper in Chicago refused to run an announcement for the 1981 New Year's Eve vigil demonstration in front of the consulate. Fourth, Pucinski "went on radio and television programs on the 31st urging people to avoid the vigil and to stay home and 'sip wine' instead" and two PAC members called people working with Pomost telling them that they would be "beaten up" if they joined the vigil. This of course is Pomost members' interpretations of the events. It illustrates, however, that they perceived the PAC as being hostile to Pomost strategies.

On February 4, 1983, Jan Kanty Miska, using PAC Washington Metropolitan Area Division stationary, wrote to Wiktor Orlikowski warning him of the suspicions he had about Pomost representative Magnus Krynski. He accused him of fiscal irresponsibility and misuse of funds, and implied that he had some alternative source of funds (the implication here was that the Polish communist government was backing Krynski). Miska asked in his letter "WHO pays for it, whom does it serve." On January 21–22, 1983, an article in the *Dziennik Związkowy*, written by Jan Krawiec, an active member of the PAC echoed Miska's accusations of Krynski. Krynski promptly contacted a lawyer who concluded that the remarks in the letter and article were indeed libelous remarks.

The divisiveness escalated as Pomost challenged the PAC's claim to be the sole representative of Polonia. Pomost leaders felt the August 31, 1984, anniversary of the Gdansk agreement (which marked the birth of Solidarity) was "too important for the particular interests" of one Polonian organization, and they sent a letter to the president of the Illinois Division offering to help co-organize the demonstration. The president declined their offer stating that the PAC was "the central political representation" of the Polish Americans, and that the demonstration "should be organized by no other than the PAC" (*Pomost Quarterly*, Winter 1983, 53). The established organization was in a position of power relative to the newcomer organization because of its size and reputation. It defined itself as the leader and central representative of Polonia, and continued its proprietary attitude toward Polish affairs. Pucinski, president of the PAC Illinois Division, stated, "anyone interested in Polish affairs should be involved in the PAC."

The PAC-Pomost conflict was precipitated by several factors. First, the bureaucratic structure of the PAC made it unable to act as quickly at Pomost. In this case, structure influenced strategy. Second, Pomost began to engage in more disruptive strategies of protest. Moderate strategies like placing candles in windows did not fit with radical strategies such as chaining oneself to a fence. Third, the disagreements were centered around activities in the Chicago arena, particularly the public sphere of demonstrations. The PAC and the new immigrants could support different organizations in Poland more easily than different activities in Chicago. Supporting different organizations in Poland did not threaten the established ethnic leaders or their organizations. But Chicago was the Polish American arena. When the new immigrants demonstrated without the permission or blessing of the PAC they challenged the authority of the established organization and its right to define the situation. Chicago was the ethnics' turf, and the PAC was their home. Pomost's behavior was ungracious, disrespectful and insulting to the host country ethnics.

The Struggle for Political Ownership

After the disagreements following martial law, Pomost decided to incorporate as an organization. The founder of Pomost said that the magazine had given them "a skeleton organization and because the Polish American Congress did not take the proper steps when martial law was started we decided to turn the magazine into an organization." While Pomost the magazine did not compete with the PAC (because the PAC was not operating in the publishing domain), when Pomost the organization began lobbying in Washington on behalf of Poland they moved into PAC territory.

The PAC and Pomost disagreed on what should be the role of a Polish lobby in the United States. Pomost leaders believed a Polish lobby should try to shape U.S. foreign policy. The PAC leaders adopted a more responsive strategy that tended to follow the lead of the State Department. In addition, Pomost's bid to become Poland's representative in America challenged the PAC's forty-year position. When the newcomer challenged the established community in this arena all cooperation ended and the PAC adopted a siege mentality.

The PAC lobbying strategy was to support the State Department and White House in administration policies toward Poland, and to serve as advisors and backers rather than agitators and dissenters. PAC newsletters over a twenty-year period (September 1969 to August 1989), note only thirty-six events that I classify as "dialogue with Washington."[5] Of these thirty-six events, only three could be described as PAC disagreements with White House policy. For example, the PAC denounced the Sonnefeldt Doctrine, which stated that Eastern European countries enjoyed "an organic relationship" with the Soviet Union. For the most part the PAC took its cue from the U.S. State Department, even if it did not agree with U.S. policy. The PAC conceded its plan of "liberation" for Poland to the U.S. strategy of "containment" in the 1950s and *détente* (tolerance and openness) in the 1970s. In 1956 "the PAC wound up supporting a substantial U.S. foreign aid commitment that could only serve to stabilize the new government and deal a seemingly fatal blow to the dream of liberation" (Pienkos 1992, 16). In 1968, when he became president of the PAC, Mazewski avoided the past PAC president Charles Rozmarek's strong rhetoric of Polish liberation and espoused instead a human rights principle of citizen's freedom consistent with the U.S. policy of détente. In general, the PAC preferred to work with the State Department, not against it. Polish American scholars (Lopata 1976; Blejwas 1981; Pienkos 1991) have argued that the PAC was never really able to influence U.S. policy and as a result they have always been a very minor player in U.S. foreign affairs.

5. Of these thirty-six events, 70 percent took place after 1980 (only 57 percent of the newsletters and bulletins were post-1980). These dialogues with Washington were events where PAC officials had some contact with U.S. public officials on a national level. I divided the events into four types: solicited consultations, unsolicited memoranda, public relations events, and shows of support. Solicited consultations ($N = 6$) were those events where Washington asked PAC leaders for advice. For example, in 1987, PAC officials were invited to the White House to brief Deputy Secretary of State Whitehead before his trip to Poland. Unsolicited memoranda ($N = 18$) were unrequested statements, letters, and appeals by the PAC to U.S. policy makers. Examples included the PAC suggesting a policy program for U.S. relations with Poland in March 1984. Public relation events ($N = 8$) were those events when representatives from the White House came to Chicago, or PAC leaders went to Washington, to present a positive U.S.-Polonia image for political campaigners. Examples included PAC leaders' attendance at the swearing in of the new ambassador to Poland, and Spiro Agnew's address to the PAC convention in 1972. Shows of support ($N = 6$) were similar to public relation events, but here the administration used the PAC to endorse a new State Department policy. One example was PAC President Mazewski's attendance at the White House when Reagan announced the lifting of the remaining economic sanctions against Poland on February 9, 1987. (The count totals thirty-eight because two events were coded as both unsolicited memoranda and shows of support.)

This conciliatory relationship between the PAC and the State Department was confirmed in interviews with PAC officials. The president of the Illinois division said that the PAC wanted to work with the State Department; they did not want to be a "counterforce." "It's just good sense to communicate with the State Department and say, 'what's your position on this question,' rather than create a counterforce. In those instances where we are not satisfied that enough is being done, we would take those [counter] positions. We would not do it in a disarming manner, we would not do it in a threatening manner." PAC officials believed that it was important to be loyal to America. One leader said being a "loyal American" means being "loyal to the State Department." The Illinois Division president said that "as Americans" they wanted to support the views of the government of the country of which they were citizens.

New immigrants were extremely unhappy with this stance. Pomost leaders wanted a lobby that would direct State Department policy, not be directed by it. One Pomost member told me that he felt that the PAC does not "represent Polonia, they represent the State Department." Another Pomost leader believed the PAC "simply does whatever those people in the State Department propose. The transmission should be a different way. We should be pressing the State Department to fulfill our will." Pomost leaders wanted a lobby that would "demand" more for the opposition in Poland and be "more aggressive" toward the communist regimes in Poland and the Soviet Union.

Pomost eventually started its own lobby. Until 1982, the majority of Pomost's funds were sent to Poland. After 1982 more money stayed in the United States to support its quarterly, radio program and lobby (Table 5.2). The progression of the destination of its funds shows the movement of the activities from mostly financial support to the opposition in 1980, to support for the building of the organization's media (in 1982), to the building of a Polish lobby (in 1984). Between 1983 and 1985, Pomost had numerous contacts with American elected officials and directors of international committees and organizations.[6] Pomost promoted policies that

6. Most of the contacts with Washington were through Pomost's Washington representative, Magnus Krynski. This example sort of argues against what I said in Chapter 4 about immigrants' not having networks to American institutions. However, the Pomost activists involved in this lobbying effort had been in the United States for twenty years, and some World War II émigrés were also involved. They were not "new" immigrants. Magnus Krynski was from the World War II cohort. He arrived in the United States as a teenager with his parents in 1939, and went on to become a professor of Slavic Studies at Duke University. Although Pomost was

enforced a strong stance against communism and lobbied against American isolationist policies that took a "hands-off" approach to Poland. Pomost supported a stronger Export Administration Act that would limit the transfer of high technology to the USSR and the Soviet bloc; and it supported the pipeline technology ban. They were not lose cannons in Washington. They played a rather safe game, looking for alliances with members in polity, trying to find something they could exchange for support (mostly votes). In one letter on November 1, 1983, Magnus Krynski, Pomost's representative in Washington, wrote to Pomost leader Krzystof Rac: "Above all, we must use moderate language, criticize from the position of friends of the Administration and not lose our access there." Even though they wanted to work inside, they nonetheless aggressively challenged U.S. policies toward Poland. The two hardest fought battles were about economic sanctions and the Yalta Treaty of 1945.

Table 5.2 Destination of funds donated to Pomost, 1979–1984

Year	Opposition Movement	Pomost Press and Radio	Lobby	Other*
1979	$596	$560	—	—
1980	9,891	2,862	—	—
1981	5,617	1,803	**$19,824	$2,078
1982	2,662	7,144	182	2,926
1983	2,417	2,569	5,801	2,404
1984	1,110	854	10,963	2,153
Totals	22,293	15,792	36,770	9,561
100%	(26%)	(19%)	(44%)	(11%)

Source: *Pomost Quarterly*, 1979–84, refers to how donations were earmarked.

*Other includes payments received from Pomost chapters in California, New York, California, and Africa, as well as unspecified funds marked "for Pomost."

**All of this money was used to place a full-page advertisement in the *New York Times* on July 10, 1981, under the title "Back the Courageous People of Poland," asking the U.S. Congress to prevent a Soviet invasion of Poland.

The conciliatory style of the PAC and the aggressive style of Pomost were evident in how the two groups acted on the issue of lifting economic

---

a new immigrant organization it also attracted World War II émigrés and some younger Polish Americans. Krynski was able to work as a lobbyist for Pomost in part because he was not a newcomer.

sanctions. Initially, Pomost, the PAC, and the opposition leaders in Poland all supported the sanctions as a sign of support for the opposition and an act of censure against the communist regime. After the 1984 amnesty in Poland, the United States began to lift the sanctions in stages; Pomost fought this every step of the way. The first debate was over restoring Poland's most-favored-nation (MFN) status. Magnus Krynski wrote a letter to Frederick Montgomery of the Trade Representatives Office, which was read into the Congressional Record on Tuesday, August 2, 1983. Krynski argued against a memorandum proposed by Mitchell Kobelinski, who argued in favor of restoring Poland's MFN status. About Kobelinski's plan Krynski wrote: "His advocacy of economic collaboration with the unpalatable Jaruzelski regime is generally rejected by the Polish-American community as morally ambiguous." Krynski argued that "all the major Polish-American organizations" including the "pro-Solidarity" Pomost are in favor of keeping the sanctions in place, even the PAC, "the organization which represents the older generations of Polish Americans and is perhaps least responsive to issues of foreign policy."

The PAC initially supported the sanctions, but then wavered and eventually altered their policy to bring it more in line with the State Department. The PAC was upset when sanctions against Poland "were lifted without any change in the military and political situation either in Afghanistan or in Poland" (*PAC Newsletter*, September 1986, 9), yet it gave verbal and public support for their removal. The PAC sent President Reagan a telegram on August 16, 1983, which asserted that even though the Polish regime continues its "policy of repression," Poland "desperately needs resumption of economic relations with Western democracies" to help its economy. PAC held to its position that "sanctions can only be removed in response to the regime's substantive moderation of its policies," yet suggested that in good faith the United States might open negotiations by removing sanctions against fishing rights and reschedule Polish debts. They concluded, however, that "this in no way changes our position since these recommendations do not affect the imposed sanctions." Pomost saw the PAC as talking out of both sides of its mouth. The PAC position, however, was very much in line with what Walesa was saying at that time. As early as December 1983, Walesa had publicly made a distinction between economic restrictions and economic aid, stating that while restrictions could be a "gesture of disapproval" he was "in favor of real foreign aid" (Walesa 1987, 289). But Pomost was also critical of Walesa for this position. On December 13, 1983, Krzystof Rac, president of Pomost, wrote to President Reagan criticizing Walesa for making the statement that sanctions should be lifted and argued forcefully to keep them in place. On January 11, 1984, Krynski wrote to Pomost supporter David Wilke stating that Pomost need not "take orders from Warsaw or Gdansk. . . . We know more about the economy of Poland and the West than Lech and Glemp and all their experts put together." Pomost was adamantly against lifting any sanctions. Pomost wanted the sanctions to remain in place in order to pressure the Polish government to relegalize Solidarity and to begin a program of social reforms. While PAC leaders believed that membership in the IMF would strengthen Poland's relations with the West and make them less dependent on the USSR, Pomost leaders felt Western aid would only give Poland a face-lift, prolong the process of economic and social decay, and delay the overthrow of the regime (*Pomost Quarterly*, Summer 1984, 49–51).

The second issue that exposed the different policies of the two groups and resulted in Washington hearing two Polonian voices was the Renounce Yalta Campaign. This campaign, started in 1982 by a member of Pomost, fought to abolish the 1945 Yalta Treaty on the grounds that it had allowed the Soviets to establish totalitarian regimes in Eastern Europe. Moreover, they argued, the Yalta agreement itself had been violated, as there had been no free elections in any of the communist satellite countries. The PAC initially worked with Pomost to collect signatures in support of renouncing Yalta. The PAC had adopted resolutions in 1983 and 1984 calling on the U.S. Congress to reexamine and renounce the Yalta agreement (*PAC Newsletter*, December 1983; August 1984). However, when it became known that President Reagan and the State Department would not support this campaign, the PAC withdrew its support. Jerzy Lerski, a prominent World War II émigré and PAC director, wrote, "Polish V.I.P.'s are simply afraid to raise this issue [renouncing Yalta] without the blessing, which seems rather unlikely, of the State Department" (Lerski 1983, 2). The PAC took the position, in agreement with the State Department, that the Yalta Treaty need not be renounced, but that its program of free elections should be enforced. Pomost, however, continued to lobby the U.S. Senate to adopt a resolution to renounce Yalta, which it eventually did in a very watered-down version.[7]

7. In 1984, Pomost enlisted the help of Congressman Tom Corcoran who was running as a Republican for an Illinois Senate seat. Corcoran agreed to support the Yalta proposal, and in return Pomost supported his Senatorial bid. Pomost wrote the resolution that called for Congress formally to renounce the Yalta Treaty and Corcoran introduced it as Resolution 435

Pomost never claimed to represent Polish Americans in the United States; it claimed to be the "voice of *Solidarność* in the West" (Zmuda 1982, 51). In a letter from Pomost member Adam Kiernik to Krynski on April 4, 1984, he claimed that Pomost was "Poland's best and truest representative in the Western World." Even though Pomost claimed to be Poland's and not Polonia's representative, in the process of trying to create a new lobby it stepped on the toes of the established organization. Pomost's attempts to secure recognition as being a viable alternative to the voice of the PAC placed them in a competitive relationship with the established organization. The two lobbying organizations competed for resources—resources that were not as easily divisible as money—such as the attention of influential American officials. This difficulty sharing resources was exacerbated by the fact that the organizations had different interpretations about what kind of lobby there should be.

It was not only Pomost's attempts to start a new lobby that antagonized the PAC, but also that in trying to justify the need for a new lobby, the Pomost leaders attacked the PAC for what they called (and tried to convince others of) an ineffective track record. Several articles in the Pomost quarterly criticized the present Polish American lobby (Kiernik 1984; Rurasz 1984). The executive director of the PAC Illinois Division said she used to receive ten- or fifteen-page letters from Pomost criticizing the PAC's lobby. A national vice-president of the PAC said that attempts to work together with Pomost came to naught because Pomost leaders "came to the conclusion that Polonia organizations, Polish American Congress and other Polonia organizations are no good; and that they will set up their own organization to lead." On November 30, 1983, Krynski wrote to Pomost president Rac that Polish Americans "deserve a better leader than such an irresponsible person as Mazewski. . . . We should call on the members of the PAC to write letters demanding the resignation of Mazewski." Pomost's biting remarks about the incompetence of PAC leaders (one Pomost member referred to it as "spitting" at them) placed them in an antagonistic relationship. It was not just the lobbying efforts that threatened the PAC, it

in the House of Representatives at the first session of the 98th Congress, in 1983. Corcoran lost the Senate race, but other Congressmen supported the bill. In 1985, Representative Jack Kemp and Senator Robert Kasten sponsored a resolution that was approved by both houses. The resolution did not renounce Yalta, but asked that the provisions of Yalta (free elections, the right to self-determination) be met (see *Pomost Quarterly* from 1983 through 1985 for continuous discussion of this issue).

was the aggressive lobbying style, the public criticism, and the unwillingness to subordinate themselves to the PAC that caused the breakdown in
relations.

In contrast to Pomost, another new organization, Studium North American Center for the Study of Polish Affairs (Studium), was involved in
independent lobbying activities yet still cooperated with the PAC. This was
possible for several reasons. First, Studium joined the PAC immediately,
something Pomost never did. Second, though the task of Studium was
ultimately to help Poland, their leaders chose to accomplish this task by
subordinating their organization to the PAC. Unlike Pomost, Studium
recognized the authority of the PAC. The chairman of Studium from
1976–87 said, "The PAC is the leading and authoritative body representing
the interests of organized Polonia in the U.S. One of the Studium's
functions is to serve the Polish American Congress, providing it with advice
and responding to its requests for assistance in the preparation of memoranda" (*Studium Papers*, October 1987, 76). Third, although Studium disagreed with particular PAC policies, it did not publicly criticize PAC or its
leaders for being inept. One Studium leader told me that if they disagreed
with the policy they attacked the particular policy statement instead of the
leaders. Because of this attitude, Studium successfully worked together with
the PAC.

Whether or not the PAC lobby was effective, most of Polonia still
recognized the PAC as the representative of Poland's and Polonia's voice in
America. The PAC lobby was in a sense, a convention; and once a convention is established, members of the group have the right to sanction those
who violate that convention (Hardin 1982, 177). Pomost broke a customary
practice by publicly attacking the PAC. Moreover, many Polonians felt that
an attack on the PAC was an attack on Polonia itself. A World War II émigré,
and member of the PAC, told me, "See, the Polish American Congress is
like my home. If somebody comes to my home he should show enough
courtesy to behave properly in my own place, otherwise I would kick him
out. They [the PAC] are the hosts here, they were here first. They have to
have some respect. These young people don't even speak English yet, but
they are kicking these old peoples' butts." Apparent in this man's quote is
the fact that Pomost members were newcomers ("they don't even speak
English yet") and therefore had no right to attack an established organization. In addition, the symbolic meaning of the language of "hosts and
guests" underscored the proprietary feelings of the Polish Americans and

some of the World War II émigrés. One émigré, a national PAC director
said:

> Pomost had people who, when they came [to America] they were
> educated, they were much more advanced [than Polish Americans].
> But [Pomost] did not want to recognize anybody from the Polish
> American Congress. People in the Polish American Congress
> couldn't be ignored, although they were maybe not such intellectual
> people. . . . Some of these people they're simple folk, but they are
> participating, they're doing their best. And because Pomost wanted
> to push them away, they said, "No I'm not going to give it away. I've
> been here thirty years, and just because I don't know how to write
> articles like the people in Pomost doesn't mean that I have to just
> be pushed outside."

PAC leaders felt that Pomost was trying to usurp their authority. They
defended their right to lead Polonia not based on merit or leadership skills
but on the fact that they were already there—the PAC and Polish Americans were established, and that gave them more power in the community.

The hostile strategy of Pomost put the PAC on the defensive. PAC leaders
defined Pomost's lobbying campaign as "counterproductive." PAC vice-
president Lukomski wrote a memo to the PAC National Directors on July
31, 1986, titled, "Pomost—A Disruptive Force in American Polonia."

> Over the past several years, Pomost has waged an aggressive cam-
> paign to foment dissension within the Polish American community,
> and undermine the credibility of the Polish American Congress as its
> broad, national representative. . . . While we recognize Pomost's
> right (in a free, pluralistic society) to pursue its own objectives, we
> feel that the appearance of token support which Pomost claims from
> the conservative elements of the administration and members of the
> U.S. Congress could be politically counterproductive by creating
> divisiveness, resentment and backlash within the main body of the
> Polish American community. (Lukomski 1986, 1)

If the complaints against the PAC were valid, then the leaders of the PAC
stood to lose some of their authority, or the PAC could have been forced to
change its structure, policy or strategies. It cost the PAC less to repress

Pomost than to bargain with them. Once Pomost began attacking it, the PAC withdrew any resources it had shared with the new organization. The most important resource the PAC had given Pomost was legitimacy. The PAC not only withdrew its legitimacy-conferring actions, it also set out to discredit the new organization. The PAC dubbed Pomost a radical fringe group, claiming it represented only a minority opinion in Polonia. In the previously mentioned memo Lukomski wrote, "Pomost represents a marginal constituency, basically limited to groups of fairly recent immigrants holding extreme right-wing positions regarding both the domestic and foreign policy issues, far removed from the thinking of mainstream Polish Americans and their responsible leaders." Pomost members were being redefined as "young turks" compared to the stalwart, responsible established Polonian leaders.

Pomost became the pariah of Polonia. Pomost member Marek Laas wrote to Krynski on September 21, 1983, describing a meeting he attended in Washington where he met a woman who was "aghast" when she learned that Laas represented Pomost. She pronounced "loudly" that she "represented the PAC" and walked away. By the late 1980s the PAC leaders acted as if Pomost had not existed, some claiming they knew nothing of the group. When I asked Pucinski, the president of the Illinois Division about Pomost he said, "I don't know who they are, I just don't know those people," even though two of Pomost's founders had been his vice presidents from 1980 to 1982. In Donald Pienkos book about Polonia's work for Poland (1991), the only mention of Pomost in over six hundred pages is in a footnote on page 540, that describes Pomost as being critical of PAC president Mazewski. Pomost challenged the PAC and lost. When the new organization presented an opposing policy and worked outside of the conventions of Polonia (that is, outside of the PAC), then they were defined as a counterforce, as a marginal constituency, and eventually dismissed altogether.

The conflict between Pomost and the PAC negatively affected solidarity between other new immigrants and Polish Americans. In 1984–85, when Freedom and Brotherhood were forming, Pomost was in ugly battle with the PAC. Polish Americans and World War II émigrés became increasingly suspicious of new immigrants. Brotherhood leader Cholodecki said, "We were identified with groups that automatically assumed that 'the old Polonia' were traitors. Mazewski stated many times that 'the young' are doing anti-Polish work here" (Krajewski 1989, 38). The new organizations made an effort to show the PAC that they wanted to work together and that they respected the position of the established leaders. Despite the initial wariness, the PAC eventually did work with them. Perhaps Pomost's extremism helped Brotherhood and Freedom once the PAC could be assured that the moderates were indeed moderates. The PAC still needed immigrants to help organize its political activities for Poland. While Freedom and Brotherhood members were not as docile and agreeable as the PAC would have preferred, still they were certainly not as aggressive and insulting in their behavior as Pomost members had become.

Brotherhood and Freedom did not compete with the PAC nor did it challenge its representative authority. Freedom and Brotherhood mostly wanted to raise money for the opposition. They did not engage in lobbying activities. Freedom leaders said that lobbying and national political activities were "not our sphere. Helping the underground is our only goal." Though Freedom did initiate petitions and send letters to officials, it did not see this as lobbying activity. Brotherhood, as an organization, also did not aspire to become a lobbying organization. Its main goal was to unite Solidarity refugees in emigration and send financial help to the underground. The limited nature of these new organizations' goals made it difficult for PAC leaders to reject them. In the first newsletter of Brotherhood, one of the leaders wrote that the organization's goal of sending "material-technical aid to the underground" was so "simple and transparent" that it had to be accepted "by everyone who is against the communist domination of Poland." Both organizations remained small with narrowly defined agendas which minimized the threat that the new organizations wanted to take over the representative role of the PAC.[8]

Perhaps more important, neither Brotherhood nor Freedom, as organizations, publicly attacked or criticized the PAC (even though many of their members disagreed with PAC policies and perceived PAC leaders to be incompetent). Freedom leaders did not consider it their place to advise or comment on PAC's relations with the State Department or the U.S. Congress. Freedom leaders believed that new organizations should cooperate with the PAC because it was older, larger and more reputable. They believed

8. One member of Brotherhood expressed the opinion that even though the PAC was a weak lobbying organization, the PAC should be supported because "it is larger, and smaller organizations have even less chance of being heard." In addition, most of the members of these organizations were not American citizens, and few were fluent in English. Pomost leaders had been in the United States longer than Freedom or Brotherhood leaders, many of them were citizens and did speak English. Moreover, Pomost included several young, outspoken Polish Americans. Pomost had a better chance of becoming a lobbying organization than did either Freedom or Brotherhood.

that attacks on the PAC only hurt Freedom's efforts to collect money for the Polish opposition. In 1989, Freedom had a radio program for a few months whose announcer, a volunteer and non-Freedom member, verbally criticized the PAC on the air. Freedom canceled the radio program because the announcer violated an organizational stipulation that maintained that "on the radio there may be no attacks whatsoever on the Polonia independence organizations, and in particular, on the PAC and its leaders," and publicly apologized for the offensive remarks (*Dziennik Związkowy* 1989c, 3). This "no-attack" policy was written into their bylaws.

Although Brotherhood as an organization often disagreed with the policies of the PAC, they never did so publicly. Between 1985 and 1989, Brotherhood preferred harmony to conflict. Hubert Romanowski, a Brotherhood leader said, "Why fight with another organization? That's just stupid. . . . State your view that Poland has to be independent, but don't fight with another organization. Fight only with arguments, not with people in another organization." In January 1987, Brotherhood and the PAC held a "conference of reconciliation." A press release written for the conference states, "For much too long we have observed with regret the relations between Poles who immigrated to the U.S. before and shortly after World War II and those who have come since Solidarity and martial law. Each group has treated the other as if they weren't true Poles." At the meeting, leaders from both groups signed an "accord to work together." This public statement of intent to cooperate stands in marked contrast to the bared-teeth antagonism of the late Pomost-PAC era. Brotherhood, as an organization, did not compete with the PAC for authority. They recognized PAC's dominant position in Poland, and reasoned the best strategy was to try and work together peaceably. Cholodecki said, "They are natives here whose voices every administrator takes seriously. And they are the only ones who . . . can open many doors for us. We could open them ourselves, but then we put ourselves at risk of old Polonia closing them in our faces out of fear of losing their monopoly" (Krajewski 1989, 41). Although some Brotherhood leaders (particularly Cholodecki) eventually engaged in rancorous fights with PAC leaders in the early 1990s, Brotherhood the organization did not. Brotherhood purposely stayed away from butting heads with the PAC. It saw the PAC as potentially useful as an ally, and as potentially dangerous as an enemy.

As established members of the community, the Polish Americans and their organizations felt that they should be the "voice" of Polonia. The new immigrants, however, often felt that as recent arrivals from Poland they were in the best position to speak for Poland. The struggle for ownership of the community (that is, the right to speak for Poland and Polonia), was often played out in the political arena as the groups debated the issue of the Polish lobby in America. Cooperation could be maintained, as it was with Brotherhood and Freedom, when the new organization did not challenge the established ethnics representative authority. When a new organization competed with the PAC for the right to define the situation and represent Poland's interests (as did Pomost), the new and established organizations competed for power. When this happened, the PAC, the larger and more established organization, won.

The Problem of Leadership

While Freedom and Brotherhood did not publicly attack Polonian leaders and their organizations, new immigrants were generally displeased with the leadership of established Polonia. New immigrants did not respect Polonian leaders whom they perceived as uneducated and ineffective. Upon arrival, many were dismayed when they found how politically weak the Polish American community was in America, often comparing it unfavorably to the Greek and Jewish communities. In the 1980s, there were no chairs of Polish literature or Polish studies at major universities, no national and few local Polish American leaders, and Polish Americans who had become successful in business often were no longer part of the ethnic community. One immigrant described the two opening speakers at a symposium on Polish-Jewish relations:

> In all my whole life I will never forget this experience, it was really something. The Poles represented the lowest possible standard of ability to communicate, to persuade others. It was really embarrassing. First Mr. Moskal [the PAC president] spoke, and he said a few jokes and that was it. Then Mr. Silverman [representing the Jewish American community], a very educated man, very good speaker spoke for thirty minutes, a prepared speech where he made some very good points and clear suggestions. It was really something, we are represented by such low standards.

One continual criticism was the low level of education of the Polonian leaders. As mentioned, the new immigrants believed they were of a higher status than the Polish American ethnics, and this was in part related to educational levels. While over a third of the Polish American population has some postsecondary education (Lieberson and Waters 1988, 107–8), immigrant perceptions of Polish Americans were strongly influenced not by the invisible Americans of Polish descent who had integrated into America's middle class, but by the visible Polish American ethnic leaders. Leaders at the helm of these large Polonian organizations were not the most educated members of the community. In 1983, only five of the thirty-five candidates for "the seventeen highest national offices" in the PNA had some college experience (Pienkos 1984, 462). Among the twelve candidates for PAC presidency described in an article in the *Dziennik Związkowy* (October 5, 1988, p. 5) only four indicated any postsecondary education. Three listed their professions as clerical personnel, and Edward Moskal, who won the election, specialized in "fixed sales." As the man quoted earlier who was defending the established leaders said, they were "maybe not such intellectual people . . . they are simple folk."

A second criticism of the PAC leaders centered on the fact that the president of the PNA fraternal has always simultaneously been the PAC president (mostly because the PNA provided the majority of money and members to the PAC and the PAC could not financially support itself). The new immigrants were not interested in these fraternal organizations, which focused mostly on promoting ethnic culture and selling insurance. The new immigrants (and many World War II émigrés) thought it unwise for the head of a fraternal insurance company to be the leader of the political wing of Polonia. One new immigrant said: "The fraternals are not effective anymore. They didn't provide us with appropriate leadership, simply. And because the PAC is based on the fraternals it's ineffective." Another woman, also a new immigrant said about Moskal, "He is a good chief of insurance, but I don't know if he is a good chief of Polonia." Another suggested "changing the rules of the game" and separating the PNA from the PAC, so that "when the PAC president will be above this fraternal organization he will be more influential."

In one scathing commentary on the Polish American community printed in a Polish-language magazine in Chicago, Maciech Wierzynski, a new immigrant, wrote that, in the Polish community, "stupidity is rampant. There is a lack of people who are able to speak intelligently on controversial topics. . . . I repeat, intellectual helplessness is a characteristic trait of

Chicago Polonia and its establishment, especially visible now when the world, Poland, and even Polonia are changing so rapidly" (1989, 11). He gave a similar opinion in an interview published in *Gazeta International* in Poland titled "We Are Simply Better," where "we" referred to the new immigrants. In answer to the question of how Polonia can help Poland, he launched into a criticism of the powerlessness of Polonia.

> You know, they don't have people in the right places, in business, in the media, or in politics. And historically it is because they have not paid enough attention to sending their kids to college. Can you imagine that the president of a Polish-American group only finished high school. So how can he be an effective partner? There are very few effective Polish-Americans. One example is Brzezinski. But I think it's going to change with the most recent influx over the last ten years. They are much better educated, they are upwardly mobile. This makes some Polish-Americans angry and jealous. (1990, 8)

Another immigrant said, "Polonia has no real leaders. This is the problem. . . . You know they have a few stupid college professors, and then almost illiterate guys, like [PAC President], who is, you know, I don't think I could ask him to work for me on the hired position as the maintenance man to clean my desk." And in another published criticism, the author also denigrated the PAC/PNA president by saying: "His qualifications and competence are not high enough for him to perform his duties well . . . his authority and influence and that of the PNA and PAC are declining quickly" (Bereszko 1989, 9).

These types of comments from the new immigrants particularly galled the Polish Americans. They had fought for decades against mainstream America's portrayal of them as "dumb Polaks." Now here was a group of "their own" deriding them with the same stereotype. These attacks undercut the authority of the PAC and, not surprisingly, created tensions within the community.

Conclusion

Conflict between new immigrants and established residents was related to competition for leadership positions in Polonia and representative authority. Blocked from policy-making positions in the organization that billed itself as "the sole representative" of both Polonia and Poland in America, some new immigrants felt their only recourse was to develop a parallel organization that inevitably competed with the PAC. Key issues that produced conflict were opposing strategies and differences in opinion about U.S. foreign policy toward Poland. New immigrants and Polish Americans had different interpretations of what were acceptable relations with Poland. New immigrants were more often against business relations with the Polish regime while some Polish Americans profited from those business deals. Conflict also arose over disagreements about how to protest in the Chicago arena. Since Polish American authority was centered in this arena, when new immigrants went against the wishes of the established leaders they challenged their authority. New immigrants challenged the PAC authority more directly when they engaged in lobbying activity, and offended the leaders most ungraciously when they publicly criticized them.

The established leaders had ownership of the community because of their history—they had been in this country longer and the new immigrants were just that, new. The proprietary feelings of the Polish Americans were reflected in their treatment of the new immigrants as outsiders. Polish Americans were hosts and the new immigrants were but guests in their organizations and community. The structure of the PAC ensured that newcomers would be old-timers by the time they assumed any positions of power in the established organizations. In the end, the asymmetric relation between the two groups gave the established community more power to label rebellious newcomers as a radical fringe. Recognizing the power of the established community, most newcomers did not challenge the old leaders. Yet the newcomers clearly recognized a divide within the community, perceived the Polish American leaders as incompetent, and claimed "we" are simply better.

6

Identity and National Loyalty: The 1989 Election

Economic conditions in Poland declined rapidly throughout the 1980s. A new wave of strikes in May and June of 1988 further crippled the Warsaw regime. Free from the threat of Soviet intervention (the Soviets were occupied with their own crises) and in the spirit of *glasnost* and *perestroika*, the Polish communist government finally sat down with the Solidarity opposition leaders and chartered out a course of social reform in early 1989. The most dramatic result of the February 1989 discussions, known as the roundtable talks, was the agreement to hold partially free elections, the first since World War II. Elections were to be held in June 1989 for a two-house parliament. The upper house senate (which had been disbanded after a rigged referendum in 1946) was restored, and all of its 100 seats were open to free election. In the lower house, 161 of the 460 seats (35 percent) were open to free election; the remaining seats were reserved for members of the Communist Party (that is, the Polish United Worker's Party) and the parties allied with the communists (the United Peasant Party and the Democratic Party). For this reason, the elections were referred to as being only partially free and were treated with some suspicion. Critics felt that the elections were merely a transparent strategy aimed at co-opting members of the opposition into the government to share the responsibility for the economic crisis. They feared that Solidarity was being set up to be the scapegoat for the disastrous economic and ecology conditions in Poland.[1] Despite these criticisms, Poles in Poland, Polish immigrants in America,

---

1. Many opposing the elections did so because the elections were not completely free; the communists and their former allies would control two-thirds of the votes in the lower house, and the lower house could override vetoes of the president or the senate with a two-thirds majority. Other criticisms of the agreements included: (1) the newly created position of President, expected to go to a Communist Party member, was too powerful; (2) the Solidarity union had agreed not to strike during this period, which crippled the union's power.

and Polish Americans were thrilled—if somewhat hesitant—about the partially free elections. Poles abroad would have the opportunity to participate directly through absentee ballots, and, in Chicago, thousands of Poles voted at the Polish consulate on June 3.

The 1989 election laid bare the distinction between foreign-born immigrants and native-born Americans of Polish heritage. The meaningfulness of the hybrid Polish American ethnic identity was diminished in this context. Instead, the salient identities were the political identities of being a Pole or an American. The election forced the issue of national loyalty to the foreground, and both immigrants and ethnics remained loyal to their countries of birth. Most immigrants were still Poles and ethnics were Americans. The "American" identity is a political identity or nationality rather than an ethnic identity (Waters 1990, 53), and negotiations in this arena centered around defining this political identity. Rather than asking who belonged to Polonia or what was the meaning of Polishness, in the spring of 1989, Chicago Polonia was trying to define who was an American and what it meant to be an American. Were Polish immigrants who came to the United States ten years before and had taken U.S. citizenship Americans? Could that American identity tolerate political activity undertaken for another nation? Donating money to help the democratic opposition movement in Poland never challenged one's loyalty to America as could voting in another nation's election.

Polonia's Involvement in the 1989 Election

Although not everyone supported the roundtable agreements and the elections, the Solidarity leaders accepted the challenge to run for the 261 seats open to them. Solidarity placed their campaign in the organizational arm of the Citizens' Committee, a group of 120 public figures who, as an informal advisory council to Lech Walesa, put together a list of 261 candidates. The opposition had only two months to choose candidates, prepare campaign platforms, and disseminate information about who to vote for and how to vote. Dissemination of information was crucial. The Polish government allowed Solidarity candidates limited access to the state-owned media: only thirty minutes of radio air time and thirty minutes of television broadcast time per week (there were no nonstate-owned radio or television channels in Poland at that time). Walesa "called back some of his troops" from abroad, as one new immigrant said, such as political satirist Jacek Federowicz to help with the campaigns. Still, the opposition needed a lot more help, mostly money to buy audiovisual materials and technical equipment. A Brotherhood member who visited Poland during the campaign described what he saw as the needs and problems: "One telephone line that was always busy, no fax machine. They didn't have even a video camera [which] they need to make video clips about the candidates' work and their opinions." Walesa and the Citizens' Committee appealed to Polonia for financial support, and Poles abroad began collecting money for the campaign.

In addition to Polonia's role as the rich Uncle Sam, Poles abroad could also directly participate in the election. The Polish constitution gave Poles abroad the right to vote. In the past, it was usually only consulate staff and other Communist Party devotees who exercised this right. In contrast, in the 1989 election, thousands of Polish citizens voted. The impetus for mobilizing the absentee vote came from political refugees in Chicago and Washington, D.C., rather than from Solidarity leaders in Poland. One refugee explained, "Solidarity in Poland was too concerned with its own problems to worry about Polonia." She was among a group of refugees who had traveled to Poland in the spring of 1989 to meet with Solidarity leaders. She said, "We tried to get them to recognize that Polonia's vote was important because we would be voting the day before they voted in Poland, and we could influence the mood of the election in Poland." The immigrants pressed the Solidarity leaders to sanction their collective efforts. In particular, they wanted Solidarity to provide a certificate that legitimated the authority of the election judges chosen by a group of new immigrants organizing the election in Chicago. In response, Walesa's Citizens' Committee faxed letters giving formal authority to these poll watchers. The Citizens' Committee also made appeals, printed in the Polonian media, asking Poles abroad to vote in the elections. In Chicago, 5,631 Poles voted, and the new immigrants took credit for what they considered to be a large voter turnout. One immigrant said, "It is because of our efforts that six thousand Poles in Chicago voted. Without the TV, press and radio campaign, most of Polonia would have seen the elections as just another communist trick." The results of the election are now known to the world: all but one of Solidarity's 261 candidates won (and the other open senate seat went to an independent candidate). In Chicago, 95 percent of the Polish voters chose Solidarity candidates (Butterini 1989, 1).

Poles and Americans

The two key issues debated in the spring of 1989 were whether to support the election in Poland and whether to support the absentee vote in Chicago. There were three stances in Polonia: (1) those who supported the election in Poland and the absentee vote in Chicago; (2) those who supported the election in Poland but were not involved in the absentee vote; and (3) those who opposed the election in Poland and the vote in Chicago (Table 6.1). The position of each organization was conditioned by which faction of the opposition they supported in Poland and whether their members were primarily Poles or Americans.

Table 6.1 Polonia groups supporting the election in Poland and Chicago

Groups	Support election in Poland	Support absentee vote in Chicago
Brotherhood, Solidarity Election Committee, Fair Elections Committee	Yes 35 percent is better than nothing	Yes Polonia's vote is important
PAC, especially PAC's Solidarity Election Fund	Yes Follow Church and Solidarity	No We are Americans
Freedom, Alliance, Committee on Behalf of Free Elections in Poland, Pomost Polish American Conservative Organization	No We want 100 percent free elections	No We want 100 percent free elections

Support From Immigrants

New immigrants supported both the election in Poland (by sending money and communication equipment) and the absentee vote in Chicago (by mobilizing voters, organizing and supervising the election process, and publicizing the campaigns). Brotherhood leaders endorsed the election immediately and, similar to the way it supported the opposition throughout the 1980s, its members gave money and supplies to local election campaigns rather than the national campaigns. In mid-April, Brotherhood members Jaroslaw Cholodecki and Hubert Romanowski traveled to Poland with money, video and audio equipment, and fax machines and distributed them in their hometowns (Wroclaw and Opole) as well as in Warsaw. The cash came from Brotherhood membership dues. The money for the tape recorders and a shot mike came from a special PAC Solidarity Election Fund, and the money for the fax machines came from two Polish American lawyers. After this initial trip to Poland, Brotherhood's material support for the election was channeled through the PAC Solidarity Election Fund.

In addition to supporting the campaign in Poland, Brotherhood members and other new immigrants organized and mobilized the absentee vote in Chicago through a newly formed organization called the Solidarity Election Committee. This committee was organized by Brotherhood leaders but incorporated new immigrants who previously had not been affiliated with any Polonian organization. This committee nominated ten election judges and two election commissioners to oversee the election in Chicago. All twelve people received individual certificates of approval from the official National Election Commission (*Państwowa Komisjia Wyborcza*) in Warsaw.[2] As mentioned above, these new migrants thought the Chicago vote was important because it would take place one day before the election in Poland. Cholodecki, one of the key organizers of this committee said: "We can make a difference. . . . If there will be a big turnout here in Chicago the day before the elections in Poland, it will be a big incentive for the people [in Poland] who still don't know whether to vote" (Cassel 1989, 8). Strategies for mobilizing voters included teaching Poles how to vote, for whom to vote, and where to vote, in order to ensure that Solidarity candidates got elected.[3] This committee put up campaign posters for

2. In addition to the two election judges and ten commissioners that received certificates of recognition from Warsaw, the president of the PAC nominated four of his own men to be election judges. These PAC-appointed men did not have letters from Solidarity's National Election Commission in Poland confirming their appointment, mostly because they were appointed too late. Yet without these letters, the PAC appointees were seen as less legitimate. One immigrant involved with the Solidarity Election Committee in Chicago said, "Because they had no certificate they were like the consulate workers," which meant that she compared them to the communists in the consulate who were running the election.

3. Voting in the elections was a complicated process. Poles abroad were allowed to vote for the three senate seats in Warsaw. Three of the thirty-two candidates for these seats were Solidarity candidates, and Solidarity instructed Poles to vote for these three. In addition, Poles abroad voted on three additional ballots for seats in the lower house. Poles were instructed to cross off the names of all communist candidates running unopposed (this included the national list of thirty-five candidates and a local list of four candidates), and to vote for the Solidarity candidate running for the *Warszawa Śródmieście* seat (the downtown district of Warsaw). Instructions given by Solidarity's National Election Commission, reprinted in the

Solidarity candidates, passed out campaign buttons, and disseminated information about Solidarity candidates and voting procedures. On election day, members of this committee organized the long lines of people voting, answered questions about how and where to vote, and passed out kielbasa, apples, and tea to people who had been waiting in line to vote for two to four hours. They also raised the Polish flag and hung a *Solidarność* banner across the street from the consulate.

Polish Americans as Americans

Polish Americans and the established ethnic organizations generally did not support the absentee vote in Chicago, and those that did, did so as Americans. Polish Americans were more forthcoming with their support for the elections in Poland than the vote in Chicago, but even then their support was tempered by reservations about the communist government's motives for allowing free elections. As a result, the PAC was guarded and sluggish with its support. After the roundtable agreements in 1989 the PAC published a declaration in the *Dziennik Związkowy* (February 24–25, 1989, 1) with the title, "The Accomplishments of the Agreement in Poland Requires Prudence and Moderation." The prudence and moderation were directives to Polonia—they did not want to hastily support something that may turn out to be a sham. The PAC made numerous statements that the elections were "not fully democratic" and that the roundtable agreements did "not completely fill the aspirations of the Polish nation"; however, it maintained that the partially free elections were a move in the right direction, and gave "its full support and trust to the position represented by Lech Walesa" (PAC 1989a, 1; PAC 1989b, 1).

The announcement of the elections came in February, but the PAC did not begin raising money to support them until late April. Six weeks before the election day, the PAC started its nationwide Solidarity Election Fund campaign. PAC national vice-president Lukomski said the money was "used to organize publicity for the candidates. Mostly it will go for communica-

---

Polish-language press in America, and handed out as instruction flyers at the election told the people exactly how to vote. The instructions explicitly directed the voters to cross off all the Communist Party candidates. It did not say "If you want"; it said "Do it," using the imperative verb form, and also reminded them to use a "horizontal line" in order to make the ballot valid. While voting at the consulate in Chicago, few people used the private voting booths. Many filled out the ballots at open tables in communal activity, helping each other, and referring constantly to the flyers or clipped newspaper articles that had the voting instructions.

tions equipment." PAC state divisions, Polonian organizations, and Polonian radio and newspapers helped disseminate information about the election and raise funds. The PAC Illinois Division raised money for Solidarity to buy "technical resources such as video equipment, tape recorders, tapes, microphones, amplifiers, copiers, paper, etc." (Solidarity Election Committee 1989, 5). The PAC Illinois Division raised $4,500, while the national campaign collected over $100,000. The PAC sent the money to a legitimate organization in Poland (Solidarity's Citizens' Committee) through legitimate channels. The PAC fund only sent money to the national election campaign, which did not require that PAC officials have any particular knowledge about the local candidates or local elections. Both national and Illinois divisions' PAC funds went to mainstream Solidarity, a sensitive point that the PAC defended by saying that it had raised money under the banner of Solidarity, meaning that the money could not go to other independent candidates. Roman Pucinski, president of the Illinois Division, said that since the appeal was for "Funds for Solidarity," the PAC was restricted in dispersing the money, "so [Leszek] Moczulski [leader of Confederation for an Independent Poland] could not get help because it would be a breach of contract with the people. We told them this was for Walesa and Solidarity."

The PAC was not overzealous in its support. In fact, Pucinski said that the fundraising was reserved: "We could have sent a lot more money but we wanted to be very careful. . . . We did not want to do anything that would give the [Polish] regime an excuse for hollering foul" (Cassel 1989, 8). PAC's prudence was in alignment with the U.S. State Department's attitude of supporting Poland's move toward democracy with broad gentle strokes, without becoming too involved in determining who the specific players would be. The United States was cautious about this first election. Poland was the first country to break away from the Soviet bloc. PAC leaders had the same thoughts. They gave some support to the general election but had a clear "wait-and-see" attitude.

While the PAC eventually supported the elections in Poland, it did not take any significant action to support the vote in Chicago. No PAC leaders came to the consulate on election day except Pucinski, who was also a Chicago alderman, who was there only for a few minutes in the evening talking to reporters. The PAC was basically indifferent to the absentee vote in Chicago. The PAC waited until the eve of the election to make a statement encouraging Poles abroad who were not U.S. citizens to vote.

This appeal was framed in a quote by Walesa, with a reference to the Roman Catholic Church, removing PAC responsibility for the endorsement.

> We are aware that these elections will not be completely free and democratic, and that they will not fulfill the hopes and desires of the Polish society. . . . The elections, however, were accepted by the legitimate representative of the Polish society, which in our understanding is Solidarity. . . . We think that it is not our responsibility nor our right to teach Polish society how they should achieve their primary goals. . . . The role of Polonia is limited to supporting the Polish society in their efforts to achieve their goals. . . .
>
> In the appeal on May 3d, Lech Walesa wrote: "The Polish nation is one—those in the country and those living outside its borders. In the name of this unity, in the name of shared concerns for the Fatherland, I summon all Poles living abroad to participate in the elections of 1989." . . .
>
> Also, the religious leaders (*Prymasowska Rada Społeczna*) summon Catholics to participate in the elections. Because of this the Polish American Congress acknowledges that it is our duty to show solidarity with the Polish society and to give support for the election. For this purpose the Solidarity Election Fund was established. To show our moral support for the Polish society we appeal to all Poles in the United States who have the right to vote to participate in the elections and support the candidates for the Senate and Sejm proposed by the Solidarity Citizens' Committee. (PAC 1989d, 1)

For the PAC, the legitimate institutions in Poland were still Solidarity (specifically Walesa's branch of the opposition) and the Roman Catholic Church. The PAC claimed that it was "limited to supporting" not directing changes in Poland, and offered this as a justification for not doing more. Furthermore, during the 1989 election the fraternal organizations chose to emphasize the business rather than ethnic nature of their organizations. The president of the PNA, Edward Moskal, said, "We can't get directly involved in the political process, even in the U.S., because we are a not-for-profit life insurance company" (Yuenger 1989, 3).

The main reason, however, for the Polish Americans' disinterested stance was that the "right" to participate in the elections was determined by who was a Pole and who was an American. The umbrella identity was split in half—each person was forced to choose one or the other side. Ethnics defined themselves as Americans. The PAC's attitude toward the absentee vote can be summed up in its statement, "As American Polonia we don't have the opportunity to participate in the elections, [but we do] have the opportunity to demonstrate our belief and support in the elections" (PAC 1989c, 1). On the eve of the election PAC vice-president Lukomski said on Cholodecki's radio program that the reason the PAC statement came out so late and was not very strong was "because basically the PAC is an American organization. So there was a problem if they should support such a political situation, which concerns only Poland, not Polish Americans." He continued by saying it was obvious that the PAC supported the elections, because of the money it had raised, but, as Americans, they could not become involved in the absentee vote. Forced to choose, Polish Americans defined themselves as Americans first.

Even Polish Americans involved in helping the absentee vote in Chicago framed their concern as Americans; they were Americans dedicated toward advancing democracy and capitalism, not Americans participating in another country's election. Two Polish American lawyers, Lawrence Leck and Tom Gobby, founded Fair Elections in Poland, Inc. In a letter sent to potential supporters, the Fair Elections president, Tom Gobby, stressed that the elections were Poland's first step toward a free market system, and for this reason they should be supported: "Fair Elections in Poland, Inc., was formed to promote and encourage fair and free elections as well as business and economic development in Poland by American citizens. . . . In short, economic progress is not possible without political progress." The Polish Americans acted publicly as "American citizens" not as Polish Americans. Fair Elections in Poland, Inc., raised money for the Solidarity campaign in Poland and disseminated information to the American public about the elections.[4] They supported the elections as Americans, however. At a fund raising booth in downtown Chicago a Polish American women was questioning Tom Gobby about the need for another organization. The women said that she had heard the PAC was sending a quarter of a million dollars

4. Fair Elections made appeals for funds to run the campaigns of Solidarity-backed candidates. The funds they collected were transmitted directly to an official foreign exchange account of the Citizens' Committee of Solidarity in Warsaw. The account was opened with the approval of the Polish government. The funds sent to Solidarity were used to produce video presentations, print election newspapers and campaign literature as well as distribute these materials, and pay support staff. Fair Elections also supported the elections in Chicago by providing shuttle buses to transport voters from the Polish neighborhoods in Chicago to the consulate on election day.

to Poland for the election and she wanted to know why Fair Elections was duplicating the service.

POLISH AMERICAN: Why are you doing this too, isn't one enough? I'm worried that all this money isn't going to get there. . . . Why don't you just have one collection? Who runs this organization?

GOBBY: (pointing to a brochure he reads the names of Polish émigrés on the Honorary Committee) Kolakowski, Milosz, Brzezinski—

POLISH AMERICAN: Never heard of them. And this president, Gobby, what kind of name is Gobby. Is that Polish?

PRESIDENT: *Ma'am, it has nothing to do with Poles, it has to do with helping Poland. We all want to help further democracy.* We're sending the money directly to the *Komitet Obywatelski*, the Citizens' Committee. There is enough need to have several groups collecting. Believe me they need all the help they can get.

A Polish American involved in Poland defined his or her activity as an American: "It has nothing to do with Poles" and a lot to do with "democracy." Even when Polish Americans acted on their sentimental ties to the ancestral homeland by becoming involved in homeland politics, they did so as Americans. Their ethnic identity did not challenge their political identity as Americans.

Cohorts United Against the Election

A group of people in Poland and Polonia opposed the 1989 election. In Polonia this group included Polish Americans, World War II émigrés, and new immigrants. They were against the elections because not all of the seats were open to free elections, and because they feared that the elections were a communist ploy to shift responsibility for Poland's economic problems to the opposition. They believed the 1989 agreement to hold partially free elections only partially fulfilled the stipulations of the Yalta accord. Freedom and other political organizations of new immigrants, such as Alliance for Independence (Alliance), conceded that the elections were a step in the right direction but argued for 100 percent free elections. Along with these Chicago groups, other new immigrants across America as well as a number of World War II émigrés opposed the elections.[5] One circle of the World War II veterans' organization, the Association of Polish Combatants, referred to the roundtable agreements as a strategy of co-optation, and urged the PAC to challenge Walesa's acceptance of only 35 percent open seats in the lower house and "demand full, democratic elections" (Declaration 1989, 3). These World War II émigrés joined forces with new immigrants in Freedom and Alliance to oppose the elections. In diplomatically worded public statements they applauded the steps toward freedom but argued that it was not enough.

The election dissenters created the Committee on Behalf of Free Elections in Poland, demanding "free, democratic and nonfalsified elections in Poland" (*Dziennik Związkowy* 1989a, 3). This committee included representatives from Polonia (leaders from Freedom, Alliance, and World War II veteran organizations) and Poland (leaders from Confederation for an Independent Poland and Fighting Solidarity). Just as Freedom and Alliance had monetarily supported these more uncompromising opposition groups in the past, they now supported their opposition to the elections. The Committee on Behalf of Free Elections in Poland sent a petition to the U.S. Congress urging its members to press the Polish government into holding completely free elections. They collected petition signatures outside churches, at Polonian meetings, and at Polish American parades. At the 1989 May 3d Polish parade in Chicago, their placards read, "Democracy not Bargains: Free Elections." Confederation for an Independent Poland and Fighting Solidarity eventually reversed their original protest against the elections and later some of their officials even ran for office.[6] As a result,

5. Several immigrants in northern California objected to the elections. One man debated whether the free seats represented a democratic choice when there was "your forty-year enemy on one side, and then those who oppose it all from one party. Of course you have to choose the other, and this again is not like free choice." Members of an organization known as "Americans for an Independent Poland" also expressed this point. One man was skeptical that the elections represented reform.

> Once all the smoke settles, the regime hopes to continue to reside firmly in the seat of power (with an air of legitimacy hitherto unknown), the discredited Solidarity will be unwittingly co-opted to blame for the economic ruin, the population will lose its heroes, and the West will loosen its purse strings to let billions of dollars trek east to be gobbled up by mankind's most inefficient and inhuman system. (Kruczkowski 1989, 6)

6. Despite its criticism of the roundtable talks and agreements, Confederation for an Independent Poland announced support for the elections in late April. It stated that although "these elections will not be free" Confederation for an Independent Poland had decided to take part because "we want confrontational elections with the government and not confron-

Freedom members, to use their own words, "privately boycotted" the elections in Chicago (they refused to participate but they also did not engage in a public display of protest).

While most of the opposition to the elections was expressed in a stance of nonaction, some groups and people actively discouraged voters. One Alliance leader announced on his radio program that *wakacjusze* who had overextended their visa (and thus were eligible for deportation) ran the risk of having their names reported to the U.S. Immigration and Naturalization Service if they voted. On election day in Chicago a dozen men picketed in front of the consulate in Chicago. One placard of a World War II émigré read, "Welcome to KGB HDQTRS" on one side (in English), and on the other side, "*Całe ZOMO głosuje, i ty też*" ("All of Zomo is voting, and you, too"—ZOMO was the hated military police reserves in Poland). One Polish American heckled the voters while handing out flyers listing his objections to the election. This protest at the consulate was led by members of the renamed Pomost, the Pomost Polish American Conservative Organization. None of the former Pomost members were in this group. Pomost had become a haven for extreme radical anticommunists in Polonia, including new immigrants, World War II émigrés, and Polish Americans. Despite the new faces, Pomost's message was still the same: "There can be no co-existing with communism. . . . [Communism] cannot be altered, modified, subdued or controlled" (*Głos Niezależnych*, 1989, 3). The most vociferous complaint from this group was that the elections represented compromise. Like the nineteenth-century Polish Romanticists, this group wanted total and complete liberation.

National Loyalty and Ethnic Identity

Throughout the campaign there was a continual need to define who *could* vote and who *should* vote. According to Poland's constitution, anyone born in Poland or who at any point in their life had had a Polish passport could vote. Even Poles who had become American citizens could legally vote, according to the Polish constitution. It was never absolutely clear, however,

---

tational elections with Solidarity" (*Dziennik Związkowy*, 1989b, 5). Fighting Solidarity also initially boycotted the elections but then some of its members ran for offices.

whether Poles who had become American citizens could, under U.S. law, vote in Poland's elections, yet there was some evidence to support such voting. Shortly before the elections, information appeared in the Polonian media indicating that, in 1967, the United States had approved the right for American citizens with Israeli citizenship to vote in the Israeli elections. Polonia leaders like Jan Nowak and Zbigniew Brzezinski also made statements confirming that Poles with American citizenship could vote, though neither said they "should" vote.

The quarrelsome issue of whether Polish immigrants who had taken American citizenship should vote was phrased as a question of loyalty: Was voting in a Polish election an act of disloyalty to one's American citizenship? PAC leaders adopted the stance that people should not vote if they were American citizens. (According to PAC bylaws, all elected PAC officials must be American citizens, so no PAC official was supposed to vote.) The PAC declared: "According to American law, persons with U.S. citizenship should not vote because that is what they agreed to when they accepted American citizenship" (PAC, 1989c). The PAC Illinois Division president said, "We considered that [voting] would have put a dent in their oath of loyalty."

The World War II émigrés most often found themselves in this betwixt and between position of being both native-born Poles (they could vote) and U.S. citizens (should they vote?). When forced to choose, most World War II émigrés defined themselves as Americans. Kazimierz Lukomski, a World War II émigré and member of the PAC board of directors, said on Cholodecki's radio program on election eve, "I don't expect people from my emigrant generation to take part in the elections. . . . They would not go to vote because well, well, well, we are Americans. So we cannot vote." No other event in this study forced immigrants to choose one political loyalty over the other the way that the absentee vote did. The World War II émigrés had lived in the United States for several decades, many had taken American citizenship, and thus the divisions between ethnic and immigrant were less distinct. In her study of World War II émigrés, Mostwin found that within a decade or two after arrival émigrés had a strong political attachment to America. One émigré wrote, "I myself feel Polish and so does my wife and so do my children (born abroad). As far as citizenship is concerned though, we feel 100 percent American, we vote, we take active part in political life, we argue with our American friends about the necessity to support the government or Nixon's policies" (Mostwin 1971, 341). By the late 1980s, their American roots were even deeper. As a result, most World

War II émigrés did not participate in the elections. While clearly still interested in the politics of the homeland, they defined their primary political identity as being American.

Recent arrivals and *wakacjusze* were least conflicted over whether they should vote because many were not American citizens. First, people must be permanent residents for five years before they can apply for citizenship. Second, the *wakacjusze* were not permanent residents and so could not become U.S. citizens. Third, many still expected to return to Poland. Other new immigrants, however, had become citizens and were torn over loyalty issues. Even some of those organizing the vote in Chicago were uncertain whether they themselves should vote, because voting was seen as a challenge to their oath of loyalty to the United States. Poles who worked for American governmental officials were advised not to be involved in the elections in Chicago. One immigrant withdrew from being an election judge for this reason. She said, "I feel very bad about it. It's very difficult. I want to show my support for Solidarity, but I have my job to think about. They don't want me to be so visible. I can't be having my name in the paper. They say it just doesn't look good." Before the election I asked one of the leaders of the Solidarity Election Committee who had just become a U.S. citizen if he would vote and he said, "That's a private question. I don't know."

There was also some hesitation about voting at the Polish consulate. Since World War II, the consul general represented a Polish communist regime and the consulate figuratively "sits on Polish soil." Many World War II émigrés considered going to the consulate to be tantamount to returning to Polish soil, and they had vowed never to return to Poland while it was under communist rule. Also, some new immigrants were struck by the contradiction of voting at a place in front of which they had previously protested. In fact, some worried that the policy of allowing Poles abroad to vote was a scheme being used by the communist regime to help legitimate the consulate in the eyes of Poles abroad. One leader of Brotherhood said, "For the first time they see the consulate as a real thing, not only a nest of spies but a place that Poles go to vote, a legitimate institution for Poles by Poles."

In addition, those factions that were ideologically against the elections in Poland tried to discourage participation by spreading rumors in Polonia about the repercussions from voting. One rumor was that voting would jeopardize one's present status as a U.S. citizen, or would ruin one's chances to become a U.S. citizen. A second rumor was that temporary migrants on overextended visas (invalid visas) would be turned over to the U.S. Immigration and Naturalization Service (INS) to be deported. A third rumor was that those eligible for permanent residency because of the 1986 Immigration Reform and Control Act (IRCA) would lose their eligibility if they voted. The PAC made public statements to dispel only the second and third rumors, and did not address the rumor about the danger to U.S. citizenship. Representatives of the PAC were uncertain about the legal issues and really did think that there was a moral question about U.S. loyalty. One Polish journalist, a new immigrant, wrote that because of these rumors, "a political discussion of the election was substituted by an exchange of statements such as whether to be scared or not, and if to fear, who to fear, the KGB, the FBI or the INS" (Wierzynski 1989, 11).

Whether it was the rumor of jeopardizing one's American citizenship, or the sincere belief that American citizens should not vote, only a few American citizens voted. In my survey of 464 voters (8.2 percent) at the Polish consulate on the day of the election, only 17 of the voters were U.S. citizens.[7] The voters also tended to be recent arrivals (90 percent of the voters surveyed had arrived in the United States after 1978, and over 60 percent after 1984). The voters were pretty evenly divided between permanent and temporary residents. There was also a relation between legal status and length of time in the United States. The longer immigrants were in the United States, the more likely they were to have a permanent legal status: 97 percent of those who came before 1982 had permanent legal status (as citizens or permanent residents) compared to only 20 percent of those who arrived after 1985 (Table 6.2). The relation between length of time in the United States and legal status can be accounted for in part by the fact that some legal statuses require a certain period of residency (for example, citizenship requires five years of permanent residency). In other cases, having been in the United States for a longer period allowed people to gain permanent residency by the IRCA amnesty act of 1986. Finally, since most temporary visas are only valid for a few years, one would expect the majority of those with legal temporary visas to have come fairly recently, as was the case. In fact, year of arrival and legal status may be measuring almost the same thing, which could be defined as strength of ties to America.

---

7. The voters in the sample ranged in ages from eighteen to eighty-five years old, with 57 percent of the voters in the thirty to forty-nine year range. The majority of the voters were men (67.5 percent). The voters resided mostly in Chicago: 98 percent of the sample lived in the Chicago metropolitan area, and 77 percent lived within the city limits. The other respondents were from Wisconsin or Indiana.

Those Poles who were less attached to the United States, as evident by temporary resident status and recent arrival, were more likely to have voted.

Table 6.2   Relation between year of arrival and legal status

Year of Arrival in U.S.		Percent U.S. Citizens	Percent Permanent Residents	Percent Temporary Residents
	N	(17)	(226)	(217)
before 1982	135	12.6	84.4	3.0
1982–85	106	0	62.3	37.7
1986–89	217	0	20.3	79.7

Note: Temporary residents include people with both valid and invalid visas. More than half of those with temporary visas admitted to having overextended (invalid) visas.

Another measure of nonpermanent attachment or weak ties to the United States was the high percentage of voters (65 percent) who said they planned to return to Poland. Only 4 percent of the voters said they did not plan to return, a low percentage in comparison to the other samples of Polish newcomers (see Appendix, Table A.2).

In summary, the opinion of the established Polonian leaders that American citizens should not vote, coupled with the data on who did vote, show that the election in Chicago was an event for new Polish immigrants. Not only did the established community remove itself from the election arena in Chicago, it also correctly assessed (and perhaps influenced) the general feeling among members of the community that those Poles who had lived in the United States for more than a decade, and especially those who had taken U.S. citizenship, should not be participants in Poland's national election. The event was for new immigrants—not ethnics—because ethnics were Americans. And the immigrants who did participate had weak ties to America, as indicated by their noncitizenship, short length of time, and desire to return to Poland.

Conclusion: Power and Legitimacy

The relatively minimal conflict between immigrants and ethnics during the election was a result of the fact that the two main identities were Pole and American. The fuzzy category of ethnicity that created the potential for an overarching identity was not salient. While immigrants and ethnics both supported the election by raising funds, they did not compete for leadership rights in the Chicago arena. For the most part, Polish Americans were defined out of the election arena in Chicago because they were Americans. The PAC, then, was not a potential player in this arena. In the vacuum left by the absence of the PAC, new organizations and immigrants had a chance to gain some prestige without stepping on the toes of the established organization.

The new immigrants gained significant exposure and legitimacy through having organized the absentee vote in Chicago. Cholodecki aptly explained the changes.

> You know, Mary, you work and you work and then someday it all begins to pay off. For five years I was working and no one noticed. I was trying to organize, making a hundred calls a day, keeping contacts, the lines open, all the small stuff with no big achievement, and now it all happens. . . . Since around the spring [the election period], people are calling, I'm on TV, in the magazines, on the radio.

The new immigrants emerged as leaders of new Polonia with local endorsement, international Polish approval, and national political and media recognition.

First, the strong support for the election morally won the new immigrant leaders the support of new Polonia. The fundraising and campaigning for Solidarity candidates gave them publicity. The Polish cable television station in Chicago followed the Solidarity Election Committee, filming its activities and people. The Committee members' appointments as election judges and election commissioners gave them legitimacy. Because the Solidarity candidates did win by a landslide, those who supported the elections came out on the side of the victors, so the supporters gained more respect and notoriety in the community than the dissenters.

Second, the new immigrants gained legitimacy in the eyes of their countrymen in Poland. The Solidarity opposition had to rely upon these new immigrants to run the campaign abroad. Also, along with the round-table accord for partially free elections came a general opening of freedom in Poland. For the first time, these new immigrants began traveling back and forth to Poland. One leader of Brotherhood went to Poland six times in 1989, after not having been in Poland since he left in 1983. This face-to-face contact with the candidates and later newly elected government officials in Poland helped him informally lobby for recognition of new Polonian leaders in Chicago. This paid off when, one year after the elections, in the fall of 1990, Hubert Romanowski, one of the election commissioners (and a founder of Brotherhood), was appointed the first noncommunist Polish consul general in Chicago since World War II.

Third, the new immigrants gained recognition from a more general American audience. When journalists went into Polonia to find information, they found that new immigrants were the ones who were knowledgeable and willing to talk.[8] Many of these calls for information first went to the PAC and PNA national offices, and people there referred the callers to the immigrants running the Solidarity Election Committee. The names of these new immigrants eventually became known among media personnel as "the ones to call." One immigrant said, "The PAC is now sending anyone who calls wanting to know something to me. Even stupid things, like what's the weather like in Poland, or what are relations between the Church and Solidarity. . . . I'm talking to people all the time, especially now. Now is an extraordinary time, now is the time to make the news." In addition to the linkages to the media, the new immigrants established links to U.S. government agencies and political groups. The Solidarity Election Committee helped send a representative from the local Democratic party to monitor the elections in Poland. Also during this time new immigrants in the Solidarity Election Committee started an English-language biweekly bulletin about Poland. The raison d'être for the bulletin stemmed from the changes in Eastern Europe created by the elections and need for "up-to-the-minute" news. They distributed the bulletin to American institutions and government officials interested in Eastern European affairs. This gave them contacts with key players in American foreign affairs without becoming lobbyists and challenging the representational role of the PAC. The immigrants over time were losing their newcomer status. There was some irony to it all—it was activities for the homeland that helped immigrants develop ties with American institutions and officials.

Although the new immigrants created a miniature coup as informational authorities on Poland, they did not secure the right to be political repre-

8. Some of the TV and radio stations and presses that contacted this group of new immigrants about the election included National Public Radio, a national TV network (NBC), local TV stations (WTTW, WGN, WBBM, WLS), newspapers (*Philadelphia Inquirer, Detroit Free Press, Chicago Tribune, Chicago Sun-Times*), national magazines (*U.S. News and World Report, Time*), and other news organizations (United Press International, Voice of America, Radio Free Europe).

sentatives of Polonia. After the elections the Bush administration continued
to call upon PAC officials to discuss Polish foreign affairs. When George
Bush was preparing for his July 1989 trip to Poland, he invited PAC leaders,
not these new immigrants, to the White House.

Yet many new immigrants felt that the inactivity of the Polish Americans
was evidence that they should not be Poland's representative in America.
New immigrants who supported the absentee vote felt that the PAC did too
little, too late. One new immigrant said, "It's just another instance showing
us that they don't really care about Poland. We are not asking them to vote,
but only to support the election, so all those who are here who are not U.S.
citizens will vote. I am very upset by their inactivity." Another new immigrant said that for the Polish Americans:

> Poland is a joke. What they need are some new Polish jokes. Then
> they will be active. If in two weeks there is a string of Polish jokes
> then these people will unite and yell and give all the money to
> defend themselves from the Polish jokes. But to help Poland, to help
> the election? No, Poland is not a real issue. The Polish jokes unite
> them, that is the real issue for the PAC.

Immigrants were more concerned with home country issues (the national
election) than were ethnics.

The new immigrants' criticisms of Polish Americans demonstrated their
lack of understanding of the issues facing ethnics. Polish jokes were a
problem on American soil, and the election of Solidarity candidates was a
problem on Polish soil. Polish Americans stood firmly on American soil.

The absentee vote in Chicago divided the community into foreign-born
immigrants and native-born ethnics. The main determinate of whether one
could vote was drawn along nativity lines—those born in Poland could vote.
However, whether one *should* vote was a matter of national loyalty. Ethnics
born in America were Americans, and their primary loyalty was to America.
For new immigrants who had only recently arrived, especially the *wakacjusze*
who intended to return home, the primary loyalty was clearly Poland.
Others, however, who had been in the United States for an extended period
of time and who had become U.S. citizens, were less certain about what they
should do.

The elections exposed the fundamental difference between the foreign
born and native born as an issue of political identity—the former were
Poles and the latter were Americans. Polish American was not an operable

identity in this situation. In the past, the ambiguous Polonian or hyphen-ated Polish American identity provided fertile ground for competition, as collective action often led to a struggle for representational rights (such as lobbying or demonstrating). The elections presented a unique situation in which mobilization on American soil did not lead to a struggle for leader-ship positions. New immigrants became leaders during this event because the PAC believed it had restrictions on its ability to act. The minimal (but not completely absent) conflict between immigrants and ethnics during the election was a result of the fact that the two main identities were Pole and American. These different political identities were less confrontational than the shared and troublesome Polonian identity.

Conclusion:
Migrations and Generations

The present understanding of ethnicity for descendants of European immigrants is that this "white ethnic" identity is largely symbolic, meaning it does not structurally order individuals' lives. Richard Alba argues that the white ethnic identity manifests itself in small cultural commitments to ethnic parades and part-time leisure activities, but it does not serve as a strong basis for solidarity (1990, 306). Mary Waters argues that for middle-class white ethnics, the ethnic identity "does not affect much in everyday life" (1990, 147). At most, it lends color to holiday customs, spice to the buffet table, and zest to the personality. This conclusion was based on interviews with "some very nice regular people in suburbs of San Jose and Philadelphia" (xiii). That is, she developed her theory about ethnic identities in the 1980s by studying nonethnic communities—just "regular" folk. Alba's data came from a random sample of people living in the Albany-Schenectady-Troy region in upstate New York in the mid-1980s. The results of both Waters's and Alba's studies reflect their methodology and research agendas. They both chose a general sample rather than targeting ethnic communities. In sampling by region or looking for "regular people" rather than sampling by ethnic community, the researchers found people who self-identified as an ethnic but did not participate in the ethnic community. In contrast, Paul Wrobel (1979) set out specifically to study a Polish neighborhood in Detroit in the early 1970s. He found that ethnicity did structure Polish Americans' behaviors, attitudes, and choices. The members of this Detroit community not only saw themselves as Polish American, but this identification had implications for gender, family, and community relations, as well as church practices. In Chicago Polonia in the 1980s, for the leaders and active members of Polonian organizations, even for those in the third generation, ethnicity did influence their social behavior and their sense of self. Their ethnicity did serve as a basis for solidarity, and it did affect their everyday lives.

In a revisitation of his symbolic ethnicity argument, Herbert Gans (1994) attempts to correct what he sees as wrong interpretations of this concept. He does not argue that a symbolic identity is meaningless, nor does he suggest that ethnicity will die out shortly. Yet, he does see ethnic cultures as fading and assimilation (the old form of slipping into a dominant cultural identity) as prevailing. In Chicago Polonia, two events interrupted this fading process by reestablishing the ethnics' attachments to the homeland. The first was actually a cluster of significant events that aroused and renewed interest in Poland—Pope John Paul II's election, the formation of Solidarity, martial law, the 1989 election, and the subsequent collapse of communism. Struggles in the homeland triggered collective action in Polonia, and this action energized and reinforced ethnic identity. Mary Kelly also found that for Lithuanian Americans "the declaration of Lithuanian independence gave their ethnic heritage new meaning" (Kelly and Nagel 1995, 12).

A second event that helped reestablish ties to Poland was the influx of new immigrants who were by nature more intimately connected to the homeland than the ethnics. The immigrants invigorated the ethnic community not simply because they spoke Polish and knew the home recipes, but because they had concrete attachments to people, organizations, and institutions in the homeland. The arrival of the new migrant cohort also contested the existing ethnic identity. The efforts Polonians exerted to defend their established positions and definitions served to strengthen, not weaken, their ethnic identity. The "transfusion" of new blood was not a simple process, and at times it appeared that Polonia would reject it. The tumultuous incorporation of the newcomers into the established community was a result of the differences between immigrants and ethnics, between Poles and Polish Americans, and between communist Poland and capitalist America.

Events in the homeland directly affected collective action in the United States. Between 1980 and 1990, changes in the character of collective action in Polonia corresponded to the changes in Poland. In 1980 the actors collected money for the striking workers; in 1982 they demonstrated against martial law; in 1984 they were concerned with the issue of sanctions; in 1986 they supported the underground publishing houses; in 1989 they worked to help elect Solidarity officials; and in 1990 the goals of Polonian political organizations were to help Poland's emerging free-market system. The splintering of Solidarity in Poland had a ripple effect in Polonia. For example, Freedom began supporting the Confederation for an Indepen-

dent Poland and Fighting Solidarity after the opposition in Poland faction-
alized. The organizational goals of Forum were directly altered by changes
in Poland: a group of new immigrants had been talking about creating a
political lobby, but then their resources were redirected into an organization that began investing in Poland's new private market. The changes in
Poland altered the framework within and the issues around which Polonians mobilized.

A more basic transformation took place in ethnic organizations after
the collapse of communism. Just as they did in the 1920s and 1960s
when Polonians rallied under the banner of "Emigrants for emigrants"
(*Wychodźstwo dla wychodźstwa*), in the 1990s Polish Americans began to call
for a more domestic-centered agenda for its organizations. An editorial in
Dziennik Związkowy titled, "Will the Concept of Emigration for the Sake of
Emigration Revive?" (December 11, 1989, 3) asked:

> If Poland gains its freedom (and everything signifies that it will),
> does it mean that Polonia will lose its basic idea that has been the
> inspiration for all its activity through the years? In a sense yes, but
> then the work of Polonia should be altered toward a part of life that
> has been neglected until now, Polonia's American life, building
> prestige and authority in the United States for Polonia.

The goals of these ethnic organizations were defined and redefined in
reference to the homeland.

The predominant model of ethnic collective action (Olzak 1983 and
1986; Nagel 1986; Hechter 1975; Enloe 1981) is a conflict model: ethnic
groups mobilize resources to compete better with other groups within the
same society. When studying ethnic communities derived from immigrant
roots, we need to broaden the concept of ethnic collective action to include
action directed toward the homeland. The homeland shapes ethnic and
immigrant communities. The politics of the homeland influences the
formation of factions within the settlement community, directs the strategies and goals of collective action, and creates new networks in the host
country. The homeland also gives meaning to the ethnic identity by helping
to define who the community is (or is not) and what its goals are (or are
not).

The studies of ethnic collective action in the United States and Canada
often fail to distinguish between immigrants and ethnics. Yet this distinction is important. Differences between individuals born in America and
those born abroad affect such things as networks, cultural capital, and

political loyalties, which in turn influence organizational ideologies, goals, and strategies. Moreover, it is often immigrants who rally the community on the homeland's behalf and reactivate and enliven the ethnic identity. To retain authority in the community, the established ethnic leaders have to either co-opt the immigrants' activities or engage in their own activities.

Another important distinction is within migrant cohorts. Not all newcomers are the same and therefore do not act similarly in emigration. Transient migrants who have little desire to assimilate may become social problems, "sore thumbs," or simply nuisances to the ethnic community. But if they remain visible to the larger society they help to renourish the cultural identity in America. People were more "aware" of Poland or the Polish community in America when they had Polish maids and nannies. But these temporary migrant workers seldom engaged in collective action for the homeland. It was the Poles who had been involved in the opposition in Poland who were more likely to be involved in political action for Poland while in emigration. Immigrant characteristics (such as prior activism, organizational and political skills, networks to other activist groups) explained involvement in ethnic collective action more so than cohort size (a variable that Olzak [1982] finds key to determining ethnic collective action). The leaders of the immigrant community were the refugees although they represented the smallest percentage within the entire new Polish cohort.

Ethnic collective action for the homeland, invigorated by an influx of new politically active immigrants, generated concrete actions, excited passions and hostilities, and influenced the behaviors of those Polish Americans who participated in the ethnic community. The new immigrants struggled against the established ethnics, contesting and twisting their ethnic identities, as each group tried to represent Poland's interests as well as their own. The ethnics were not just defending a symbolic identity but concrete leadership positions and organizational coffers.

The Struggle for Cultural Ownership

The new immigrants and established ethnics struggled over who was a "real" Pole. As one second-generation ethnic told me when recommending a restaurant, "It's run by *real* Poles. I mean Poles that recently came over. So they have a good kitchen." The PAC Illinois Division president introduced the leader of Freedom at a demonstration on August 31, 1988, as "a real

Polish worker" whose "ties to Poland are not sentimental but real." If Polish immigrants were the "real Poles" what were Polish Americans, impostors? Polish Americans had to define the boundaries of the community broadly enough to include themselves. After reading the minutes at a June 1988 meeting of the Polish-American Women's Coalition, the recording secretary asked for any corrections or deletions. One of the members stood up and said, "We are the Polish *American* Women's Coalition. You keep saying Polish Women's Coalition." The presence of both new immigrants and Polish Americans within Forum led to numerous discussions about whom Forum represented. Whether or not Forum was representative of Polonia depended on how Polonia was defined. Because Forum was composed mostly of new immigrants, the Polish Americans did not think that it was representative of Polonia; for the same reason, the new immigrants thought it was representative. Forum's immigrant president once said about Forum, "We are the Polonia group that is considered the most active and the biggest; we are Polonia's group." In response, the Polish American chairman said, "We haven't even touched Polonia, only about three percent of Polonia. Polonia is not these newcomers." Pointing to those present at the meeting he continued, "Polonia is me and Andrew and Celia and Chris and Mary, this is Polonia." All mentioned were second- to fifth-generation Polish Americans. Later he repeated, "I want to stress that this is not an organization of the newest immigrants in Polonia. Polonia is more than this."

The Polish American ethnic identity was a cultural identity formed in America from an attachment to the ancestral homeland. The presence of these new immigrants, whose cultural identity as Poles could not be doubted, accentuated just how non-Polish the ethnics actually were. The cultural identity for the immigrants represented what Werner Sollors calls a "descent identity." They were Poles precisely because the had been born in Poland. The cultural identity for the older-generation ethnics in America was more tenuous. For Polish Americans, the Polish identity was not a "given," certainly not the same way it was for newly arrived immigrants. The ethnics had to claim their identity, and in many cases because of intermarriage, the ethnic identity was chosen from a variety of options (Waters 1986). The ethnic identity was built more on what Sollors refers to as the language of consent, "which stresses our abilities as mature free agents and 'architects of our fates' to choose our spouses, our destinies, and our political systems" (1986, 6). Sollors, however, defines the ethnic identity in America as a descent identity and the American identity as the constructed and self-made consent identity. This may in fact look true when cross-group comparisons are made between ethnics and Americans. However, in Chicago Polonia in the 1980s, identity was being negotiated within community, and compared to the strength with which the immigrants could claim Polish as a descent identity, the ethnic identity resembled more of a consent identity.

The struggle for cultural ownership was, for Polish Americans, a struggle for cultural survival. George de Vos and Lola Romanucci-Ross argue that ethnicity is a past-oriented identity. Connected to an ancestral heritage, the ethnic identity gives the individual "a sense of continuity in which one finds to some degree the personal and social meaning of human existence. . . . To be without a sense of continuity is to be faced with one's own death" (1975, 364). The immigrants brought with them new symbols, language, patterns of behavior, and cultural interpretations that challenged and sometimes mocked the Polish American traditions, thereby threatening their connection to the past. Were they to accept the immigrants' definition of the situation, Polish Americans symbolically faced their own death. Instead, they fought back with "Polonia is not these newcomers, Polonia is me, and Celia and Mary." They claimed loudly: WE are Polonia! WE third- and fourth- and fifth-generation Americans are Polonia!

Both the newcomers and the established folks argued over the right to define the meaning of Polishness, the right to represent Poland in America, the right to cultural ownership. These turf wars resembled what Sollors calls "biological insiderism" wherein "the relativist position of ethnic insiderism uses ethnicity to wrap a cloak of legitimacy and authenticity around the speaker who invokes it" (1986, 13). The Polish Americans based their claims for community ownership on their established identity—they had been here longer, they had a right to the position. The newcomers based their claim for ownership on their newness—they had just come from Poland, they better understood what Poland needed and what the Polish identity meant in late twentieth-century Poland. Ethnics could undervalue the descent identity of the immigrants by stressing their own consent identity; the immigrants eclipsed the ethnics' consent identity by claiming ownership via descent.

Immigrants and Ethnics

At the heart of the borders within community was the qualitative difference between first-generation foreign-born immigrants and the native-born later-generation ethnics. Immigrants and ethnics were socialized in different societies; and immigrants did not live in the society in which they were socialized. Pedraza-Bailey writes, "The immigrants' preparation for adult roles in society takes place in their country of origin, although they will live these lives . . . in the new society to which they immigrated" (1990, 48; 1985, 10). Moreover, the two societies differed. Polish Americans were raised in America, a democratic-capitalist system, a system very different from either pre- or postwar Poland. These different contexts produced different patterns of social behavior as well as different frames of reference for interpreting this behavior. Moreover, the cultural identity for each group was shaped on different continents—while Polish immigrants, of course, had attachments to Poland's historical national symbols, their cultural identity was shaped in a contemporary Poland. In contrast, the ethnic identity originated in rural peasant culture and was transformed in a working-class American culture.

"Immigrant" is not a cultural category, it is a social identity. The structural nature of this identity is reflected in the immigrants' bounded networks, social needs, and involuntary status. First, immigrants have fewer connections and less experience in America than ethnics. Although they usually have some attachments in the new country, the resources immigrants initially have available to them through their networks are limited. Most new immigrants do not get positions in America that are equal to the positions they held in the homeland, and for them immigration represents downward mobility. Until they learn the host country language, immigrants' networks are bounded by the linguistic community, which restricts both information and opportunities. Second, the process of moving from one society to another reduces the value of human capital. Language skills become less useful (speaking Polish well will not necessarily help someone get into graduate school), and professional training is devalued (law degrees from Poland are inapplicable, medical residency programs must be redone, midwife training counts for almost nothing in the United States). As a result, the newcomer has a narrower range of networks, information sources, and opportunities in the new society than does the established resident. New immigrants experience these limitations because they are immigrants, not because they are Polish.

The ethnic identity does not create the same structural constraints. Polish Americans speak English and are educated in American institutions. Their sources of information are not limited to the Polish-speaking or even the ethnic community. Their degrees and training in the United States are not devalued. Moreover, by the 1980s, while having suffered discrimination in the past, the structural indicators of occupation, education, and income were on an aggregate level similar to other white groups in this country (Lieberson and Waters 1980).

The structural nature of the immigrant identity is also reflected in social needs. In general, the immigrant focuses on immediate needs (such as jobs and language). The ethnic focuses on the needs of the ethnic community (cultural maintenance and defamation). Polish Americans have to negotiate a Polish identity, and immigrants have to negotiate an American identity.[1] The immigrants needed job retraining and English-language courses. Ethnic cultural needs were satisfied by folk dances and funds for ethnic events.

A third indicator of the structural nature of the immigrants' identity is the nonvoluntary nature of that identity. The newcomer status is not something the immigrant can take out only on special occasions the way that third-generation Polish Americans can choose to emphasize their Polishness on holidays or at weddings. The immigrant identity—visible to others because of the Polish accent—is involuntary. No one asks the third-generation Polish American "Where are you from?" but the immigrant is subjected to this question even by strangers. Polish Americans have the optional, voluntary identity of other white ethnics (one exception is the ethnic indicator within some surnames, but one can more easily change a name than skin color or accent). While the immigrant identity is the primary social identity (for many even a master status) that shapes behavior, opportunities, and networks, the cultural identity of the ethnic competes with myriad social identities. John Bukowczyk notes that, for the third and fourth generations, the Polish American identity

> was an occasional identity, one that coexisted with other, often more compelling, identities and the cultures and associations that accompanied them—musician, engineer, American, Democrat, socialist, writer, softball team member, or historian. Culturally, little about these young men and women was identifiably Polish or Polish-American. Homogenized—or, for the upwardly mobile,

1. Hurtado et al.'s study of first-generation Mexican immigrants, *Mexicanos*, and second- and later-generation Mexican Americans, *Chicanos*, found that the groups have different problematic identities: "For the newcomer *Mexicanos*, the especially problematic labels involving the United States were part of what it means to be a Mexican American or American of Mexican descent, while for the later generation *Chicanos*, it was the problematic relation to Mexico that was part of the dual identity" (1994, 147).

assimilated—they were Polish-Americans only when they wanted to be. (Bukowczyk 1987, 144–45)

The white ethnic's optional identity can be modified to fit the occasion. As Mary Waters (1990) notes, most third-and fourth-generation Americans have several ancestral choices. In this research project, I alternated between my fifth-generation Polish American identity (especially when I was with Polish Americans) and my fourth-generation Dutch ancestry (when I was with new immigrants, especially those who defined Polish Americans in harshly derogatory terms). White ethnics can even at times "invent" or redefine ancestors. For example, one day I was visiting my cousin Charlie in New York. He was living near Coney Island, which has a significant number of new Russian immigrants. One January day, while walking down a central street in this district lined with Russian merchants, Charlie in his large Russian fur hat said something like, "I feel right at home here being Russian and all." I gasped, "Charlie you're Irish and Polish!" He then told me about how one of our great-great-grandparents came from Russia (actually that ancestor was Polish from the Russian Partition). This optional nature of the ethnic identity contrasts greatly with the nonvoluntary nature of the immigrant identity.

The final difference between immigrants and ethnics is that the immigrant identity is tied more concretely to the homeland—as expressed in networks and political loyalties. Immigrants are more intimately connected to the homeland: they are more likely to send remittances, to visit the homeland, to correspond with family and friends in the homeland, and to be involved in the political and economic developments of the homeland. In contrast, ethnics have a more sentimental attachment to the culture and history of the homeland. For immigrants, the Polish identity is a political identity; for ethnics the Polish identity is a cultural identity. When oriented toward nationalistic action for the homeland, a political identity demands more energy than a cultural identity. Herbert Gans maintains that white ethnics have a nostalgic allegiance to culture and homeland that requires very little effort. "Old countries are particularly useful as identity symbols because they are far away and cannot make arduous demands on American ethnics" (1979, 11). When the new immigrants came to Chicago, however, the old country was no longer so far away. The momentous events in Poland as well as the arrival of new immigrants pressured the Polish American ethnic leaders and their organizations to augment their symbolic sentiments with concrete political action. Nonetheless, the immigrants always had more concrete ties to the homeland than the ethnics. This was best illustrated when they engaged in collective action for Poland. The Polish American ethnics could not draw on personal and informal ties but instead relied on formal, institutional ties to mainstream national groups. In contrast, the new immigrants had contacts with regional and local opposition groups and lesser known opposition organizations.

In the case of Poland's struggle for independence, ethnics were loyal to an idea and were helping a cause; immigrants were loyal to a nation and were helping friends and families. While actions on behalf of Poland strengthened the ethnic identity, they did not challenge the American identity. Polish Americans were first and foremost Americans. Pienkos states the importance of Polonia's efforts for Poland was not that Polonia could or did influence Washington, but the actions for Poland "perpetuated a sense of identification with Poland, which helped to strengthen feelings of ethnic consciousness and pride in what Polish Americans stood for as *Americans*" (1993, 20; emphasis mine). Activity for Poland was done by Polish Americans as Americans, illustrated succinctly by the Polish American leader of the Fair Elections in Poland organization, who said they were supporting the elections as American citizens to advance the spread of democracy and capitalism. At one point, Zbigniew Brzezinski told Polonia to use its strength as voting Americans to help Poland. He urged Polish Americans to use more "political leverage" to check to make sure that their elected representatives have Polish Americans on their staff, to monitor how the representative votes on such issues as immigration or the National Endowment for Democracy, an institution that supported Solidarity (*PAC Newsletter*, September 1986, 6–7). Brzezinski stressed the American-based behavior of the identity. Political action for Poland by Polish Americans was done in an American political context. Immigrants, on the other hand, by voting in Poland's national election, demonstrated they still had a political identity as Poles.

While interest in Poland stimulated the ethnic identity, Polish Americans were also concerned with domestic issues such as cultural celebration, defamation, and discrimination. These were ethnic concerns and immigrants were not as interested in pursuing this agenda. The immigrants perceived this activity as a substitute for, not a complement to, activity for Poland. The immigrants wanted more resources and energy devoted to Poland's cause; and conversely the ethnics saw Poland's needs as secondary to the needs of the ethnic community in America. One immigrant said the ethnic organizations are only concerned with "Polish Americans who live here, who are born here; they think just most about situation of Polish Americans in America, not about Poland. They send some money, they send some medicine, but not about political action." The newcomers unfairly criticized Polish American leaders for being more interested in the "Polish joke" than in Poland's fate. Immigrants had simply not been in the United States long enough to appreciate the Polish American's sensitivity to the "dumb Polak" stereotype.

On an episode of *NYPD Blue*, Sipowicz—the good-hearted, but racist, Polish detective who constantly doubts the honesty, integrity, and intelligence of blacks, Latinos, and Arabs—finally investigates a case involving Polish Americans who all call themselves Polaks ("It's OK for us Polaks to call each other dat, right?"). These Polaks pronounce their "ths" like "ds" and use a lot of double negatives and few polysyllabic words. Sipowicz is offended when someone implies Poles are stupid, and he acts out a caricature of the dumb Polak; yet while solving the case, Sipowicz himself cannot decide if the Polaks are "stupid idiots or devious geniuses." Immigrants have not lived here long enough to know why that stereotypical portrayal of the Polish American as dim-witted, racist, and uncouth in manners is offensive. (Or perhaps, Polish immigrants do in fact see Polish Americans that way, and they do not think of it as a negative statement about themselves but about the ethnics.)

Newness is a perishable attribute. The wearing away of newness is related to the immigrant's length of time in the host country, the age at arrival, and the degree of integration into ethnic and host communities. Immigrants who arrive in the host country after their teen years often retain, to some degree, an immigrant identity (see Eva Hoffman's [1989] poignant recounting of the problems of transferring her self and soul to a new culture). One World War II émigré said, "Once born a foreigner, you are in the United States always a foreigner . . . You can not enter into this society and be one of them." Perhaps this is true, but immigrants can, over time, begin to construct an ethnic identity. What this means is that their behavior and values come to align with those shared by members of the ethnic community; needs change as they become less preoccupied with immediate resettlement concerns and more preoccupied with long-term issues related to cultural maintenance and the social status of the group in America; and finally, networks extending back to the homeland weaken and become less concrete while ties to American institutions and groups become more extensive.

The transition from immigrant to ethnic occurs along three levels: within the community, within organizations, and within the individual. The community usually undergoes the transition when the second generation reaches adulthood, and the transition in organizations usually follows the transition in the group, as illustrated by the changes in Polonia and its organizations in the 1920s and the 1930s. How this transition occurs within the individual is murkier. Immigrant parents have ethnic children, and the parents are often pulled into ethnic activity when they engage in the process of transferring language and history to their children. But when are immigrants no longer newcomers?; when they learn English?; when their refugee cash assistance runs out?; when they become citizens? There is no sharp cut-off between immigrants and ethnics, which is why I often use the most centered group in each category (new immigrants and later-generation ethnics) to make many of my points. The transitional gray region between the immigrant and ethnic was evident in both the World War II cohort and among those immigrants who arrived in the 1960s.

Immigrants begin to look like ethnics when they start to establish stronger networks in the United States. Over time, the immigrants cultivated a more productive network of ties to American institutions—Pomost's lobby was run mostly by immigrants who had been in the United States for twenty to forty years; Cholodecki, who arrived in the early 1980s, had connections to American politicians and American media sources by the late 1980s. The weakness of the immigrants' ties to America and the strength of their ties to Poland are what define and shape their behavior and relations. The strength of each of these networks changes after the immigrant has been out of the homeland and in America for many years.

The failure to distinguish between immigrant and ethnic identities was the cause of much tension and misunderstanding within Polonia. Immigrants reached out to ethnic organizations asking for social services that these ethnic organizations did not have; the ethnics interpreted this request as a behavioral legacy of communism. The newcomers felt the organizations should help them because of the bond of Polishness. For the same reason, the ethnic leaders thought the new immigrants should join their organizations. The affinity that Poles and Polish Americans shared, based on a common ancestral homeland, made both groups think they ought to work together, but the differences between immigrants and ethnics created divisions within the community. Even so, various subgroups within Polonia were able to work together to achieve collective goals. The lines of solidarity were formed across migrant cohorts and through generations.

Solidarity Among Migrations and Generations

Ethnic solidarity is often considered a necessary precondition to ethnic collective action.[2] For culturally disparate groups, however, defining the collective interest as well as a collective identity can be problematic.[3] Only a few studies have focused on identity formation as a function of ethnic collective action (Schiller 1977; Padilla 1985). In Chicago, sharing an ancestral heritage created the potential for allegiance, but it was not a sufficient condition. Polish immigrants and Polish Americans had problems acting as a collective, often defining themselves as two groups—old Polonia (*stara Polonia*) and new Polonia (*nowa Polonia*)—rather than as a unified whole. In this community, the collective identity did not exist prior to collective action but emerged from the cohorts' efforts to work together.

While consensus within the community was never achieved, a solidarity of interests formed along migrational and generational lines. For example, Karen Majewska, a third-generation Polish American, is a graduate student of English and a member of the Polish American Historical Association (PAHA). She is studying turn-of-the-century Polish women writers in Polonia such as Helena Męczynska Stas. At the 1993 PAHA meetings in Chicago, Karen offered to take some conference attendees to the South Side Polish bars in her old neighborhood, the *górale* bars, for some "real dancing." These bars were built around the turn of the century and were maintained and modified over the decades by the descendants of these immigrants. This is Karen's heritage. Her attraction to this older cohort does not end with her scholarly interest in Stas, nor her social interest in *górale* bars. Karen also writes "Cute Girl" comic books that have Polish themes that represent her grandmother's Polishness, which is now her own Polishness. In one series, the Cute Girl goes to her grandmother's house, greets her with "*dzień dobry*," helps her make *pierogi*, and then listens to the Polka Hour

---

2. For a discussion of the relation between ethnic solidarity and ethnic collective action, see Hechter, Friedman, and Appelbaum 1982; Olzak 1983 and 1986; Nagel 1986; Hannan 1979; Hechter 1978; Bonacich 1972; Yancey, Eriksen, and Juliana 1976.

3. Jenkins notes that in the resource mobilization models of the 1970s "collective interests are assumed to be relatively unproblematic and to exist prior to mobilization, instead of being socially constructed by the mobilization process" (1983, 549). More recently, social scientists have analyzed the influence of culture, consciousness, and solidarity (Fantasia 1988) and symbolic struggles and political cultures (Gamson 1981 and 1988) on mobilization and collective interests. Scholars focusing on "new social movements" (such as the ecology and peace movements) view collective identity as the central issue to be explained (Melluci 1980 and 1989; Cohen 1985; Eder 1985; Dalton et al. 1990; Inglehart 1990).

on the radio. In another, entitled *"Pamiątki Polki"* (Polka Memories) the Cute Girl remembers waking up Sunday morning and listening to the Polka radio program, watching her mom and aunt polka together at weddings, and her father, who "danced with abandon," trying to teach her to polka as a young girl.

Karen is a third-generation Polish American. Her Polishness is defined in part by her grandparents' generation and the rural Poland they left one hundred years ago. Her Polishness differs from the Polishness of Sasha, the son of a concentration camp survivor. Sasha does not know how to polka. He has little interest in turn-of-the-century Polish culture but a great interest in World War II and present-day communist Poland. Sasha is of the second generation and he understands the children of the newest Polish cohort in a way that Karen never will. The second generation shares some similar problems. Their immigrant parents want them to retain their native language, so they send them to Saturday Polish school. The children are often reluctant to attend. As ten-year-olds they would prefer to spend their Saturday mornings watching cartoons like other American kids or playing football. As adults, these second-generation children tell stories about how they outwitted their parents and teachers to avoid going to Saturday school. When these children get together they talk about the wonders of white bread (their parents only had the dark Polish bread in their houses) and the problems of communicating with parents whose first language was Polish. The second generation understands what it is like to have immigrant parents—though they have come from different migrant cohorts they have similar generational experiences.

Migrants also share the bond of similar experiences. Even if the process of migration differs, migration itself is a uniquely transforming experience; those who have had this experience know what it feels like to pack up and move from one society to another. In the 1980s, this solidarity among migrants was evident in the links between the World War II émigrés and the newest immigrants. Not only did the World War II émigrés and new immigrants both share the experience of migration, but within these two cohorts existed similar subgroups of political activists—the World War II veterans, especially those involved in the Home Army during World War II, and the Solidarity refugees. The World War II veterans and the Solidarity refugees shared three common experiences: (1) both groups had been involved in opposition activity to help liberate their homeland, and their opposition networks in Poland served as bases for creating new organizations in America; (2) both groups experienced the disruption of emigration; (3) both groups felt the tensions between their migrant cohort and the Polish

American ethnic community. These shared experiences moderated the migrant cohort differences and produced cross-cohort solidarity. As one World War II émigré wrote about the Solidarity refugees, "Personally, I have no problem with finding a common language with these people and feel absolutely no generational gap" (Nowak 1989, 3).

Both the Solidarity activists and the World War II veterans belonged to politically-minded generations and felt morally obligated to continue political activity on behalf of Poland while in emigration. Both had undergone what McAdam refers to as an "alternation" resulting from participation in social movement activity, which produces an identity transformation that persists throughout life (1989, 746). Poles from both cohorts thought it was their duty to help Poland. Continued activity for Poland's cause while in emigration repaid a perceived debt to the Fatherland. Jan Nowak, a prominent World War II veteran wrote:

> Among the Solidarity emigration there are many brilliant and valued people who have the feeling of a mission for Poland. . . . The hope that is associated with them is that they will continue Polonia's political work, because the post-WWII emigration (which I, myself, belong to) is leaving the stage. We should help them so that they can step into the existing Polonian structures and play some role in them. (1989, 3)

The World War II émigrés' recognition that the Solidarity refugees shared "a mission for Poland" made them more eager to work together with this new political generation.

The veterans felt that the Solidarity refugees were the first wave of Poles to come to America with whom they could identify. PAC vice-president Lukomski said, "The way I look at it, our World War II immigration is decidedly political, and their immigration, the post-Solidarity immigration, truly is the first political immigration which came to this country [since us]." Denoting the political cohort by the Solidarity date, the World War II veterans discounted the political worth of the earlier 1960s and 1970s immigrants who created Pomost. As a result, this link to the World War II veterans was not as strong with Pomost members, who were for the most part not political refugees, and strongest with the Solidarity refugees in Brotherhood and Freedom. In addition, World War II émigrés made a distinction between *wakacjusze* and refugees in terms of political activity. One World War II veteran said the *wakacjusze* were only in the United States "to make money and they did not care about their nation's destiny." He praised the "post-Solidarity immigration, the refugees" with whom they worked together. Another World War II veteran, lamenting the fact that the new immigrants in general were not involved in Polonia, mentioned that there was a "small group, politically active, and there is no problem with them. We understand them and we try to help them." The refugees earned the respect of the World War II émigrés not only because of their past actions in Poland but because, unlike most *wakacjusze*, they were politically active for Poland in the United States.

The World War II émigrés and Solidarity refugees also shared the experience of trying to coordinate this political action within the Polish American organizational arena. In the mid-1980s, the World War II émigrés, cognizant of their own experience with the PAC and still smarting from the Pomost affair, were aware that the newcomers could become frustrated with the PAC's organizational and ideological conservatism. The World War II émigrés instructed the new immigrants about how to work within the PAC. Below is an excerpt of a letter PAC vice-president Lukomski wrote to the Solidarity refugees who participated in the PAC-Brotherhood conference of reconciliation in January 1987. The letter takes the tone of a mentor, revealing the writer's sensitivity toward the status declination experienced by political refugees and his understanding of the rigid hierarchy within the PAC structure.

> I realize the disproportion of your situation resulting from the fact that many of you held directorships and positions of responsibility in the hierarchy of Solidarity, while, here, in emigration, you are entering an already established structure and hierarchy in which you must still make a position for yourself, which will depend on what you can contribute toward the PAC divisions and not on your past Solidarity achievements and activities. . . . I am talking from my own, and from my friends' experiences. We had to swallow many bitter pills in our time.

This shared history—oppositional activity, emigration, and entry into the Polish American community—created a bond between the World War II veterans and the Solidarity refugees.[4]

---

4. Mostwin also notes similarities between Solidarity refugees and the soldiers emigration (1991, 156–58). While there were similarities, there were also differences because the two

   In Chicago Polonia, the political organizations active on Poland's behalf
were composed mostly of Poles who were members of these two political
migrations. The World War II émigrés dominated the PAC committees that
dealt with issues relating to Poland—the Polish Affairs Committee (on
both the national and divisional level) and the committees to support
democratic opposition. These were also the committees that attracted new
immigrants. Informal linkages between the World War II veterans in the
PAC and the Solidarity refugees underscored most of Polonia's collective
action for Poland. In several interviews, new immigrants said there was no
Freedom-PAC cooperation, or Brotherhood-PAC cooperation, yet they
would describe instances of cooperation with members of the PAC. One
member of Brotherhood said "I'm in touch with Mr. Lukomski, and we
discuss things, but only like a private discussion, never in some official
meeting." Another Brotherhood leader told me that when the PAC needed
to prepare position papers on Poland, PAC leaders asked Brotherhood
leaders for help. I mentioned that it sounded like Brotherhood leaders
were advisors, and he said, "I can't say that. We are like friends of Mr.
Lukomski, not political advisors, because nobody except him wants our
advice." Jan Nowak was also a strong ally for all the new immigrant groups,
even Pomost, for whom he wrote a public statement of support (1980).

   The new immigrants were brought into the PAC through the patronage
of the World War II émigrés. One member of the Brotherhood said,
"Lukomski tried to include us [in the PAC] as the representatives of the
younger generation." Lukomski invited Brotherhood leaders to national
Polish Affairs Committee meetings as well as informal meetings with PAC
policy makers. He also suggested that the PAC appoint a new immigrant as
one of the PAC national directors. Freedom leaders had the patronage of
Julian Witkowski, the chairman of the Polish Affairs Committee in the
Illinois division in the late 1980s. There were a half-dozen other patrons
(including Jan Morelewski, Jan Jurewicz, and Bonaventure Migala). These
men—all World War II émigrés—were prominent players in the PAC,
strongly supported the newcomers in their activities, and "walked the bases
for them" when the PAC balked at cooperative efforts. In March 1988,
Brotherhood leaders organized a banquet to honor these patrons (specifi-

---

groups migrated in different time periods. One of the key differences had to do with attitudes
toward and types of assistance programs available to each group upon arrival. When the World
War II émigrés arrived the welfare state was not as developed as it was for the post-1980
refugees.

cally Lukomski, Morelewski, Migala, and Jurewicz) for their actions in support of Solidarity and their work with the new immigrants.

The World War II émigrés became a liaison between the Solidarity refugees and the Polish Americans. In order to be effective liaisons, the émigrés needed to understand both sides. While they shared a fierce loyalty for the homeland with the post-1980 refugees, these émigrés, who by the 1980s had been in the United States for thirty years, were also sympathetic to the needs of the Polish American ethnic group. Even though they advocated to push Polish affairs to the forefront of the PAC agenda, the World War II émigrés empathized with the Polish Americans' need for a domestic agenda and the concerns of the ethnic community. Furthermore, they understood that the PAC did not want to be overrun with newcomers and that the traditional structure of PAC was unlikely to be changed. The World War II émigrés used this insight to educate the new immigrants in an effort to curb what Nowak had called the newcomers' "pretensions toward their predecessors" (1989, 3). Understanding both sides, the World War II émigrés acted as arbitrators at times of misunderstanding and discord.

One example of arbitration occurred in the winter of 1988 during the demonstration for a priest killed in Poland. The PAC Illinois Division, on the urging of Witkowski, agreed to cosponsor the demonstration with Brotherhood and Freedom. While the PAC Illinois Division supported the demonstration, Polish American leaders of the national PAC were against the demonstration. The demonstration did take place, and the World War II émigrés did their best to mediate the tensions caused by the disagreements between the Polish Americans and the new immigrants. Witkowski said that when he wrote the newspaper article about the event, he tried to avoid conflict by choosing to praise Pucinski, the president of the PAC Illinois Division who sanctioned the event, rather than criticize Moskal, the national PAC president who was against the event. He said it was better "to be positive and praise good actions than to criticize bad actions." In so doing, this émigré showed by example how diplomacy defused a potentially explosive situation. In contrast to this form of diplomacy, the new immigrants wanted to protest against the actions of Moskal, the PAC president. The newcomers circulated a petition that criticized Moskal for his attempt to censor information and stop the demonstration. They also planned to hold a demonstration in front of Moskal's PNA office. Although the protest letter was read on the radio, Lukomski prevented the letter from being sent to the PAC president. Lukomski was also able to convince the newcomers not to picket the PNA building in protest.

Chicago Polonia in the 1980s represented a heterogeneous community with contested borders. The "us-them" divide, along which identity was constructed, was an in-house border. Within Polonia, diverse cultural groups struggled to create a working collective identity. They believed they ought to cooperate because they had the same goal; but differences among generations and migrations led to internecine conflict. Some groups were not so dissimilar—for example, veterans from the World War II cohort found common understanding with the post-1980 Solidarity refugees. Other identities, however—in particular, the ethnic and immigrant identities—were on opposite poles in a community struggling to define the meaning of Polishness in America.

Bibliography

Alba, Richard. 1990. *Ethnic Identity: The Transformation of White America.* New Haven: Yale University Press.

Allen, Theodore W. 1994. *The Invention of the White Race.* Vol. 1: *Racial Oppression and Social Control.* New York: Verso.

Amnesty International Reports. 1983. London: Amnesty International Publications.

Annual Report of the Immigration and Naturalization Service. See U.S. Department of Justice, Immigration, and Naturalization Service.

Annual Report of the Polish Welfare Association. 1989. Chicago, Ill.

Ascherson, Neil. 1981. *The Polish August.* New York: Penguin Books.

Ash, Timothy Garton. 1983. *The Polish Revolution.* New York: Vintage Books.

Aveni, Adrian. 1978. "Organizational Linkages and Resource Mobilization: The Significance of Linkage Strength and Breadth." *Sociological Quarterly* 19 (Spring): 185–202.

Baganha, Maria Ioannis Benis. 1991. "The Social Mobility of Portuguese Immigrants in the United States at the Turn of the Nineteenth Century." *International Migration Review* 25 (2): 277–302.

Barth, Frederik. 1969. "Introduction." In *Ethnic Groups and Boundaries: The Social Organization of Cultural Difference,* ed. Frederik Barth, 9–39. Boston: Little Brown and Company.

Bell, Derrick. 1992. *Race, Racism and American Law,* 3d ed. Boston: Little, Brown and Company.

Bereszko, Jerzy. 1989. "Teatr absurdu" (Theater of the absurd). *Kurier,* May 9, p. 9.

Best, Paul J. 1982. "Polish-American Scholarly Organizations." In *Pastor of the Poles,* ed. Stanislaus Blejwas and Mieczyslaw B. Biskupski, 153–65. New Britain, Conn.: Polish Studies Program Monograph.

Bethell, Nicholas. 1969. *Gomulka: His Poland and His Communism.* London: Longmans, Greeb, and Company.

Bialasiewicz, Wojciech. 1989. "Przegląd Prasy Polonijnej" (A look over Polonian press). *Kalejdoskop Tygodnia,* in *Dziennik Związkowy,* July 4, p. 16.

Blau, Peter. 1963 (1955). *The Dynamics of Bureaucracy: A Study of Interpersonal Relations in Two Government Agencies,* 2d ed. Chicago: University of Chicago Press.

Blejwas, Stanislaus. 1981. "Old and New Polonias: Tension Within an Ethnic Community." *Polish American Studies* 38 (2): 55–83.

Bobinska, Celina. 1975. "Introduction." In *Employment Seeking Emigrations of the Poles World-Wide, Nineteenth and Twentieth Century,* ed. Celina Bobinska and Andrzej Pilch, 7–27. Krakow: Jagiellonian University.

Bodnar, John. 1981. "Ethnic Fraternal Benefit Associations: Their Historical Development, Character and Significance." In *Records of Ethnic Fraternal Benefit*

Associations in the United States: Essays and Interviews, 5–14. St. Paul: Immigration History Research Center, University of Minnesota.

Bodnar, John, Roger Simon, and Michael Weber. 1982. *Lives of Their Own: Blacks, Italians and Poles in Pittsburgh,* 1900–1960. Chicago: University of Illinois Press.

Bohlen, Charles. 1973. *Witness to History: 1929–1969.* New York: Norton and Company.

Bonacich, Edna. 1972. "A Theory of Ethnic Antagonism: The Split Labor Market." *American Sociological Review* 37 (October): 547–59.

———. 1973. "A Theory of Middlemen Minorities." *American Sociological Review* 38 (October): 583–94.

Boulding, Kenneth. 1941. *Economic Analysis,* 3d ed. New York: Harper and Row.

Bourdieu, Pierre. 1989. "Social Space and Symbolic Power." *Sociological Theory* 7 (1): 14–25.

Briggs, Michael, and Michael Cordts. 1981. "Envoys Hit 'Vandals' in Polish Protest." *Chicago Sun-Times,* December 29, p. 3.

Brozek, Andrzej. 1985. *Polish Americans: 1854–1939.* Translated by Wojciech Worsztynowicz. Warsaw: Interpress.

Buechler, Steven. 1990. *Women's Movements in the United States.* New Brunswick, N.J.: Rutgers University Press.

Bukowczyk, John J. 1984. "Polish Rural Culture and Immigrant Working Class Formation, 1880–1914." *Polish American Studies* 41 (2): 23–44.

———. 1987. *And My Children Did Not Know Me: A History of Polish-Americans.* Bloomington: Indiana University Press.

Bukowski, Jerzy. 1989. "Emigruj Albo Strzelaj" (Emigrate or shoot). *Dziennik Związkowy,* April 3, p. 4.

Butturini, Paula. 1989. "Solidarity Off to Solid Start at the Ballot Box." *Chicago Tribune,* June 5, p. 1.

Carrer, Jean. 1970. *Across the Continents in Search of Justice.* Chicago: Alliance Press.

Carter, Bob, Marci Green, and Rick Halpern. 1996. "Immigration Policy and the Racialization of Migrant Labour: The Construction of National Identities in the USA and Britain." *Ethnic and Racial Studies* 19 (1): 135–57.

Cassel, Andrew. 1989. "Chicago's Poles Are Key Players in Polish Vote." *The Philadelphia Inquirer,* June 2, p. 8.

Chow, Rey. 1993. *Writing Diaspora: Tactics of Intervention in Contemporary Cultural Studies.* Bloomington: Indiana University Press.

Cichon, Donald, Elzbieta Gozdziak, and Jane Grover. 1986. *The Economic and Social Development of Non-Southeast Asian Refugees.* Vol. 2: *Chicago Poles.* Washington, D.C.: U.S. Department of Health and Human Services, Office of Refugee Resettlement, GPO.

Ciechanowski, Jan. 1947. *Defeat in Victory.* New York: Doubleday.

Cisek, Andrzej M. 1989. "Polish Elections Won't Be Free." *Gannett Westchester Newspapers,* April 20, p. 8.

Claremont de Castijello, Irene. 1972. *Knowing Woman: A Feminine Psychology.* New York: Harper and Row.

Conzen, Kathleen Neils, David A. Gerber, Ewa Morawska, George Pozzetta, and

Rudolph Vecoli. 1990. "The Invention of Ethnicity: A Perspective from the USA." *Altreitalie 3* (April): 37–63.

Crockatt, Richard. 1995. *The Fifty Years War: The United States and the Soviet Union in World Politics, 1941–1991.* New York: Routledge.

Curtis, Russell, and Louis Zurcher. 1973. "Stable Resources of Protest Movements: The Multi-Organizational Field." *Social Forces* 52 (September): 53–61.

Dalton, Russell, Manfred Kuechler, and Wilhelm Burklin. 1990. "The Challenge of New Movements." In *Challenging the Political Order: New Social and Political Movements in Western Democracies*, ed. Russell Dalton and Manfred Kuechler, 3–22. Cambridge: Polity Press.

Davies, Norman. 1982. *God's Playground: A History of Poland.* Vol. 2. New York: Columbia University Press.

———. 1986. *Heart of Europe: A Short History of Poland.* New York: Oxford University Press.

Declaration. 1989. "O Temat Manifestacji 3 Majowej" (About the May 3d manifestation). *Dziennik Związkowy*, March 14, p. 3.

De Vos, George, and Lola Romanucci-Ross. 1975. "Ethnicity: Vessel of Meaning and Emblem of Contrast." In *Ethnic Identity: Cultural Continuities and Change*, ed. George De Vos and Lola Romanucci-Ross, 363–90. Palo Alto, Calif.: Mayfield Publishing Company.

di Leonardo, Micaela. 1984. *The Varieties of Ethnic Experience: Kinship, Class and Gender Among California Italian-Americans.* Ithaca, N.Y.: Cornell University Press.

Dziennik Związkowy. 1988. "12-letnia Służba Ruchóm Demokratycznych w Polsce" (Twelve years of service to the democratic movement in Poland). December 2–3, p. 9.

———. 1989a. "Do Polaków Na Emigracji" (To Poles abroad). March 6, p. 3.

———. 1989b. "Apel do Polaków w Kraju i Na Obczyźnie" (An appeal to Poles in the homeland and in foreign lands). April 24, p. 5; reprinted, May 18, p. 5.

———. 1989c. "Oświadczenie Freedom for Poland" (Declaration of Freedom for Poland). October 10, p. 3.

Easterlin, Richard, David Ward, William Bernard, and Reed Ueda. 1982. *Immigration.* Cambridge, Mass.: Belknap Press.

Enloe, Cynthia. 1981. "The Growth of the State and Ethnic Mobilization: The American Experience." *Ethnic and Racial Studies* 4 (2): 123–36.

Eder, Klaus. 1985. "The 'New Social Movements': Moral Crusades, Political Pressure Groups, or Social Movements?" *Social Research* 52 (4): 871–90.

Erdmans, Mary P. 1992a. "The Social Construction of Emigration As a Moral Issue." *Polish American Studies* 49 (1): 5–25.

———. 1992b. "Émigrés and Ethnics: Patterns of Cooperation Between New and Established Organizations in Chicago's Polish Community." Ph.D. dissertation, Northwestern University, Evanston, Ill.

———. 1995. "Immigrants and Ethnics: Conflict and Identity in Polish Chicago." *The Sociological Quarterly* 36 (1): 175–95.

———. 1996a. "Home Care Workers: Polish Immigrants Caring for American Elderly." *Current Research on Occupations and Professions* 9: 267–92. Greenwich, Conn.: JAI Press.

———. 1996b. "Nielegalni imigranci i domowa opieka pielęgniarska: Pozarynkowe warunki osiągania zadowolenia z pracy" (Illegal immigrant home care workers: The non-market conditions of job satisfaction). *Przegląd Polonijny* 22 (2): 53–69.

———. 1997. "The Transformation of the Polish National Alliance: From Immigrant to Ethnic Organization." In *Ethnicity-Culture-City: Polish-Americans in the USA*, ed. Thomas Gladsky, Adam Walaszek, and Malgorzata M. Wawrykiewicz. Warsaw: Oficyna Naukowa.

Espiritu, Yen Le. 1996. "Colonial Oppression, Labour Importation and Group Formation: Filipinos in the United States. *Ethnic and Racial Studies* 19 (1): 29–49.

Fantasia, Rick. 1988. *Cultures of Solidarity: Consciousness, Action, and Contemporary American Workers.* Berkeley and Los Angeles: University of California Press.

Fernandez, Roberto, and Doug McAdam. 1989. "Multiorganizational Fields and Recruitment to Social Movements." In *International Social Movement Research*, 2:315–43. Greenwich, Conn.: JAI Press.

Fernadez-Kelly, Patricia, and Richard Schauffler. 1994. "Divided Fates: Immigrant Children in a Restructured U.S. Economy." *International Migration Review* 28 (4): 662–89.

Flam, Helena. 1996. "Anxiety and the Successful Oppositional Construction of Societal Reality: The Case of KOR." *Mobilization* 1 (1): 103–21.

Foreign Relations of the United States: Cairo and Tehran. 1943. Washington, D.C.: GPO.

Frankenberg, Ruth. 1993. *White Women, Race Matters: The Social Construction of Whiteness.* Minneapolis: University of Minnesota Press.

Freeman, Jo. 1973. "The Origins of the Women's Liberation Movement." *American Journal of Sociology* 78 (4): 792–811.

Galush, William. 1974. "American Poles and the New Poland: An Example of Change in Ethnic Orientation." *Ethnicity* 1 (3): 209–21.

Gamson, Josh. 1989. "Silence, Death, and the Invisible Enemy: AIDS Activism and Social Movement 'Newness.'" *Social Problems* 36 (4): 351–67

Gamson, William. 1975. *The Strategy of Social Protest.* Homewood, Ill.: Dorsey Press.

———. 1981. "The Political Culture of Arab-Israeli Conflict." *Conflict Management and Peace Science* 5 (2): 79–94.

———. 1988. "Political Discourse and Collective Action." In *International Social Movement Research*, 1:219–44. Greenwich, Conn.: JAI Press.

Gans, Herbert. 1974. "Forward." In *Ethnic Identity and Assimilation: The Polish American Community*, by Neil Sandberg, vii–xiii. New York: Praeger Publishers.

———. 1979. "Symbolic Ethnicity: The Future of Ethnic Groups and Cultures in America." *Ethnic and Racial Studies* 2 (1): 1–19.

———. 1994. "Symbolic Ethnicity and Symbolic Religiosity: Towards a Comparison of Ethnic and Religious Acculturation." *Ethnic and Racial Studies* 17 (4): 577–92.

Gazeta International. 1990. "A Pole Is a Human Being, Too." Week 24, no. 15, p. 2.

Geertz, Clifford. 1963. "The Integratice Revolution: Primordial Sentiments and Civil Politics in the New States." In *Old Societies and New States*, ed. Clifford Geertz, 105–57. New York: Free Press.

Giddings, Paula. 1984. *Where and When I Enter: The Impact of Black Women on Race and Sex in America*. New York: Bantam Books.

Glazer, Nathan. 1959. "The Immigrant Groups and American Culture." *Yale Review* 48 (3): 382–97.

———. 1990. "Hansen's Hypothesis and the Historical Experience of Generations." In *American Immigrants and Their Generations: Studies and Commentaries on the Hansen Thesis After Fifty Years*, ed. Peter Kivisto and Dag Blanck, 104–13. Urbana: University of Illinois Press.

Glazer, Nathan, and Daniel P. Moynihan. 1970. *Beyond the Melting Pot: The Negroes, Puerto Ricans, Jews, Italians and Irish of New York City*. Cambridge, Mass.: MIT Press.

Głos Niezależnych. 1989. "Stop Helping Communists." June 16, p. 3.

Goffman, Erving. 1974. *Frame Analysis*. New York: Harper & Row.

Golab, Caroline. 1977. *Immigrant Destinations*. Philadelphia: Temple University Press.

Goldfarb, Jeffrey. 1982. *On Cultural Freedom: An Exploration of Public Life in Poland and America*. Chicago: University of Chicago Press.

Gordon, Milton. 1964. *Assimilation in American Life*. New York: Oxford University Press.

Grant, Madison. 1916. *The Passing of the Great Race*. New York: Charles Scribner's Sons.

Greeley, Andrew M. 1974. *Ethnicity in the United States: A Preliminary Reconnaissance*. New York: John Wiley and Sons.

Greene, Victor. 1975. *For God and Country: The Rise of Polish and Lithuanian Consciousness in America, 1860–1910*. Madison: State Historical Society of Wisconsin.

———. 1990. "Old-Time Folk Dancing and Music Among the Second Generation, 1920–1950." In *American Immigrants and Their Generations: Studies and Commentaries on the Hansen Thesis After Fifty Years*, ed. Peter Kivisto and Dag Blanck, 142–66. Chicago: University of Illinois Press.

Gross, Felix. 1976. "Notes on the Ethnic Revolution and the Polish Immigration in the U.S.A." *The Polish Review* 21 (3): 150–72.

Haiman, Miecislaus. 1946. "Polish Americans Contributions to WWII." *Polish American Studies* 3 (1–2): 35–39.

Handlin, Oscar. 1952. *The Uprooted*. Boston: Little Brown and Company.

———, ed. 1966. *The Children of the Uprooted*. New York: George Braziller.

Hannan, Michael. 1979. "The Dynamics of Ethnic Boundaries in Modern States." In *National Development and the World System*, ed. John W. Meyer and Michael Hannan, 253–75. Chicago: University of Chicago Press.

Hardin, Russell. 1982. *Collective Action*. Baltimore: Johns Hopkins University Press.

Harriman, Averell, and Elie Abel. 1976. *Special Envoy to Churchill and Stalin, 1941–1946*. London: Hutchinson & Co.

Hechter, Michael. 1975. *Internal Colonialism: The Celtic Fringe in British National Development, 1536–1966*. London: Routledge & Kegan Paul.

———. 1978. "Group Formation and the Cultural Division of Labor." *American Journal of Sociology* 84 (2): 293–318.

Hechter, Michael, Debra Friedman, and Malka Appelbaum. 1982. "A Theory of Ethnic Collective Action." *International Migration Review* 16 (2): 412–34.

Hein, Jeremy. 1993. "Rights, Resources and Membership: Civil Rights Models in France and the United States." *The Annals of the American Academy of Political and Social Science* 530 (November): 97–108.

Higham, John. 1973. *Strangers in the Land: Patterns of American Nativism, 1860–1925.* New York: Atheneum Press.

Hoffman, Eva. 1989. *Lost in Translation: A Life in a New Language.* New York: Penguin Books.

Hondagneu-Sotelo, Pierrette. 1994. *Gendered Transitions: Mexican Experiences of Immigration.* Berkeley and Los Angeles: University of California Press.

hooks, bell. 1992. *Black Looks: Race and Representation.* Boston: South End Press.

Hunter, Albert, and Suzanne Staggenborg. 1986. "Communities Do Act: Resource Mobilization and Political Action by Local Community Organizations." *The Social Science Journal* 23 (2): 169–80.

Hurtado, Aida, Patricia Gurin, and Timothy Peng. 1994. "Social Identities—A Framework for Studying the Adaptations of Immigrants and Ethnics: The Adaptations of Mexicans in the United States." *Social Problems* 41 (1): 129–51.

Index on Censorship. 1985. Vol. 14, no. 3. Washington, D.C.: GPO.

Inglehart, Ronald. 1990. "Values, Ideology, and Cognitive Mobilization in New Social Movements." In *Challenging the Political Order: New Social and Political Movements in Western Democracies,* ed. Russell Dalton and Manfred Kuechler, 43–66. Cambridge: Polity Press.

Ignatiev, Noel. 1995. *How the Irish Became White.* New York: Routledge.

INS Statistical Yearbook. See U.S. Department of Justice, Immigration and Naturalization Service.

Jacobson, Matthew Frye. 1995. *Song of Sorrows: The Diasporic Imagination of Irish, Polish, and Jewish Immigrants in the United States.* Cambridge, Mass.: Harvard University Press.

Janowska, Halina. 1975. "An Introductory Outline of the Mass Polish Emigrations, Their Directions and Problems." In *Employment-Seeking Emigrations of the Poles World-Wide, Nineteenth and Twentieth Century,* ed. Celina Bobinska and Andrzej Pilch, 121–45. Krakow: Jagiellonian University.

Januszewski, David G. 1985. "Organizational Evolution in a Polish American Community." *Polish American Studies* 42 (1): 43–58.

Jenkins, Craig. 1983. "Resource Mobilization Theory and the Study of Social Movements." *Annual Review of Sociology* 9: 527–53.

Jenkins, Craig, and Charles Perrow. 1977. "Insurgency of the Powerless: Farm Workers Movements, 1946–1972." *American Sociological Review* 42 (April): 249–68.

Kanter, Rosabeth Moss. 1977. *Men and Women of the Corporation.* New York: Basic Books.

Kantowicz, Edward. 1975. *Polish-American Politics in Chicago, 1988–1940.* Chicago: University of Chicago Press.

———. 1977. "Polish Chicago: Survival through Solidarity." In *The Ethnic Frontier,* ed. Melvin Holli and Peter Jones, 180–209. Grand Rapids, Mich.: William B. Eerdmans Publishing Co.

Kazal, Russell A. 1995. "Revisiting Assimilation: The Rise, Fall, and Reappraisal of a Concept in American Ethnic History." *American Historical Review* 100 (April): 437–71.

Keil, Charles. 1979. "Class and Ethnicity in Polish-America." *Journal of Ethnic Studies* 7 (2): 37–46.

Kelly, Mary E., and Joane Nagel. 1995. "Ethnic Re-identification: Native Americans and Lithuanian Americans." Paper presented at the Midwest Sociological Society meeting, Chicago.

Kibria, Nazli. 1994. "Household Structures and Family Ideologies: The Dynamics of Immigrant Economic Adaptation among Vietnamese Refugees." *Social Problems* 41 (1): 81–96.

Kieniewicz, Stefan. 1969. *The Emancipation of the Polish Peasantry.* Chicago: University of Chicago Press.

Kiernik, Adam. 1984. "A Time for the Western Political Captive Nation Community to Be Reborn." *Pomost Quarterly* 24 (Fall): 40–43.

Kivisto, Peter, and Dag Blanck, eds. 1990. *American Immigrants and Their Generations: Studies and Commentaries on the Hansen Thesis after Fifty Years.* Chicago: University of Illinois Press.

Klandermans, Bert. 1989. "Introduction." In *International Social Movement Research,* 1:301–14. Greenwich, Conn.: JAI Press.

Klandermans, Bert, and Dirk Oegema. 1987a. "Campaigning for a Nuclear Freeze: Grassroots Strategies and Local Governments in the Netherlands." In *Research in Political Sociology,* vol. 3, ed. Richard G. Braungart. Greenwich, Conn.: JAI Press.

———. 1987b. "Potentials, Networks, Motivations, and Barriers: Steps Toward Participating in Social Movements." *American Sociological Review* 52 (4): 519–32.

Kleeman, Janice. 1985. "Polish-American Assimilation: The Interaction of Opportunity and Attitude." *Polish American Studies* 42 (1): 11–26.

Kobylanski, Julia. 1980. "Demonstrations." *Pomost Quarterly* 8 (Fall): 52.

Krajewski, Andrzej. 1989. *Region USA: Działacze "Solidarności" o kraju, o emigracji, o sobie* (Region USA—"Solidarity" activists on the homeland, emigration, and themselves). London: Aneks Publisher.

Kromkowski, John. 1986. "Eastern and Southern European Immigrants: Expectations, Reality, and a New Agenda." *Annals of the American Academy of Political and Social Science* 487 (September): 57–78.

———. 1990. "A Compendium of Social, Economic and Demographic Indicators for Polish Ancestry and Selected Populations in the United States of America." *Polish American Studies* 47 (2): 5–74.

Kruczkowski, Zenon. 1989. "The Story Behind Poland's Reforms." *Transcript-Telegram* (Holyoke, Mass.), March 18, p. 6.

Krynski, Magnus. 1983. "W odpowiedzi na memorandum" (A response to the memorandum). *Pomost Quarterly* 19 (Summer): 9.

———. 1984. "The Economy As a Component of Foreign Policy: The Need for a Long-Range Trade Build-Down with the Soviet Bloc." *Pomost Quarterly* 21 (Winter): 45-51.

Kubik, Jan. 1994. *The Power of Symbols Against the Symbols of Power: The Rise of Solidarity and the Fall of State Socialism in Poland.* University Park: Pennsylvania State University Press.

Kula, Marcin. 1996. "Emigration from a Communist Country—Both Economic and Political: A Post-Communist Perspective." *Journal of American Ethnic History* 16 (1): 47–54.

Kuniczak, Walter. 1968. *The Silent Emigration.* Chicago: Polish Arts Club.

Kurier. 1989. "Jeden cel—pomóc Polsce" (One goal—help Poland). 20 (64): 4–7.

Kusak, Teresa. 1989. "Kusak Questionnaire: Results of Questionnaire from the Inaugural Meeting of the Polish American Economic Forum." Unpublished document.

Lane, Arthur Bliss. 1948. *I Saw Poland Betrayed.* New York: Bobbs-Merrill Co.

Lerski, Jerzy. 1983. "Co o Jałcie pamiętać należy?" (What should we remember about Yalta?). *Pomost Quarterly* 18 (Spring): 2–6.

Lerski, Jerzy, Kazimierz Lukomski, Jan Nowak, and Boleslaw Wierzbianski. 1988. "Pięć Minut Przed Dwunastą: O Jutro Kongresu Polonii Amerykańskiej" (Five minutes to midnight: On the future of the Polish American Congress." *Dziennik Związkowy,* November 12, p. 3.

Li, Gertraude Roth. 1982. "The Polish People: The Challenge of Sponsorship." World Relief, Ethnic Profile. New York: Refugee Services Division.

Lieberson, Stanley, and Mary Waters. 1988. *From Many Strands: Ethnic and Racial Groups in Contemporary America.* New York: Russell Sage Foundation.

Lipski, Jan Jozef. 1985. *KOR: A History of the Workers' Defense Committee in Poland, 1976–1981.* Berkeley and Los Angeles: University of California Press.

Lipsky, Michael. 1968. "Protest As a Political Resource." *American Political Science Review* 62 (4): 1144–58.

Local Community Fact Book, Chicago Metropolitan Area 1960. 1963. Edited by Evelyn M. Kitagawa and Karl E. Taeber. Chicago Community Inventory, University of Chicago.

Lopata, Helena. 1964. "The Functions of Voluntary Associations in an Ethnic Community: 'Polonia.' " In *Contributions to Urban Sociology,* ed. Ernest W. Burgess and Donald Boque, 203–23. Chicago: University of Chicago Press.

———. 1976. *Polish Americans: Status Competition in an Ethnic Community.* Englewood Cliffs, N.J.: Prentice-Hall

Los, Miaria. 1988. *Communist Ideology: Law and Crime.* New York: St. Martin's Press.

Luciuk, Lubomyr Y. 1986. "Unintended Consequences in Refugee Resettlement: Post-War Ukrainian Refugee Immigration to Canada." *International Migration Review* 20 (2): 467–83.

Lukas, Richard. 1978. *The Strange Allies: The United States and Poland, 1941–1945.* Knoxville: University of Tennessee Press.

Lukomski, Kazimierz. 1986. "Pomost—A Disruptive Force in American Polonia." Memo sent to the members of the National Council of Directors of the PAC, presidents of the State Divisions and Chapters, and members of the Polish Affairs Committee.

Mannheim, Karl. 1952. "The Problem of Generations." In *Essays on the Sociology of Knowledge*, ed. Paul Kecskemeti, 276–321. New York: Oxford University Press.

Margolis, Maxine L. 1990. "From Mistress to Servant: Downward Mobility Among Brasilian Immigrants in New York City." *Urban Anthropology* 19 (3): 215–32.

Massey, Douglas, Rafael Alarcon, Jorge Durand, and Humberto Gonzalez. 1987. *Return to Aztlan: The Social Process of International Migration from Western Mexico.* Berkeley and Los Angeles: University of California Press.

McAdam, Doug. 1989. "The Biographical Consequences of Activism." *American Sociological Review* 54 (5): 744–61.

McCarthy, John, and Mayer Zald. 1973. *The Trend of Social Movements.* Morristown, N.J.: General Learning Press.

———. 1977. "Resource Mobilization and Social Movements: A Partial Theory." *American Journal of Sociology* 82 (6): 1212–41.

McGreevy, John T. 1996. *Parish Boundaries: The Catholic Encounter with Race in Twentieth-Century Urban North.* Chicago: University of Chicago Press.

Mead, Margaret. 1942. *And Keep Your Powder Dry: An Anthropologist Looks at America,* chap. 3. New York: William Morrow and Company.

Melucci, Alberto. 1980. "The New Social Movements: A Theoretical Approach." *Social Science Information* 19 (2): 199–226.

———. 1989. *Nomads of the Present: Social Movements and Individual Needs in Contemporary Society.* Philadelphia: Temple University Press.

Michnik, Adam. 1985. *Letters from Prison and Other Essays.* Berkeley and Los Angeles: University of California Press.

Miller, Kerby A. 1985. *Emigrants and Exiles: Ireland and the Irish Exodus to North America.* New York: Oxford University Press.

———. 1990. "Class, Culture, and Immigrant Group Identity in the United States: The Case of Irish-American Ethnicity." In *Immigration Reconsidered: History, Sociology, and Politics,* ed. Virginia Yans-McLaughlin, 96–129. New York: Oxford University Press.

Miller, Paul W. 1987. "Aspects of Occupational Mobility and Attainment Among Immigrants in Australia." *International Migration Review* 21 (1): 96–113.

Morawska, Ewa. 1985. *For Bread with Butter: The Life Worlds of East Central Europeans in Johnstown, Pennsylvania, 1890–1940.* Cambridge: Cambridge University Press.

———. 1990. "The Sociology and Historiography of Immigration." In *Immigration Reconsidered: History, Sociology, and Politics,* ed. Virginia Yans-McLaughlin, 187–238. New York: Oxford University Press.

Morris, Aldon. 1984. *The Origins of the Civil Rights Movement: Black Communities Organizing for Change.* New York: The Free Press.

Moskal, Edward. 1991. "To Reply or Not to Reply." *Zgoda* (Chicago), February 1, p. 5.

Mostwin, Danuta. 1971. "The Transplanted Family: A Study of Social Adjustment of the Polish Immigrant Family to the United States after the Second World War." Ph.D. dissertation, Columbia University, New York, N.Y.

———. 1991. *Emigranci polscy w USA* (Polish immigrants in the USA). Lublin, Poland: Catholic University of Lublin Press.

Nagel, Joane. 1986. "The Political Construction of Ethnicity." In *Competitive Ethnic Relations*, ed. Susan Olzak and Joane Nagel, 93–112. New York: Academic Press.

———. 1994. "Constructing Ethnicity: Creating and Recreating Ethnic Identity and Culture." *Social Problems* 41 (1): 152–76.

———. 1995. "American Indian Ethnic Renewal: Politics and the Resurgence of Identity." *American Sociological Review* 60 (6): 947–65

Nahirny, Vladimir C., and Joshua A. Fishman. 1965. "American Immigrant Groups: Ethnic Identification and the Problem of Generations." *Sociological Review* 13 (3): 311–26.

Nee, Victor, Jimy M. Sanders, and Scott Sernau. 1994. "Job Transitions in an Immigrant Metropolis: Ethnic Boundaries and the Mixed Economy." *American Sociological Review* 59 (6): 849–72.

Newman, Barry. 1987. "Solidarity's Legacy: Underground Culture Pervades Polish Life, But Can It Survive Lack of Repression?" *Wall Street Journal*, July 23, p. 1.

Nielson, Francois. 1985. "Toward a Theory of Ethnic Solidarity in Modern Societies." *American Sociological Review* 50 (April): 133–49.

Novak, Michael. 1971. *The Rise of the Unmeltable Ethnics: Politics and Culture in the Seventies*. New York: Macmillan.

Nowak, Jan. 1980. "Pomost." *Pomost Quarterly* 5 (Winter): 3–4.

———. 1986. "The Polish American Congress and the U.S. Policy of Sanctions." *Studium Papers* 10 (2): 50–56.

———. 1989. "Emigracja jest dla mnie misją" (Emigration is a mission for me). *Kurier*, March 14, p. 3.

Oberschall, Anthony. 1973. *Social Conflict and Social Movements*. Englewood Cliffs, N.J.: Prentice-Hall.

Obidinski, Eugene. 1975. "American Polonia: Sacred and Profane Aspects." *Polish American Studies* 32 (1): 5–18.

Obidinski, Eugene, and Helen Stankiewicz Zand. 1987. *Polish Folkways in America: Community and Family*. New York: University Press of America.

Ogbu, John U. 1992. "Understanding Cultural Diversity and Learning." *Educational Researcher* 21 (8): 5–14.

Olzak, Susan. 1982. "Ethnic Mobilization in Quebec." *Ethnic and Racial Studies* 5 (3): 253–75.

———. 1983. "Contemporary Ethnic Mobilization." *Annual Review of Sociology* 9: 355–74.

———. 1986. "A Competitive Model of Ethnic Collective Action in American Cities, 1877–1889." In *Competitive Ethnic Relations*, ed. Susan Olzak and Joane Nagel, 17–46. New York: Academic Press.

PAC. 1989a. "Osiągnięcie Porozumienia w Polsce Wymaga Rozwagi i Umiaru: Oświadczenie K.P.A." (Accomplishing the agreement in Poland requires prudence and moderation: Declaration of the PAC). *Dziennik Związkowy*, February 24, p. 1.

———. 1989b. "Porozumienie Ustanawia Układ Stosunków Społeczno-Politycznych w Polsce: Oświadczenie K.P.A." (Agreement establishes sociopolitical relations in Poland: Declaration of the PAC." *Dziennik Związkowy*, April 6, p. 1.

———. 1989c. "Kto Może Głosować?" (Who can vote?). *Dziennik Związkowy*, May 22, p. 3.

———. 1989d. "Kongres Polonii Amerykańskiej w Sprawie Wyborów" (Polish American Congress on election affairs). *Dziennik Związkowy*, June 2, p. 1.

PAC Bulletin. 1980–81. Chicago: Polish American Congress.

PAC Illinois Division Bulletin. 1974–79. Chicago: Illinois Division of the Polish American Congress.

PAC Newsletter. 1969–79, 1981–90. Vols. 10–20, 1–18. Chicago: Polish American Congress.

Pacyga, Dominic. 1987. "Polish America in Transition: Social Change and the Chicago Polonia, 1945–1980." *Polish American Studies* 44 (1): 39–55.

———. 1991. *Polish Immigrants and Industrial Chicago: Workers on the South Side, 1880–1922*. Columbus: Ohio State University Press.

———. 1996. "To Live Amongst Others: Poles and Their Neighbors in Industrial Chicago." *Journal of American Ethnic History* 16 (1): 55–73.

Padilla, Felix. 1985. *Latino Ethnic Consciousness: The Case of Mexican Americans and Puerto Ricans in Chicago*. Notre Dame: University of Notre Dame Press.

Padgett, Deborah. 1980. "Symbolic Ethnicity and Patterns of American Identity Assertion in American-Born Serbs." *Ethnic Groups* 3 (1): 55–77.

Park, Robert, and Herbert Miller. 1921. *Old World Traits Transplanted*. Chicago: University of Chicago Press.

Parot, Joseph John. 1981. *Polish Catholics in Chicago, 1850–1920*. DeKalb: Northern Illinois University Press.

———. 1975. "The Racial Dilemma in Chicago's Polish Neighborhoods, 1920–1970." *Polish American Studies* 32 (2): 27–38.

Patterson, Orlando. 1975. "Context and Choice in Ethnic Allegiance: A Theoretical Framework and Caribbean Case Study." In *Ethnicity: Theory and Experience*, ed. Nathan Glazer and Daniel Moynihan, 305–48. Cambridge, Mass.: Harvard University Press.

Pcar, Robert. 1988. "U.S. Helping Polish Underground with Money and Communication." *New York Times*, October 1, p. 8.

Pedraza-Bailey, Silvia. 1985. *Political and Economic Migrants in America*. Austin: University of Texas Press.

———. 1990. "Immigration Research: A Conceptual Map." *Social Science History* 14 (1): 43–67.

The People of Chicago: Who We Are and Where We Have Been. 1976. Chicago: City of Chicago, Department of Development and Planning.

Pfeffer, Max J. 1994. "Low Wage Employment and Ghetto Poverty: A Comparison of African-American and Cambodian Day-Haul Farm Workers in Philadelphia." *Social Problems* 41 (1): 9–29.

Pienkos, Donald E. 1984. *PNA: A Centennial History of the Polish National Alliance of the United States of America*. Boulder, Colo.: East European Monographs.

———. 1991. *For Your Freedom Through Ours: Polish American Efforts on Poland's Behalf, 1863–1991*. Boulder, Colo.: East European Monographs.

————. 1993. "Polish Americans and Poland: A Review of the Record." Fiedorczyk Lecture in Polish American Studies, Central Connecticut State University, New Britain, April 25.

Pilch, Andrzej. 1975. "Migration of the Galician Populace at the Turn of the Nineteenth and Twentieth Centuries." In *Employment Seeking Emigrations of the Poles World-Wide, Nineteenth and Twentieth Centuries*, ed. Celina Bobinska and Andrzej Pilch, 77–103. Krakow: Jagiellonian University.

Pinkowski, Edward. 1978. "The Great Influx of Polish Immigrants and the Industries They Entered." In *Poles in America: Bicentennial Essays*, ed. Frank Mocha, 303–70. Stevens Point, Wisc.: Worzalla Publishing Company.

Polish National Alliance (PNA). 1980. *PNA: In the Mainstreams of American Life*. Chicago: Alliance Printers and Publishers.

Pomost Quarterly. 1979–84. Vols. 1–24. Chicago: Pomost Social-Political Movement.

Portes, Alejandro, and Robert Bach. 1985. *Latin Journey: Cuban and Mexican Immigrants in the United States*. Berkeley and Los Angeles: University of California Press.

Portes, Alejandro, and Robert Manning. 1986. "The Immigrant Enclave: Theory and Empirical Examples." In *Competitive Ethnic Relations*, ed. Susan Olzak and Joane Nagel, 47–68. New York: Academic Press.

Portes, Alejandro, Samuel A. McLeod Jr., and Robert N. Parker. 1978. "Immigrant Aspirations." *Sociology of Education* 51 (October): 241–60.

Portes, Alejandro, and Ruben Rumbaut. 1990. *Immigrant America: A Portrait*. Berkeley and Los Angeles: University of California Press.

Prymasowska Rada Społeczna. 1988. "Emigracja młodych Polaków" (The emigration of young Poles). *Dziennik Związkowy*, March 18–19, pt. 2, p. 1 (first printed in *Tygodnik Powszechny*, February 15, 1988, p. 1).

Pula, James. 1980. "American Immigration and the Dillingham Commission." *Polish American Studies* 37 (1): 5–31.

————. 1992. "Polish-Black Relations: Ethnic Tensions During the Civil Rights Movement." Fiedorczyk Lecture in Polish American Studies. Central Connecticut State University, New Britain, April 23.

————. 1995. *Polish Americans: An Ethnic Community*. New York: Twayne Publishers.

————. 1996. "Image, Status, Mobility, and Integration in American Society: The Polish Experience." *Journal of American Ethnic History* 16 (1): 74–95.

Radzilowski, Thaddeus. 1986. "The Second Generation: The Unknown Polonia." *Polish American Studies* 43 (1): 5–12.

————. 1990. "Immigrant Women and Their Daughters." Fiedorczyk Lecture in Polish American Studies, Central Connecticut State University, New Britain, April 19.

Reed, John Shelton. 1974. *The Enduring South: Subculture Persistence in Mass Society*. Chapel Hill: University of North Carolina Press.

Refugee Resettlement Program, Report to Congress. 1983. Office of Refugee Resettlement, U.S. Department of Health and Human Services, Washington, D.C.

Remy, Gemima M. 1996. "Haitian Immigrants and African-American Relations: Ethnic Dilemmas in a Racially Stratified Society." *Trotter Review* 10 (1): 13–16.

Renkiewicz, Frank. 1980. "The Profits of Nonprofit Capitalism: Polish Fraternal and Beneficial Insurance in America." In *Self-Help in Urban America*, ed. Scott Cummings, 113–29. Port Washington, N.Y.: Kennikat Press.

Rocznik Statystyczny. 1989. Warsaw: Zaklad Wydawnictw Statystycznych.

Roediger, David R. 1991. *The Wages of Whiteness: Race and the Making of the American Working Class*. New York: Verso.

———. 1994. "Whiteness and Ethnicity in the History of 'White Ethnics' in the United States." In *Towards the Abolition of Whiteness: Essays on Race, Politics, and Working Class History*, chap. 11. New York: Verso.

Rurasz, Zdzislaw. 1984. "The True Meaning of Yalta." *Pomost Quarterly* 21 (Winter): 42–44.

Rumbaut, Ruben. 1994. "The Crucible Within: Ethnic Identity, Self-Esteem, and Segmented Assimilation Among Children of Immigrants." *International Migration Review* 28 (4): 748–94.

Sacks, Karen Brodkin. 1994. "How Did Jews Become White Folks?" In *Race*, ed. Steven Gregory and Roger Sanjek, 78–103. New Brunswick, N.J.: Rutgers University Press.

Said, Edward. 1978. *Orientalism*. New York: Vintage Books.

Sandberg, Neil C. 1974. *Ethnic Identity and Assimilation: The Polish-American Community*. New York: Prager Publishers.

Sanjek, Roger. 1994. "Intermarriage and the Future of Races in the United States." In *Race*, ed. Steven Gregory and Roger Sanjek, 103–30. New Brunswick, N.J.: Rutgers University Press.

Sarna, Jonathan. 1978. "From Immigrants to Ethnics: Toward a New Theory of Ethnicization." *Ethnicity* 5: 370–78.

Schiller, Nina Glick. 1977. "Ethnic Groups Are Made Not Born: The Haitian Immigrants and American Politics." In *Ethnic Encounters and Contexts*, ed. George Hicks and Phillip Leis, 23–35. North Scituate, Mass.: Duxbury Press.

Schneider, Jo Anne. 1990. "Defining Boundaries, Creating Contacts: Puerto Rican and Polish Presentation of Group Identity Through Ethnic Parades." *Journal of Ethnic Studies* 18 (1): 33–58.

Selznick, Philip. 1988 (1966). *TVA and the Grass Roots: A Study in the Sociology of Formal Organization*. Berkeley and Los Angeles: University of California Press.

Shils, Edward. 1957. "Primordial, Personal, Sacred, and Civil Ties." *British Journal of Sociology* 8 (2): 130–45.

Shokeid, Moshe. 1988. *Children of Circumstance: Israeli Immigrants in New York*. Ithaca, N.Y.: Cornell University Press.

Shulgasser, Barbara, and David S. Robinson. 1981. "Enough Protests, Polish Consulate Neighbors Say." *Chicago Sun-Times*, December 30, p. 5.

Sieredzki, Jozef. 1989. "O emigracji młodych Polaków" (The emigration of young Poles). *Dziennik Związkowy*, January 4, p. 3.

Slayton, Robert A. 1986. *Back of the Yards: The Making of a Local Democracy*. Chicago: University of Chicago Press.

Snow, David, and Robert Benford. 1988. "Ideology, Frame Resonance, and Partici-
    pant Mobilization." In *International Social Movement Research*, 1:197–217.
    Greenwich, Conn.: JAI Press.
Snow, David, Burke Rochford, Steven Worden, and Robert Benford. 1986. "Frame
    Alignment Processes, Micromobilization, and Movement Participation."
    American Sociological Review 51 (4): 464–81.
Snow, David, Louis Zurcher, and Sheldon Ekland-Olson. 1980. "Social Networks and
    Social Movements: A Microstructural Approach to Differential Recruit-
    ment." *American Sociological Review* 45 (5): 787–801.
Solidarity Election Committee. 1989. "Do wszystkich Polaków na emigracji" (To
    all Poles abroad). Communique dated April 15, 1989, was printed in *Kurier*,
    May 9, p. 5.
Sollors, Werner. 1986. *Beyond Ethnicity: Consent and Descent in American Culture*. New
    York: Oxford University Press.
Staggenborg, Suzanne. 1987. "Life Style Preferences and Social Movement Recruit-
    ment: Illustrations from the Abortion Conflict." *Social Science Quarterly* 68 (4):
    779–97.
Staniszkis, Jadwiga. 1984. *Poland's Self-Limiting Revolution*. Princeton: Princeton
    University Press.
Statistical Abstracts of the United States, 1925. Washington, D.C.: U.S. Department of
    Commerce, Bureau of Census.
Statistical Yearbook of the Immigration and Naturalization Service. 1977–93. See U.S.
    Department of Justice, Immigration and Naturalization Service.
Stinchcombe, Arthur. 1968. *Constructing Social Theories*. Chicago: University of
    Chicago Press.
Studium Newsletters. 1988–90. Ann Arbor, Mich.: The North American Study Center
    for Polish Affairs.
Studium Papers. 1976–90. Vols. 1–14 (from 1976–1982 published as *Studium News
    Abstracts*). Ann Arbor, Mich.: The North American Study Center for Polish
    Affairs.
Symmons-Symonolewicz, Konstantyn. 1966. "The Polish American Community:
    Half a Century After *The Polish Peasant*." *The Polish Review* 11 (3): 65–89.
Taylor, Verta. 1989. "Social Movement Continuity: The Women's Movement in
    Abeyance." *American Sociological Review* 54 (5): 761–75.
Templeton, Ann. 1984. "The Chicago Project: A Demonstration Refugee Resettle-
    ment Program Aimed at Self-Sufficiency." Chicago: Catholic Charities of
    Chicago.
Thomas, William, and Florian Znaniecki. 1958 (1918). *The Polish Peasant in Europe
    and America*. Chicago: University of Chicago Press.
Tierny, Kathleen. 1982. "The Battered Women Movement and the Creation of the
    Wife Beating Problem." *Social Forces* 29 (3): 207–20.
Tyszkiewicz, Stefan. 1993. "Janitoring." *Tygodnik Podhalański* 21 (May 30): 7–8.
U.S. Census of the Population, 1950: Subject Reports: Nativity and Parentage, Vol. 4
    (3A). Washington, D.C.: GPO.

U.S. Census of the Population, 1960: Subject Reports: Nativity and Parentage, Vol. 2 (1A). Washington, D.C.: GPO.

U.S. Census of the Population, 1980. Ancestry of the Population by State. Washington, D.C.: U.S. Department of Commerce, Bureau of Census, 1983.

U.S. Census of the Population, 1980. Characteristics of the Population. General Social and Economic Characteristics, Illinois. Washington, D.C.: U.S. Department of Commerce, Bureau of Census, 1983.

U.S. Census of the Population, 1980. Detailed Population Characteristics. Part 1. U.S. Summary. Washington, D.C.: U.S. Department of Commerce, Bureau of Census, 1983.

U.S. Census of the Population, 1990. Detailed Ancestry Groups for States. Washington, D.C.: U.S. Department of Commerce, Bureau of Census, 1993.

U.S. Census of the Population, 1990. The Foreign-Born Population in the United States. Washington, D.C.: U.S. Department of Commerce, Bureau of Census, 1993.

U.S. Census of the Population, 1990, Social and Economic Characteristics, Illinois. Washington, D.C.: U.S. Department of Commerce, Bureau of Census, 1993.

U.S. Census of the Population and Housing, 1990, Summary Tape File 1A. The Foreign-Born Population in the United States. Washington, D.C.: U.S. Department of Commerce, Bureau of Census, Data User Services Division, 1992.

U.S. Department of Justice, Immigration, and Naturalization Service. 1947–1976. *Annual Report of the Immigration and Naturalization Service.* Washington D.C.: GPO.

U.S. Department of Justice, Immigration, and Naturalization Service. 1977–1993. *Statistical Yearbook of the Immigration and Naturalization Service.* Washington D.C.: GPO.

U.S. Department of State Bulletin, August 1981. Washington, D.C.: GPO.

U.S. Department of State Bulletin, February 1982. Washington, D.C.: GPO.

U.S. Department of State Bulletin, December 1982. Washington, D.C.: GPO.

Vecoli, Rudolph J. 1973. "European Americans: From Immigrants to Ethnics." In *The Reinterpretation of American History and Culture,* ed. William H. Cartwright and Richard L. Watson Jr., 81–112. Washington, D.C.: National Council for the Social Studies.

Walaszek, Adam. 1992. "'How could it all appear so rosy?'—Re-emigrants from the United States in Poland, 1919–1924." *Polish American Studies* 49 (2): 43–60.

Walesa, Lech. 1987. *A Way of Hope.* New York: Henry Holt and Company.

Walsh, Edward. 1981. "Resource Mobilization and Citizen Protest in Communities Around Three Mile Island." *Social Problems* 29 (1): 1–21.

Walsh, Edward, and Rex Warland. 1983. "Social Movement Involvement in the Wake of a Nuclear Accident: Activists and Free Riders in the TMI Area." *American Sociological Review* 48 (December): 764–80.

Waters, Mary. 1990. *Ethnic Options.* Berkeley and Los Angeles: University of California Press.

———. 1994. "Ethnic and Racial Identities: Black Immigrants in New York City." *International Migration Review* 28 (4): 795–820.

Waters, Tony. 1995. "Towards a Theory of Ethnic Identity and Migration: The Formation of Ethnic Enclaves by Migrant Germans in Russia and North America." *International Migration Review* 28 (4): 515–44.

Whyte, William Foote. 1981. *Street Corner Society*, 3d ed. Chicago: University of Chicago Press.

Wicrzynski, Maciej. 1989. "Dno" (Bottom). *Kurier*, July 4, p. 11.

———. 1990. "We Are Simply Better." *International Gazette*, June 21, p. 8.

Wiewel, Wim, and Albert Hunter. 1985. "The Interorganizational Network As a Resource: A Comparative Case Study on Organizational Genesis." *Administrative Science Quarterly* 30 (4): 482–96.

Wilson, William Julius. 1978. *The Declining Significance of Race: Blacks and Changing American Institutions*. Chicago: University of Chicago Press.

Wlodarczyk, Wlademar. 1980. "Pomost After One Year." *Pomost Quarterly* 6 (Spring): 40–42.

Wytrwal, Joseph. 1961. *America's Polish Heritage*. Detroit: Endurance Press.

Wrobel, Paul. 1979. *Our Way: Family, Parish, and Neighborhood in a Polish-American Community*. Notre Dame: University of Notre Dame Press.

Yancey, William, Eugene Ericksen, and Richard Juliano. 1976. "Emergent Ethnicity: A Review and Reformulation." *American Sociological Review* 41 (3): 391–403.

Yinger, Milton. 1985. "Ethnicity." *Annual Review of Sociology* 11: 151–80.

———. 1994. *Ethnicity: Source of Strength? Source of Conflict?* Albany: State University of New York Press.

Yuenger, James. 1989. "Polish Vote Fever Infects Few Wallets in Chicago." *Chicago Tribune*, May 14, p. 3.

Zachariasiewicz, Walter. 1976. "Organizational Structure of Polonia." In *Poles in America: Bicentennial Essays*, ed. Frank Mocha, 627–70. Stevens Point, Wisc.: Worzalla Publishing Company.

Zerubavel, Eviator. 1991. *The Fine Line: Making Distinctions in Everyday Life*. Chicago: University of Chicago Press.

Zglenicki, Leon. 1937. *Poles of Chicago, 1837–1937*. Chicago: Polish Pageant.

Zhou, Min, and Carl L. Bankston III. 1994. "Social Capital and the Adaptation of the Second Generation: The Case of Vietnemese Youth in New Orleans." *International Migration Review* 28 (4): 821–45.

Zmuda, James. 1982. "An Interview with Mr. James Genden, President of the Chicago Chapter of the Afghanistan Relief Committee." *Pomost Quarterly* 14 (Spring): 50–54.

Zubrzycki, Jerzy. 1953. "Emigration from Poland in the Nineteenth and Twentieth Centuries." *Population Studies* 6 (3): 248–72.

Appendix

Table A.1 Data sources for the study

Source	Year(s)	N	Instrument	Description of sample and data
Interviews	1986–89	59	interview schedule	I interviewed individuals who were members, leaders, or employers of ethnic and immigrant Polonian organizations (see Table A.3 for a list of the organizations): 49 interviewees lived in Chicago and 10 in Northern and Southern California. Over 61 percent of the new immigrants in the sample were refugees. In the Chicago sample, I interviewed 12 Polish Americans, 8 World War II émigrés, 25 new immigrants, and 4 Americans working in agencies that resettled Polish refugees. Interviews were taped and mostly in English. This sample provides information on immigrants and ethnics working for Poland. The California interviews are used only in Chapter 2 to discuss the characteristics of the new immigrant cohort.
Fieldwork	1986–90	n/a	partipant observation	From 1986 to 1990, I attended lectures, festivals, masses, demonstrations, parades, balls, organizational meetings, conventions, fundraisers, conferences, plays, private parties, and weddings. I shopped in the Polish neighborhood, taught English to Polish immigrants, and read Polish newspapers. I gained access to the backstage behavior of some new immigrant groups (for example, Brotherhood,

Table A.1 Data sources for the study (*continued*)

Source	Year(s)	N	Instrument	Description of sample and data
				KIK, and Forum) but only participated in public activities for the Polish American organizations and other new immigrant groups. In the summer of 1987, I lived in Poland and met with members of the underground opposition, and in 1990 I taught English in Poland through the Chicago-based Polish University Abroad (PUNO).
Election	June 1989	464	questionnaire	I surveyed Poles who voted in the June 3, 1989, election through absentee ballots at the Polish consulate in Chicago. This was the first partially free election in Poland since World War II. The survey was given face-to-face and the questionnaire was in Polish. The sample represents 8.2 percent of the voters. The sample includes a large number of temporary migrants (the *wakacjusze*): 48 percent had temporary visas and more them half of these were invalid.
Forum	November 1989	109	questionnaire	I surveyed members of the Polish-American Economic Forum, an organization created in 1989 to assist Poland's emerging free market. The sample represents 25 percent of its 436 members; 72 percent of the sample completed the questionnaire at a Forum convention in November 1989, the rest completed the questionnaire through the mail. The sample includes 92 members from the new immigrant cohort, 8 from the post-World War II cohort, and 9 Polish Americans. The questionnaire for foreign-born Poles was in Polish and a different questionnaire in English was given to native-born Polish Americans. This sample provides

				information mostly on immigrants involved in action for Poland.
PUNO	1988–90	70	questionnaire	This represents a sample of immigrants who attended English as a Second Language (ESL) courses at the Polish University Abroad (PUNO) in Chicago. I taught ESL at PUNO from 1988–90. All of the respondents were students in my classes, and they were all new immigrants.
Jackowo	Summer 1989	183	questionnaire	I surveyed the businesses in *Jackowo*, the Polish immigrant neighborhood in Chicago. The surveys were conducted face-to-face in Polish and English. There were 183 businesses (including 9 vacant stores) on the first floor of buildings on Milwaukee Avenue between Belmont and Diversey, and of them 91 percent had mostly Polish customers, 74 percent had mostly Polish workers, and 61 percent were owned by Polish immigrants and Polish Americans.
Home Health Care Workers	Summer 1992	35	interview schedule	I interviewed thirty-five Polish immigrants working as home health care workers for the elderly. Over 90 percent of the workers were working illegally or had worked illegally as home care workers. The sample represents temporary migrant workers (*wakacjusze*). The information is used only in Chapter 2 to discuss the characteristics of the new immigrants.

Table A.2 Characteristics of the New Polish Cohort

Sample	N	Status at Arrival Percent		Status at Time of Interview or Survey Percent	Percent Men	Percent Age at Time of Arrival	Mean Age at Arrival	Year of Arrival Percent	Mean Years in the U.S.	Percent Post-secondary Education	Percent Occupation in the U.S.	Percent Size of City of Emigration	Percent Plan to Return to Poland
	(1)	(2)		(3)					(4)	(5)	(6)	(7)	(8)
		Refugees	Temporary										
Interviews (activists)	31	61	29	Citizen = 23 Resident = 65 Val temp = 13 Inv temp = 4	84	20s = 35 30s = 35 40s = 31 50+ = 0	35.0	1980s = 74 1970s = 16 1960s = 10	7.0	92	Prof = 41 Skill = 19 Unsk = 7	all city and town	Yes = 16 No = 50 DK = 33
Election (voters)	457	n/a	n/a	Citizen = 3 Resident = 49 Val temp = 23 Inv temp = 25	68	20s = 25 30s = 31 40s = 27 50+ = 15	37.3	1980s = 82 1970s = 16 1960s = 2	5.2	38	Prof = 6 Skill = 45 Unsk = 28	City = 61 Town = 23 Vill = 16	Yes = 65 No = 4 DK = 31
Forum (members)	92	17	51	Citizen = 39 Resident = 46 Val temp = 4 Inv temp = 12	88	20s = 38 30s = 44 40s = 11 50+ = 2	31.8	1980s = 71 1970s = 18 1960s = 11	10.0	64	Prof = 32 Skill = 34 Unsk = 13	City = 67 Town = 21 Vill = 12	Yes = 22 No = 32 DK = 47
PUNO (students)	70	n/a	n/a	Citizen = 2 Resident = 40 Val temp = 21 Inv temp = 38	24	20s = 47 30s = 31 40s = 10 50+ = 6	31.7	1980s = 93 1970s = 7 1960s = 0	3.8	78	Prof = 6 Skill = 31 Unsk = 15	City = 48 Town = 43 Vill = 8	Yes = 12 No = 56 DK = 33
Home Care Workers (*wakacjusze*)	35	0	94	Citizen = 0 Resident = 26 Val temp = 9 Inv temp = 65	23	20s = 40 30s = 20 40s = 34 50+ = 6	35.4	1980s = 95 1970s = 5 1960s = 0	4.0	91	all home health care workers for the elderly	City = 73 Town = 21 Vill = 6	Yes = 63 No = 20 DK = 17

(1) Numbers: The numbers represent those in each sample who arrived after 1960. Interview repondents represent new immigrants active in political organizations. This represents 53 percent of the people I interviewed. I include here those people from the new cohort who were involved in political activity in Chicago ($N = 21$) or in California ($N = 10$). This sample of interviews does not include Polish American ethnics (that is, native born, $N = 12$), World War II émigrés ($N = 8$), Americans (of no Polish heritage, $N = 4$), or new immigrants who were not politically active ($N = 4$). For the other samples, using a cut-off date of 1960, the total numbers represents 98 percent of the Election sample, 92 percent of the Forum sample, and 100 percent of the PUNO and Home Care Worker samples. For a description of the data sources see Table A.1.

(2) Status at Arrival: This gives the percentage of immigrants in each sample who arrived in the United States as refugees and those who arrived on temporary visas. The percent of temporary visas is an indicator of the number of *wakacjusze* in the sample on arrival. In the Interview sample, all of the refugees arrived after 1980 (after the introduction of the Refugee Act).

(3) Status at Time of Interview or Survey: This refers to the immigrants' legal status at the time of the interview or survey. The Interviews took place between 1987–90, the Election survey was June 1989, the Forum survey was November 1989, the PUNO questionnaires were collected between 1988 and 1990, and the Home Care Workers were interviewed in the summer of 1992. In the PUNO sample, 20 percent of the students received permanent residency through IRCA. The notations refer to: Citizen = U.S. citizen; Resident = permanent resident status; Val temp = a valid temporary visa; Inv temp = an expired temporary visa. Those with temporary visas represent the *wakacjusze*.

(4) Mean Years: Mean number of years the sample has been in the United States at the time of the interview or survey. The mean years in the Interview sample was inflated by five outliers who had fourteen to twenty-seven years in the United States. Taken out of the sample, the activists were here on average five years.

(5) Education: Percentage of sample who had some post-secondary education. Most of them earned their degrees in Poland.

(6) Occupation: Percentage in occupational categories in the United States at the time of the interview or survey. Prof = professional (for example, chemists, accountants, media personnel, editors, engineers, musicians), Skill = skilled (draftsman, electrician, machinist, printer), Unsk = unskilled. Not included here are those employed in clerical positions (Interviews, $N = 8$; Forum, $N = 7$), those who are small business owners (Forum, $N = 9$), or those working in domestic service (PUNO = 29 employed as childcare and elder care workers). In the Election questionnaire, respondents were given the following categories to choose from: professional, skilled, unskilled, student, not working. In the other samples it was an open-ended question.

(7) City Size: Percentage of the sample that came from each of the following three areas: City equals metropolitan area, usually the provincial capital, Town is a city other than the provincial capital, Village (Vill) is smaller than a town. In all but the Interview sample, the respondents had to chose between one of the three categories. The city was the city of last residence before departure from Poland.

(8) Return: This reflects the answer to the question asked at the time of the interview, "Do you plan on returning to Poland?" For the PUNO sample, only half of the sample answered this question.

Table A.3 Polonia organizations in Chicago related to the study

Organization	Cohort*	Founded	Size	Description of Organization	Interviews	Other sources of information: PO = participant observer, O = observer, A = archival
Brotherhood of Dispersed Solidarity Members (Brotherhood)	post-1980 refugees	1984	national = 20–30; Chicago = 10	to unite the Solidarity refugees dispersed throughout the U.S.; to support the opposition in Poland	2 founders, 2 members	PO: planning meetings, private parties, demonstrations, parades; A: organizational literature, founding letters, budgets
Freedom for Poland (Freedom)	new immigrants, mostly post-1980	1985	100 Illinois	to help the opposition in Poland	3 founders	O: demonstrations, fundraising; A: organizational literature on activities and history
Pomost	mostly new (1960s and 1970s) immigrants	1979	peak 1984 was 1000 nationally	to support the opposition in Poland; incorporated in 1982.	2 founders, 6 members/former members	A: periodicals (1979–1984)
Alliance for Independent Poland (Alliance)	new immigrants	1988	20 in 1989	to help the opposition in Poland; most members were former members of Pomost	1 founder, 4 members	O: demonstrations and public meetings
Klub Inteligentsia Katolickie (KIK)	post-1980 immigrants, some World War II émigrés	1987	100 on a list in 1989; 30–40 active	discussion/social group for new immigrants; worked closely with Brotherhood (overlapping membership)	9 members	PO: meetings, parties, parade
Fair Elections in Poland	Polish Americans and new immigrants	1989	a few organizers	to help free elections in Poland	0	PO: fundraiser, O: elections
Committee on Behalf of Free Elections in Poland	new immigrants and World War II émigrés	1989	unknown	to help free elections in Poland	0	A: Polish newspapers

Organization	Cohort*	Founded	Size	Description of Organization	Interviews	Other sources of information: PO = participant observer; O = observer; A = archival
Polish-American Economic Forum (Forum)	90 percent new, some World War II émigrés and Polish Americans	1989	436 members in March 1990	promote free market activity in Poland, economic liaison between Poland and the United States	1 founder 4 members	PO: organizational meetings, office, convention A: founding documents
Polish University Abroad (PUNO)	new immigrants, mostly post-1980	1978	1988: 10 teachers, over 100 students per semester	offered English-language, computer and business courses to new immigrants; run by new immigrants	1 founder	PO: taught English in Chicago for 2 years, and 1 summer in Poland
Polish American Congress (PAC)	mostly Polish Americans and some World War II émigrés	1944	umbrella organization, mid-1980s represented over 3000 organizations in the United States	to help Poland regain independence and to promote and defend Polish Americans; help for Poland done mostly in the Committee for Support of Democratic Opposition in Poland founded in 1976; the PAC Illinois State Division in Chicago also works for Poland and Polish Americans	1 President 2 admin. 5 members 1 Pres. IL Div 1 Dir. IL Div	O: national convention 1989, conferences, parades and festivals A: national newsletters (1969–90), PAC Illinois Division newsletters 1974–79, and founding documents; Polish- and English-language newspapers
Polish National Alliance (PNA)	mostly Polish Americans	1880	mid-1980s over 1000 lodges and close to 300,000 members	national fraternal insurance organization that supports ethnic activities	1 president 2 directors 1 editor newspaper	O: conferences, festivals, and events A: Polish- and English-language newspapers, organizational documents
Polish Roman Catholic Union	mostly Polish Americans	1873	mid-1980s over 700 lodges members	national fraternal insurance organization that supports ethnic activities	1 former president	A: Polish-language newspapers, organizational documents
Polish Women's Alliance	mostly Polish Americans	1898	mid-1980s, over 800 lodges and 100,000 members	national fraternal insurance organization that supports ethnic activities	1 president	A: Polish-language newspapers, organizational documents

Organization	Cohort*	Founded	Size	Description of Organization	Interviews	Other sources of information: PO = participant observer O = observer A = archival
Polish Welfare Association	American, Polish American and new Polish immigrants	1921	7500 clients in 1988, mostly Polish immigrants	social service organization; in 1988, 45 percent government funding, 8 percent from Polish American organizations	2 exec directors 1 administrator	A: Polish-language newspapers, community meetings, organizational documents
Copernicus Foundation	Polish Americans	1972	mailing list 14,000 (1987)	provide community culture and civic center; preserve Polish heritage and culture	2 directors of Copernicus Cultural and Civic Center	PO: language classes, festivals A: Polish- and English-language newspapers

*Immigrant in this category is an inclusive term that refers to refugees, quota immigrants, and *wakacjusz.* For the most part, refugees were the active participants and leaders.

**The number of interviews add up to over 49 (the number conducted in Chicago) because some people were members of several organizations. I interviewed individuals as leaders, founders, and members of organizations. Others I interviewed as representatives of organizations, but whose organizations are not listed here include: a Polish American director working for Catholic Charities in Chicago, which helps resettle refugees; the director of World Relief in Chicago, an organization which resettles refugees; and the director of the Illinois Office for Refugee Resettlement the main governmental agency for refugees. I also interviewed the pastors at St. Stanislaus Kotska Church (centered in the old Polish immigrant neighborhood) and St. Hyacinth (*Św. Jacek*—centered in *Jackowo*, the new Polish immigrant neighborhood). Other groups that the interviewees were members of included PNA lodges of new immigrants including: *Sierpień 80* (Brotherhood's lodge); *Giewont* (Freedom's lodge); and *Pokolenia* (Pomost's lodge).

Index